EDUCATIONAL RESEARCH: CURRENT ISSUES

This reader is one part of an Open University integrated teaching system and the selection is therefore related to other material available to students. It is designed to evoke the critical understanding of students. Opinions expressed in it are not necessarily those of the course team or of the University.

EDUCATIONAL RESEARCH: CURRENT ISSUES

Edited by

Martyn Hammersley

at The Open University

Published in association with
The Open University

P·C·P

Paul Chapman
Publishing Ltd

Paul Chapman Publishing Ltd
144 Liverpool Road
London
N1 1LA

British Library Cataloguing in Publication Data

Hammersley M.
Educational Research: Current Issues
I. Hammersley, Martyn
370.7

ISBN 1 85396 243 0

Typeset by Inforum, Rowlands Castle, Hants.
Printed and bound by
Athenaeum Press Ltd., Newcastle upon Tyne

A B C D E F G H 9 8 7 6 5 4 3

CONTENTS

ACKNOWLEDGEMENTS

We thank those listed below for their permission to use copyrighted material:

Ch. 1   Reprinted with permission from G. de Landsheere (1988) History of educational research, in J. P. Keeves (ed.) *Educational Research, Methodology and Measurement: An International Handbook,* Pergamon, Oxford.

Ch. 2   P. Atkinson, S. Delamont and M. Hammersley (1988) Qualitative research traditions, from *Review of Educational Research,* Vol. 58, no. 2, pp. 231–50.

Ch. 3   S. J. Ball (1990) Self-doubt and soft data: social and technical trajectories in ethnographic fieldwork, from *International Journal of Qualitative Studies in Education,* Vol. 3, no. 2, pp. 157–71.

Ch. 4   E. Eisner (1992) Objectivity in educational research, from *Curriculum Inquiry,* Vol. 22, no. 1, pp. 9–15, Basil Blackwell, Cambridge, Mass.

Ch. 5   D. C. Phillips (1989) Subjectivity and objectivity: an objective inquiry, reprinted by permission of the publisher from E. W. Eisner and A. Peshkin (eds.) *Qualitative Inquiry in Education: The Continuing Debate,* Teachers College Press, New York (© 1989 by Teachers College, Columbia University. All rights reserved) pp. 19–37.

Ch. 6   J. Hage and B. F. Meeker (1988) How to think about causality, from J. Hage and B. F. Meeker, *Social Causality,* Unwin Hyman, London.

Ch. 7   J. W. Schofield (1989) Increasing the generalizability of qualitative research, reprinted by permission of the publisher from E. W. Eisner and A. Peshkin (eds.) *Qualitative Inquiry in Education: The Continuing Debate,* Teachers College Press, New York (© 1989 by Teachers College, Columbia University. All rights reserved) pp. 201–32.

Ch. 8   C. Lacey (1976) Problems of sociological fieldwork: a review of the methodology of *Hightown Grammar,* from M. Shipman (ed.) *The Organisation and Impact of Social Research,* pp. 63–81, 83–8, Routledge & Kegan Paul, London.

Ch. 9   J. Nias (1991) Primary teachers talking: a reflexive account of longitudinal research, from G. Walford (ed.) *Doing Educational Research,* Routledge, London.

Ch. 10   P. H. Hirst (1983) from *Educational Theory and its Foundation Disciplines,* Routledge & Kegan Paul, London.

Ch. 11   W. Carr (1987) What is an educational practice?, from *Journal of Philosophy of Education,* Vol. 22, no. 2, pp. 163–75, Carfax, Oxford.

Ch. 12   S. Kemmis (1988) Action research, from J. P. Keeves (ed.) *Educational Research Methodology and Measurement: An International Handbook,* Pergamon, Oxford, pp. 42–9.

Ch. 13   A. Gitlin, M. Siegel and K. Boru (1989) The politics of method: from leftist ethnography to educative research, from *Qualitative Studies in Education,* Vol. 2, no. 3, pp. 237–53.

Ch. 14   M. Hammersley (1993) On the teacher as researcher, first published in *Educational Action Research,* Vol. 1, no. 3.

The editor would also like to thank his fellow members of the E824 Course Team: Roger Gomm and Peter Woods, for their assistance in compiling this volume.

INTRODUCTION

Educational research in Britain is undergoing profound changes at the present time. These changes arise from a variety of sources. One is the educational reforms of the late 1980s and early 1990s, which have introduced new pressures and constraints but have also created new opportunities. Above all, though, they have highlighted the question of the function of research in relation to policy-making, and to educational practice in general. Reflection on these and other matters has also been stimulated by internal developments and debates within educational research. Particularly important here has been the shift from the dominance of quantitative approaches to the increasing use of qualitative method. This is not simply a matter of change in technique, though that is not unimportant. It has also involved change at a deeper level, in terms of ideas about the nature and purpose of research. In the course of this, debates have arisen about methodological concepts, such as objectivity and validity, that were previously taken as largely unproblematic, or at least as primarily technical matters.

It is worth emphasizing that these external and internal factors are at odds with one another in some key respects. Recent government educational policy has for the most part flown in the face of the findings of educational research. More than this, though, recent policy has been premised on a belief in the necessity for, and availability of, quantitative indicators of the quality of educational outputs, inputs and processes. Yet the move to qualitative method within educational research arose in large part from doubts about the validity of standardized quantitative indicators. There is, then, a direct conflict not just between findings of much educational research and the direction in which national educational policy is going but also between the methodological assumptions built into that policy and those now characteristic of much educational research.

At the same time, the methodological debates surrounding educational re-search go beyond the conflict between qualitative and quantitative approaches. Some recent discussions have engaged in radical questioning of fundamental presuppositions that have shaped not just quantitative but also much qualita-tive research. For instance, doubts have been expressed about whether research can simply document the facts about educational policy and practice – whether they do not in some sense construct the 'facts' they present. Questions have also been raised about the sort of theory that research produces and its relation to educational practice. Indeed, where previously the function of educational research was seen primarily in terms of providing information of value to policy-makers and practitioners, it is now seen by some as needing to have a much more 'critical' orientation and to be much more closely involved with, if not integrated into, educational practice.

In all these various respects, opinion about methodology among educational researchers is probably more divided on fundamental issues today than it has ever been. We live in 'interesting' times, in more ways than one. The articles in this book explore these important issues, from diverse points of view. The first two chapters go some way to placing the current state of educational research in historical context. In Chapter 1 de Landsheere provides a brief account of its early history, noting how it originated in psychology, and tracing the ways in which it has developed since then. In particular, he shows how it has been influenced by the attempt to apply scientific method to resolve educational problems. His account stops in the 1970s,[1] and as a result focuses for the most part on quantitative research. By contrast, Atkinson, Delamont and Ham-mersley adopt a much narrower and more recent focus, concentrating on the emergence and development of qualitative educational research in Britain in the 1970s and 1980s. They stress its diversity, even at the beginning, and trace something of its subsequent history.

In Chapter 3, Stephen Ball considers the role of the researcher's self in ethnographic fieldwork. He argues that reflexivity provides the basis of rigour in ethnography; it is the means by which the social relations involved in re-search are related to its more technical features. He illustrates this through discussion of the various social trajectories of fieldwork, including the negotia-tion of entry, relations in the field (with particular reference to gender and ethnicity) and naturalistic sampling (covering places, persons and times). These social aspects of research make considerable demands on the researcher, not only in terms of negotiative skills but also in capacity for reflexive analysis. Finally, Ball considers the issue of whether ethnography is art or science. He is critical of accounts that reduce data collection and analysis to mere tech-nicalities, and that omit consideration of the researcher as social participant. Data are a product of the skills and imagination of the researcher and of the interface between researcher and researched. He argues that for this reason research reports should contain information about the social process that pro-duced the data, for example in the form of research biographies. The readings by Lacey and Nias included in this volume are extended examples of this.

In the next chapter, Eisner questions the role the concept of objectivity has played in educational research. He identifies two interpretations of this term: what he calls ontological and procedural objectivity. The first concerns the goal of research, portraying this as the represention of an objective reality. Procedural objectivity, on the other hand, refers to the idea that researchers should follow procedural rules in order to minimize the influence of their subjective preferences and preconceptions. Eisner rejects both of these conceptions of objectivity, on the grounds that perception and understanding are always dependent on a framework of presuppositions that actually constitute what we see, and prevent us from seeing other things. He argues that fear of the consequences of abandoning objectivity is misplaced because even without it we can still differentiate among our beliefs in terms of which are more or less sound. He also questions educational researchers' commitment to a literal conception of truth, as against the sort of truth characteristic of literature and art. His aim is to broaden educational research, to escape what he sees as the straitjacket that has been imposed on it as a result of its aspiration to scientific status.[2]

Phillips (Chapter 5) takes a contrasting view. He criticizes Eisner explicitly, arguing that Eisner's position leaves no basis for making reasonable judgements about the relative validity of competing knowledge claims. He acknowledges the failure of the foundationalism that Eisner criticizes, in which beliefs are tested against a bedrock of evidence that is beyond all possible doubt. But Phillips argues that the relativist position that Eisner seems to adopt does not automatically follow from the abandonment of foundationalism, and that there are good reasons for rejecting it. For him, objectivity is an important regulative ideal in educational research, and in social research generally.[3]

The second part of the book is concerned with more practical aspects of the research process. A feature of much educational research, both quantitative and qualitative, is a concern with identifying causal patterns. In Chapter 6 Hage and Meeker explore what is involved in this, looking at various features of causal relationships, including the role of time and asymmetry, and distinguishing among reciprocal, indirect, conditional and spurious causation. They conceptualize causality in terms of networks, and illustrate the role of diagrams in modelling these, discussing several examples from educational research.

Schofield focuses on a different issue, generalizability; but again one that arises in the context of both quantitative and qualitative research. Interestingly, her focus is on the latter. She examines several attempts to conceptualize this problem, and identifies the different sorts of generalization with which qualitative researchers are concerned. Particularly useful is her discussion of the strategies that can be used to pursue these forms of generalization, their advantages and disadvantages. She illustrates her discussion with examples from her own research.

The other two chapters in Part 2 are concerned with the practical experience and problems involved in carrying out particular pieces of research.

Lacey provides an inside account of what has become recognized as a classic sociological study in the field of education, his investigation of Hightown Grammar school (Lacey, 1970). His focus in that work was the differentiation of pupils in the school, both in the form of streaming and of differential treatment in the classroom on the basis of teachers' judgements of ability and behaviour. He argued that both forms of differentiation had the effect of polarizing pupils' attitudes towards school, and thereby their levels of academic achievement. Lacey primarily used a qualitative approach, in the form of participant observation, but he also collected quantitative data of various kinds. In his chapter he discusses problems of bias and role conflict, and displays the evaluative, interpretational and interactional processes involved in research. His account of how he came to combine methods and integrate them into the analysis deals with a particularly difficult problem encountered by many qualitative researchers.

In Chapter 9, Jennifer Nias reflects on the research that went into the making of her book, *Primary Teachers Talking* (Nias, 1989). She explains that it arose from an evaluation of a course she was teaching, and how she began with set ideas about what she wanted to find out. However, she found that the teachers she was interviewing were giving her rich descriptions of their experiences of work, of a kind that she had not met with before. From there the research developed along lines indicated by the data, becoming a longitudinal study of major proportions. Nias discusses various methodological features of the research, such as sampling, validity and the search for grounded theory. The account is notable for the way in which her own feelings are reflected upon, and for the frank description of hazards and problems. She explains how the major themes emerged from the data, describing the typical worrying sensation of drowning in the data, but then finding an unexpected reef beneath her feet. As her teachers conveyed their experiences of living through their work, so Nias re-lives here her experience of the research in all its excitement, difficulty, complexity and reward.

The final part of the reader is concerned with the relationship between educational research and practice. This is another area of sustained debate and deep differences in view among educational researchers. Chapter 10 by Hirst maps out one such disagreement: between those who see research as producing scientific theories which should form the basis for educational practice, and those who (like Hirst himself) regard educational theory as practical rather than scientific in character. He explores the implications of the latter view for the relationship between research in such disciplines as the psychology, sociology and philosophy of education, on the one hand, and the practical theory on the basis of which teachers operate on the other.

In Chapter 11 Carr develops this theme further, providing a philosophical analysis of the nature of educational practice. He looks at several different views: the idea that theory and practice are opposed, that practice is dependent on theory, and that theory is dependent on practice. He argues that each of these has some force, but that none of them is satisfactory. What is required in order to understand the problem, he suggests, is a historical reconstruction of the concept of educational practice, and in pursuit of this he provides an explication of Aristotle's conception of practice. He sees the philosophy of education as a species of practical philosophy whose task should be the re-establishment of the classical concept of educational practice in the modern world.

Kemmis's chapter is concerned with the nature of action research. He traces its origins, and outlines how more recent versions have diverged from Lewin's original conception. He examines the purposes, objects and methods of action research, and outlines the criteria by which he believes it should be judged. He concludes by looking at how action research can be facilitated by outsiders, and examines the relationship between it and other kinds of educational research. He specifically highlights what he calls 'emancipatory action research', seeing this as a form of critical social science, and explains why he believes it to be desirable.

Gitlin, Siegel and Boru are also concerned with a form of action research. They begin by criticizing the 'educational left' for its selective use of anthropology, and general failure to examine issues of method. This has led, they suggest, to a reliance on a particular version of ethnography in which are embodied social relationships of a kind that are in conflict with the values that are fundamental for the left: equality and democracy. They discuss recent criticisms of conventional ethnography within cultural anthropology, and go on to recommend what they call 'educative research'. This is based on collaboration between researchers and teachers, and is explicitly committed to achieving emancipation from social inequality.

In the final chapter Hammersley assesses the arguments that have provided the basis for advocacy of action research by teachers. He examines the criticisms of conventional educational research frequently made in this context, such as that its findings are irrelevant to practice, or are invalid because the researcher is not involved as a participant in the events he or she is studying, as well as the claims that such research is undemocratic and exploitative. In the second half of the chapter he assesses the criticisms of more traditional forms of teaching that are involved in the proposal that teachers should become researchers. Hammersley finds both these sets of criticisms less than convincing, at least in so far as they are intended to support the replacement of conventional forms of educational inquiry with collaborative and practitioner research.

CONCLUSION

In this book we have collected together articles that address many of the methodological issues about which there is currently fundamental disagreement. These issues have serious implications for the nature and function of educational research. The articles included here display a wide range of views, and address methodological problems that arise in a variety of sorts of educational research. We hope that the book will contribute to the clarification and eventual resolution of the problems that it addresses.

NOTES

1. In its original form his account extended a little further, into the 1980s (see de Landsheere, 1988).
2. Eisner develops these arguments in his book, *The Enlightened Eye* (Eisner, 1991).
3. See also Phillips (1987, 1992).

REFERENCES

de Landsheere, G. (1988) History of educational research, in J. P. Keeves (ed.) *Educational Research, Methodology and Measurement: An International Handbook*, Pergamon, Oxford.
Eisner, E. (1991) *The Enlightened Eye*, Macmillan, New York, NY.
Lacey, C. (1970) *Hightown Grammar*, Manchester University Press.
Nias, J. (1989) *Primary Teachers Talking: A Study of Teaching as Work*, Routledge, London.
Phillips, D. C. (1987) *Philosophy, Science and Social Inquiry*, Pergamon, Oxford.
Phillips, D. C. (1992) *The Social Scientist's Bestiary*, Pergamon, Oxford.

PART 1:

The nature of educational research

1

HISTORY OF EDUCATIONAL RESEARCH

G. De Landsheere

In tracing the development of educational research this article will examine the successive periods: pre-1900 era, 1900 to 1930s, 1930s to late 1950s, the 1960s and 1970s [. . .]

PRE-1900

It is certainly not incidental that within a period of about 25 years empirical educational research was born and began to tackle most of the pervasive educational problems which are today still under study throughout the Western world. The foundations for this sudden rise were laid during centuries of educational experience and philosophical thinking, and were inspired by the explosion of the natural sciences during the nineteenth century. More specifically, longitudinal observations of individual children were recorded during the nineteenth century and attained a high-quality level with the pioneering study, in 1882, by Preyer, *Die Seele des Kindes* (*The Mind of the Child*). This was the first textbook on developmental psychology. The idea of an experimental school and of experimentation in education is present in the writings of Kant, Herbart, and Pestalozzi, but this idea implied field experiences and not experimentation according to an elaborated design.

In the second part of the nineteenth century, several signs show that developments in the natural sciences slowly began to influence psychology and education. In 1859, in *The Emotions and the Will*, Bain considered the construction of aptitude tests. Five years later, G. Fisher proposed, in his *Scalebook*, a set of scales for the rating of ability and knowledge in major school subjects including handwriting. Fisher also introduced statistics into educational research by using the arithmetic mean as an index of achievement of a group of students. In 1870,

Bartholomaï administered a questionnaire to 2,000 children entering primary school in order to know the 'content of their mind' at that moment. Three years later, the first experimental study of attention was published by Miller in Göttingen. In 1875, James opened the first psychological laboratory of the United States at Harvard in order to carry out systematic observation, but not experimentation. The year 1879, saw the publication of Bain's *Education as a Science*.

It is clear that the immediate origin of modern educational research (and of experimental psychology) is not to be found in the emerging social sciences, but in the natural sciences. With his *Origin of Species* (1859), Darwin linked research on humans with physics, biology, zoology, and geography. Six years later, Bernard published his *Introduction to the Study of Experimental Medicine*, the guide to modern scientific research. In 1869, Galton suggested, in *Hereditary Genius*, applying statistics to the study of human phenomena and began work on the concepts of standardization, correlation, and operational definition. Carroll (1978) saw in Galton's *Inquiry into Human Faculty and its Development* (1883) the invention of the concept of mental testing.

Experimental psychology – soon to be followed by experimental pedagogy – was created in German physics laboratories by scholars with a strong philosophical background. Wundt, a student of one of these scholars, Helmholtz, founded the first laboratory of experimental psychology in 1879. Wundt's laboratory had a considerable impact, and the scientific leadership of the German universities at the end of the 1800s must be recognized in order to understand what happened between 1880 and 1900. At that time, many students, particularly from the United States, completed their advanced education at the universities of Berlin, Leipzig, Heidelberg, or Jena. This explains the extraordinarily rapid dissemination of Wundt's ideas: Cattell, Hall, Judd, Rice, and Valentine were among his students. His work was immediately known in France by Ribot and Binet, in Russia by Netschajeff, in Japan by Matsumoto, in Santiago, Chile by Mann, and in Argentina by Mercante. Psychological laboratories were soon opened on both sides of the Atlantic.

In the meantime, certain key events were associated with the birth of modern educational research:

1885 Ebbinghaus's study on memory drew the attention of the education world to the importance of associations in the learning process.

1888 Binet published his *Etudes de Psychologie Experimentales*; at that time he was already working in schools.

1890 The term mental test was coined by Cattell.

1891 Stanley Hall launched the review *Pedagogical Seminary*.

1894 Rice developed a spelling test to be administered to 16,000 pupils. He published the results of his testing in his *Scientific Management of Education* in 1913.

1895 In the United States, the *National Society for the Scientific Study of Education* was founded (initially called the National Herbart Society for the Scientific Study of Teaching).

1896 In Belgium, Schuyten published a report of his first educational research study on the influence of temperature on school children's attention.

Dewey, a student of Stanley Hall, opened a laboratory school at the University of Chicago.

1897 Thorndike studied under James at Harvard and there discovered the works of Galton and Binet.

Ebbinghaus published his so-called completion test to measure the effect of fatigue on school performance. This can be considered to be the first operational group test.

In the same year Binet began to work on his intelligence scale.

1898 Lay suggested distinguishing experimental education from experimental psychology.

Binet and Henri condemned traditional education in their book *La Fatigue Intellectuelle* and indicated the need for experimental education.

1899 Schuyten opened a pedological laboratory in Antwerp (Belgium) to study experimentally, among other things, group teaching methods.

[. . .] Many American authors regard Rice as the founder [of 'experimental pedagogy'] because of his research on the effect of spelling drills (1895–1897), but other names: Binet, Lay, Mercante, or Schuyten, could also qualify. As for the term itself, it was coined by Meumann (Wundt's former student) in 1900, in the German *Zeitschrift für Pädogogik* where he dealt with the scientific study of schooling. In 1903, Lay published his *Experimentelle Didaktik* where he made his famous statement about '. . . experimental education will become all education'. In 1905, Lay and Meumann together published the review *Die Experimentelle Pädagogik*. Subsequently, Meumann's three-volume work *Einführung in die Experimentelle Pädagogik* (1910, 1913, 1914) emphasized both the strict scientific and quantitative side of the laboratory, while Lay continued to emphasize both quantitative and qualitative approaches (empathy, intention) in classroom research.

When did modern educational research appear in France? There is no doubt that Binet inspired it. In his introduction to his book *La Fatigue Intellectuelle* (1898), he wrote:

Education must rely on observation and experimentation. By experience, we do not mean vague impressions collected by persons who have seen many things. An experimental study includes all methodically collected documents with enough detail and precise information to enable the reader to replicate the study, to verify it and to draw conclusions that the first author had not identified. (Simon, 1924, p. 5)

It is obvious throughout the whole psychological work of Binet that he had a strong interest in education. In 1905, he founded the School Laboratory in rue Grande-aux-Bettes in Paris. With him were Vaney, who in 1907 published the first French reading scale and Simon, the coauthor of the *Intelligence Scale*

(1905) and later author of the *Pédagogie Expérimentale*. Binet and Simon's *Intelligence Scale* presented in Rome at the 1905 International Conference of Psychology was the first truly operational mental test covering higher cognitive processes. Like Wundt's ideas, Binet's test became known throughout the world within a very few years. But beyond its intrinsic value, this test had a far greater historical significance. It was now acknowledged that a test could be a valid measurement instrument both in psychology and education.

In 1904, Claparède, a medical doctor, founded the Laboratory for Experimental Psychology at the University of Geneva with his uncle Flournoy. In 1892, Claparède had visited Binet in Paris and in the following year was, for a short time, Wundt's student in Leipzig. In 1905, he published the first version of his *Psychologie de l'enfant et pédagogie expérimentale* that was the only French educational research methods handbook until 1935 when Buyse published his *Expérimentation en Pédagogie*. In 1912, Claparède established the J. J. Rousseau Institute in Geneva which over the next fifty years was to make a marked contribution to child study and education through the work of Jean Piaget. However, Claparède remained mostly psychologically and philosophically oriented. With his theory of functional education, he was the European counterpart of John Dewey. Together they were seen as the two main leaders of progressive education.

Among many interesting features in the work of Claparède (following Dilthey's work in 1892 on *Verstehen* vs. *Erklären*) is his analysis, in 1903, of the explaining (positivist, nomothetic approach) versus the understanding (hermeneutic) approach. This elicited a debate which still lasts today.

At the end of *Les Idées modernes sur les enfants*, Binet (1924, p. 300) mentioned that 'it is specially in the United States that the remodelling of education has been undertaken on a new, scientific basis'. In fact, at the beginning of the century, education research advanced at an extraordinarily quick pace in the United States.

At Columbia University, Cattell, who had obtained his Ph.D. under Wundt and had known Galton in Cambridge, had, in 1890, as mentioned above, coined the term mental test in the philosophical journal *Mind*. In 1891, he established his psychological laboratory just above the laboratory for electricity. Under his supervision Thorndike completed his Ph.D. in 1898 on animal intelligence. Like many psychologists of the time he soon developed a keen interest in education. In this period, so much attention was focused on objective measurement that the experimental education movement was sometimes called 'the measurement movement' (Joncich, 1962).

Thorndike can be considered as the most characteristic representative of the scientific orientation in education. During the following decades, he dealt with all aspects of educational research. He was the first person to conceive of teaching methods in terms of an explicitly formulated and experimentally tested learning theory. In so doing, he opened a new teaching era. The influence of Thorndike in the field of educational research can probably be compared with the influence of Wundt in experimental psychology.

THE FLOURISHING OF QUANTITATIVE RESEARCH, FROM 1900 TO 1930

During this period, most educational research was quantitatively oriented and geared to the study of effectiveness. For a while, Taylorism and the study of efficiency, became a component of educational thinking. The behaviouristic and antimentalist study of human behaviour was regarded as the best weapon against the formalism of the past.

The following aspects of research activities, although not comprehensive, are representative illustrations of the era.

Statistical theory

It has sometimes been said that there is an inconsistency between the limitations of measurement in the social sciences and the rapidly increasing sophistication of the statistical techniques resorted to. However, it can be argued that many statistical advances were achieved by researchers in education precisely because they were aware of the complexity and the instability of most phenomena they had under study and had to look for increasingly sophisticated methods to obtain sufficient validity of measurement or else indicate the limitations of their conclusions.

The applicability of the Gaussian probability curve to biological and social phenomena was suggested at the beginning of the 1800s by Quetelet, who coined the term statistics. Galton was the first to make extensive use of the normal curve to study psychological problems. He sometimes preferred to express the same distributions with his ogive because this representation gave a better picture of the hierarchy of characteristics. Galton also suggested percentile norms. In 1875, he drew the first regression line, and developed the concept of correlation in 1877. In 1896, Pearson, who worked under Galton, published the formula for the product–moment correlation coefficient. In the first decade of the 1900s, the essentials of the correlational method, including the theory of regression, were well-developed, especially by British statisticians, Pearson and Yule. In the same period, Pearson developed the chi-square technique and the multiple correlation coefficient. Reliability was measured with the Spearman–Brown Formula. In 1904, Spearman published his analysis of a correlation matrix to sustain his two-factor theory [of intelligence] and factor analysis began to emerge.

Researchers were also aware of the statistical significance of differences. They used rather crude methods indeed, but did not take many chances. Carroll has written:

> Fortunately, American psychologists in the early days, tended to employ such a conservative standard in testing statistical differences (a 'critical ratio' of four times the probable error, corresponding to $p < 0.007$) that

at least it can be said that they only infrequently made 'Type 1 errors'. (Carroll, 1978, p. 20)

In 1908, under the name of Student, Gossett showed how to measure the standard error of the mean and the principle of the *t*-test was formulated.

Experimental design was also used. In 1903, Schuyten used experimental and control groups. In 1916, McCall, a student of Thorndike and probably the first comprehensive theorist of experimentation in education, recommended the setting up of random experimental and control groups. In a research study with Thorndike and Chapman (Thorndike *et al.*, 1916), he applied 2 × 2 and 5 × 5 latin square designs. This was 10 years before the work of R. A. Fisher in England.

The contribution of Sir Ronald Fisher was critical. With the publication of his *Statistical Methods for Research Workers* in 1925, small-sample inferential statistics became known, but were not immediately utilized. In the same work, Fisher reinforced Pearson's chi-square by adding the concept of degrees of freedom, demonstrated the *t*-test, and explained the technique of analysis of variance. In 1935, Fisher crowned his scientific career with his famous *The Design of Experiments*, originally conceived for agriculture, and not widely applied in educational research before the late 1940s.

A look at some of the statistical texts available in the 1920s is often a surprise for today's students: Thorndike (1913), McCall (1922), Otis (1925), Thurstone (1925) in the United States; Yule (1911), Brown and Thomson (1921) in the United Kingdom; Claparède (1911) in Switzerland; Decroly and Buyse (1929) in Belgium had a surprisingly good command of descriptive parametric statistics and also a keen awareness of the need for testing the significance of differences.

Testing and assessment

It has been shown that both mental and achievement tests already existed at the turn of the century. Between 1895 and 1905 tests were administered in schools in the United States, Germany, France, Belgium, and many other countries. Perhaps the critical moment was the appearance in 1905 of Binet and Simon's test, the first valid and operational mental measurement instrument. Group testing began in England in Galton's laboratory in 1905, and Burt and Spearman assisted him. In 1911, the United States National Education Association approved the use of tests for school admission and final examinations. A breakthrough occurred with the development and wide-scale, efficient use of tests by the United States Army, which were quickly constructed in 1917 mostly by drawing upon existing mental tests. Soon after the war, these tests were modified for school use (Carroll, 1978).

The 1918 *Yearbook* of the National Society for the Study of Education was entirely devoted to the measurement of educational products. In 1928, about

1,300 standard tests were available in the United States. By the 1930s, normative-test construction techniques could be considered to be fully developed: item formats, order of items, parallel forms, scoring stencils and machine scoring, norms, reliability, and validity. The psychometric advance of the United States, at that time, was such that standardized tests were often referred to as 'American tests'.

Mental tests were soon used in all industrialized countries. In particular, Binet's scale was used in Europe, North and South America, and Australia, and was tried out in some African countries. This was far from being the case with achievement tests. Some fairly crude tests were used as research instruments but frequently remained unknown to the classroom teacher. It is, for instance, surprising to observe the lack of sophistication of the achievement tests developed in France after Binet and Simon. This continued until the 1940s, and the situation is particularly well-illustrated in the book by Ferré, *Les Tests a l'école*, a fifth edition of which appeared in 1961. It is all the more surprising since in the 1930s traditional examinations (essay and oral tests) were sharply criticized in England and in France where Piéron coined the French word *docimologie*, meaning 'science of examinations'. Lack of validity, of reliability, and sociocultural bias were denounced with documented evidence. In Continental Europe, standardized achievement tests were not extensively used in schools.

Administrative and normative surveys

Among educational research endeavours, surveys are the oldest. In 1817, Marc Antoine Jullien de Paris became the founder of comparative education by designing a 34-page national and international questionnaire covering all aspects of national systems of education. The questions were posed, but unfortunately not answered, at that time.

The modern questionnaire technique was developed by Stanley Hall at the end of the 1800s to show, among other things, that what is obvious for an adult is not necessarily so for a child. This observation has, of course, direct educational implications.

In 1892, Rice visited 36 towns in the United States and interviewed some 1,200 teachers about curriculum content and teaching methods. Subsequently he carried out a spelling survey (1895–1897) on 16,000 pupils and found a low correlation between achievement and time invested in drill. This survey was repeated in 1908 and in 1911 (Rice, 1913). Thorndike's 1907 survey of dropouts was followed by a series of other surveys of school characteristics: differences in curricula, failure rate, teaching staff qualifications, school equipment and the like. The most comprehensive survey of the period was the Cleveland Schools Survey undertaken in 1915–16 by L. P. Ayres and a large team of assistants. The study was reported in 25 volumes each dealing with different aspects of urban life and education.

In Germany, France, Switzerland, and Belgium, similar but smaller surveys were carried out by 'pedotechnical' offices such as that opened in 1906 in the Decroly School in Brussels.

Several large-scale psychological surveys were undertaken: the Berkeley Growth Study (1928), the Fell's Study of Human Development (1929), and the Fourth Harvard Study (1929). In 1932, the Scottish Council for Research in Education carried out its first *Mental Survey* on a whole school population which provided a baseline for later surveys and for determining the representativeness of samples of the population of the same age.

A landmark in the history of experimental education was the *Eight-Year Study* (1933–1941) conducted in the United States by the Progressive Education Association. The initial purpose of the study, which was carried out using survey research methodology, was to examine to what extent the college entrance requirements hampered the reform of the high-school curriculum and to demonstrate the relevance and effectiveness of progressive ideas at the high-school level. In this study students from 30 experimental schools were admitted to college irrespective of subjects they had studied in high school. The by-products of this project were probably more important than the project itself. Tests covering higher cognitive processes and effective outcomes were developed by an evaluation team directed by Ralph Tyler. The careful definition of educational objectives was advanced. In 1950, influenced by the *Eight-Year Study*, Tyler wrote *Basic Principles of Curriculum and Instruction*, in which he presented his model for the definition of objectives. It was followed by Bloom's first taxonomy in 1956 (see *Taxonomies of Educational Objectives*), and this marked the beginning of contemporary thinking on the definition of objectives and on curriculum development and evaluation.

Curriculum development and evaluation

Curriculum was one focus of attention of empirical educational research from its very beginning. The article, in 1900, in which Meumann used the term *'experimentelle Pädagogik'* for the first time dealt with the scientific study of school subjects. Shortly afterwards, Thorndike introduced a radical change in curriculum development by conceptualizing teaching methods in terms of a 'psychology of school branches', and by demonstrating through his work on the transfer of learning the lack of validity of the prevailing theories of formal education, and how it ignored the needs of contemporary society. This psychological approach was perfectly compatible with the new pragmatic philosophy and the attempts to rationalize work and labour. Some years later, Decroly and Buyse hoped to 'taylorize instruction to save time for education'. The psychology of school subjects was also dealt with by other leading scholars such as Judd. But, as far as research on curriculum in the broad sense of the word is concerned, the work of Thorndike on content, teaching methods, and evaluation of material is second to none.

During the same period, the progressive movement, partly inspired by Dewey, remained in close contact with these specific developments, although it soon rejected – as William James had done earlier – a strictly quantitative experimental approach to educational phenomena. According to Thorndike's scientific approach, there could only be one standard curriculum at a given time, the best one that scientific research could produce. Most important to the movement was the rejection of formalism for functionality. The main criteria for curriculum content became individual needs in a new society, as conceived by liberal, middle-class educators of the time.

In 1918, Bobbitt published *Curriculum*, soon to be followed by Charters' *Curriculum Construction* (1923). This led to a series of studies with increasingly strong emphasis on a systematic and operational definition of educational objectives. On the European side, the Belgian *Plan d'études* (1936), written by Jeunehomme, can be considered as a curricular masterpiece, built on contributions of both strict empirical research and the progressive philosophy.

FROM THE 1930s TO THE LATE 1950s

The economic crisis of the 1930s made research funds scarce. The need for a new social order was interpreted differently: fascism in some countries (Germany, Italy, Japan); socialism in others (the *front populaire* in France and Spain). Progressivism, advocated by the New Education movement outside the United States, seemed to be an obvious educational solution in most democratic countries and a guarantee for the future of democracy.

The Second World War and the years immediately following froze most educational research activities in European countries. Freedom of research was (and still is) not acceptable to dictators. In the Soviet Union, the utilization of tests (as incompatible with political decisions) and more generally the 'pedological movement' were officially banned in 1936 by a resolution of the Communist Party, and this situation lasted until Stalin's death. However, other forms of research continued, arising from the publication in 1938 of *Thought and Language* by L. S. Vygotsky four years after his death in 1934, and the subsequent work of his associates such as Luria and Leontief in the development of Pavlov's ideas. In occupied countries, school reorganization was planned by underground movements which tried to draw conclusions from previous experiments and to design educational systems for peace and democracy. The *Plan Langevin–Wallon*, for the introduction of comprehensive secondary education in France is an example.

Conditions were different in the United States, Australia, and in Sweden. Even if no spectacular advances occurred in educational research in those countries, the maturation of ideas went on and prepared the way for the postwar developments. Warfare had again raised problems of recruitment and placement and the role of military psychology and the development of selection tests is exemplified by the work of Guilford in the United States and Husén and Boalt (1968) in Sweden.

The strong field of interest in the 1940s and 1950s was without doubt in sociological studies. The seminal investigations were those concerned with social status and its impact on educational opportunity. A series of studies in the United States showed the pervasive existence of the school's role in maintaining social distinctions and discriminatory practices. From this research it was argued that schools and teachers were the purveyors of middle-class attitudes and habits. These effects of schooling were particularly evident at the high-school stage, and this trend of research became closely linked to the study of adolescent development. This work spread to England in the mid-1950s and subsequently to other parts of the world and led to challenging the maintenance of selective schools and to establishing comprehensive high schools. This research emphasis on issues associated with educational disadvantage has continued subsequently, with concern for disparities in the educational opportunities provided for different racial and ethnic groups, for inner urban and rural groups and, in particular, for girls.

THE 1960s AND 1970s

During the first part of the 1960s in affluent countries educational research enjoyed for the first time in its history the massive support necessary for it to have a significant impact. This development was particularly marked in the United States. At that time money for research and curriculum development, particularly in mathematics and science, was readily available in the United States. In 1954, federal funds were first devoted through the Cooperative Research Act to a programme of research and development in education (Holtzman, 1978). The big, private foundations also began to sponsor educational research on a large scale. The civil rights movement, Kennedy's New Frontier, and Johnson's Great Society continued the trend.

In 1965, the Elementary and Secondary Education Act was passed which authorized funding over a five-year period for constructing and equipping regional research and development (R & D) centres and laboratories. President Johnson implemented developments that had been planned under Kennedy and in 1968, federal support for educational research reached its peak: 21 R & D centres, 20 regional laboratories, 100 graduate training programmes in educational research, and thousands of demonstration projects, represented a total federal investment of close to 200 million dollars per year.

On a much smaller scale, a similar development took place in England. Wall (1968, p. 16) wrote:

> In 1958, it was possible to demonstrate that expenditure of all kinds on research relating to education represented no more than 0.1 per cent of all expenditure on education: in 1967 the proportion may well be thirty times as much and will probably grow over the next decade.

A similar expansion took place in the Soviet Union. Between 1960 and 1970 the professional staff engaged in educational research increased considerably. In 1966, the Soviet Academy of Pedagogical Sciences took on its present status. Initially under the name of the Academy of the Russian Republic it was founded in 1943. In 1967, the *Institut Pédagogique Nationale* of France, for the first time, received significant funding for educational research. Girod de l'Ain (1967) considered 1967 as the Year 1 of educational research in France.

By the late 1960s, all highly industrialized countries were in the midst of a cultural crisis which had a deep impact on scientific epistemology and thus affected the research world. There was also talk about a 'world crisis' (Coombs, 1968) in education which applied in the first place to the imbalance between demand and supply of education, particularly in Third World countries. Deeply disappointed in their hope for general peace, wealth, and happiness, people realized that neither science and technology nor traditional – mostly middle-class – values had solved their problems. An anti-intellectualist counterculture developed, emphasizing freedom in all respects, rejecting strict rationality, glorifying community life. The value of 'traditional' education was questioned. 'Deschooling', nondirectivity, group experience, and participation seemed to many the alpha and omega of all pedagogy. This trend did not leave socialist countries unaffected. In May 1976, a group of researchers in the Soviet Union regretted a too rationalistic approach in educational research (Novikov, 1977).

At the same time, scholars also began to question science, some with great caution and strong argumentation, others superficially in the line of the Zeitgeist. Kerlinger (1977) condemned the latter with ferocity: 'mostly bizarre nonsense, bandwaggon climbing, and guruism, little related to what research is and should be.'

This was not the case in the crucial epistemological debate inspired by scholars like Polanyi, Popper, Kuhn, and Piaget. Fundamentally, the world of learning acknowledged both the contemporary 'explosion' of knowledge and the, still very superficial, comprehension of natural, human phenomena.

While Piaget (1972) showed in his *Epistémologie des sciences de l'homme*, that nomothetic and historical (anthropological) approaches are not mutually exclusive but complementary, in 1974, two of the best-known American educational researchers Cronbach (1974) and Campbell (1974), without previous mutual consultation, chose the annual meeting of the American Psychological Association to react against the traditional positivist emphasis on quantitative methods and stressed the critical importance of alternative methods of inquiry.

Since the 1960s, the computer has become the daily companion of the researcher. For the first time in the history of humankind, the amount and complexity of calculation are no longer a problem. Already existing statistical techniques, like multiple regression analysis, factor analysis, multivariate analysis of variance, that previously were too onerous for desk calculation suddenly became accessible in a few moments. Large-scale research projects became feasible. Simultaneously, new statistical methods and techniques were developed.

Huge surveys, such as Project Talent in the United States and the mathematics and six subject surveys of the International Association for the Evaluation of Educational Achievement (IEA) would have been unthinkable without powerful data processing units. Campbell and Stanley's (1963) presentation of experimental and quasiexperimental design for educational research can be considered to be a landmark.

Scientific developments in the field of educational research were not only stimulated by access to funds and to powerful technology, but also by the 'explosion' of knowledge in the physical and social sciences, especially in psychology, linguistics, economics, and sociology.

Many scientific achievements in the field of education can be mentioned for the 1960s: the new ideas on educational objectives, the new concepts of criterion-referenced testing, formative and summative evaluation, teacher–pupil interaction analysis, research on teacher effectiveness, compensatory education for socioculturally handicapped children, the study of cognitive and affective handicaps, research into the importance and methods of early education, social aspects of learning aptitudes, deschooling experiments, adult education, the development of new curricula and of an empirical methodology of curriculum development and evaluation, and developments in research methodology.
[. . .]

BIBLIOGRAPHY

Binet A 1924 *Les Idées modernes sur les enfants.* Flammarion, Paris

Brown W, Thomson G H 1921 *The Essentials of Mental Measurement.* Cambridge University Press, Cambridge

Campbell D T 1974 Qualitative knowing in action research. Paper, American Psychological Association, Los Angeles, California

Campbell D T, Stanley J C 1963 Experimental and quasi experimental designs for research on teaching. In: Gage N L (ed.) 1963 *Handbook of Research on Teaching.* Rand McNally, Chicago, Illinois, pp. 171–246

Carroll J B 1978 On the theory–practice interface in the measurement of intellectual abilities. In: Suppes P (ed.) 1978 *Impact of Research on Education.* National Academy of Education, Washington, DC

Claparède E 1911 *Psychologie de l'enfant et pédagogie expérimentale,* Vol. 2: *Les Méthodes.* Delachaux and Niestlé, Neuchâtel

Connell W F 1980 *A History of Education in the Twentieth Century World.* Teachers College Press, New York

Coombs P H 1968 *The World Educational Crisis: A Systems Analysis.* Oxford University Press, London

Cronbach L J 1974 Beyond the two disciplines of scientific psychology. Paper, American Psychological Association, Los Angeles, California

Cronbach L, Suppes P (eds.) 1969 *Research for Tomorrow's Schools: Disciplined Inquiry for Education: Report.* Macmillan, New York

Decroly O, Buyse R 1929 *Introduction à la pédagogie quantitative: Eléments de statistiques appliqués aux problèmes pédagogiques.* Lamertin, Brussels

de l'Ain G 1967 L'an I de la recherche pédagogique. *Le Monde* 5th Sept. 1967

De Landsheere G 1982 *La Recherche expérimentale en éducation*. International Bureau of Education, UNESCO, Geneva

Holtzman W H 1978 Social change and the research and development movement. In: Glaser R (ed.) 1978 *Research and Development and School Change*. Erlbaum, Hillsdale, New Jersey, pp. 7–18

Husén T, Boalt G 1968 *Educational Research and Educational Change: The Case of Sweden*. Wiley, New York

Husén G, Kogan M 1983 *Researchers and Policy-Makers in Education*. Pergamon, Oxford

Joncich G 1962 Wither thou, educational scientist? *Teach. Coll. Rec.* 64: 1–12

Kerlinger F N 1977 *The Influence of Research on Educational Practice*. University of Amsterdam, Amsterdam

McCall W A 1922 *How to Measure in Education*. Macmillan, New York

Novikov L 1977 Probleme der Planung und Organisation der pädagogischen Forschung in der Sowjetunion. In: Mitter W, Novikov L (eds.) 1977 *Pädagogische Forschung und Bildungspolitik in der Sowjetunion: Organisation, Gegenstand, Methoden*. Deutsches Institut für Internationale Pädagogische Forschung, Frankfurt/Main

Otis A S 1925 *Statistical Method in Educational Measurement*. World Book, Yonkers-on-Hudson, New York

Papert S 1972 Teaching children thinking. *Program. Learn. Educ. Technol.* 9: 245–55

Piaget J 1972 *Epistémologie des sciences de l'homme*. Gallimard, Paris

Rice J M 1913 *Scientific Management in Education*. Hinds, Noble and Eldredge, New York

Simon T 1924 *Pédagogie expérimentale: Ecriture, lecture, orthographe*. Colin, Paris

Thorndike E L 1913 *An Introduction to the Theory of Mental and Social Measurements*, 2nd edn. Teachers College Press, New York

Thorndike E L, McCall W A, Chapman J C 1916 *Ventilation in Relation to Mental Work*. Teachers College Press, New York

Thurstone L L 1925 *The Fundamentals of Statistics*. Macmillan, New York

Wall W D 1968 The work of the National Foundation for Educational Research in England and Wales. In: Butcher H J (ed.) 1968 *Educational Research in Britain*. University of London Press, London, pp. 15–32

Yule G U 1911 *An Introduction to the Theory of Statistics*. Griffin, London

2

QUALITATIVE RESEARCH TRADITIONS

P. Atkinson, S. Delamont and M. Hammersley

[...]

There are several published accounts of British qualitative research in education.[1] Here we recapitulate some major landmarks in the development of British school and classroom research [...], focusing on the different social networks that were instrumental in establishing qualitative educational methods in academic life.

Qualitative research on education developed in Britain in the late 1960s and early 1970s. This was facilitated by the expansion of the university and college sectors at a time when there was widespread questioning of educational and other orthodoxies. Among the substantial number of new scholars in the field, there was a reaction against the theoretical and methodological approaches that had previously been dominant – notably psychometrics, systematic observation, survey research, and structural functionalism. Nonstandard forms of sociology and psychology were drawn on, notably symbolic interactionism and phenomenology, as well as social and cultural anthropology. Approaches to educational research were developed which refused to take conventional educational wisdom for granted and set out to explore what happens in schools from the point of view of the participants.

One early example of this development was an initiative in the combined sociology and social anthropology department at the University of Manchester to apply anthropological methods to the study of British institutions. Two main programs of research were set up, one focusing on factory life, the other concerned with schools. It was from this latter program that the studies of D. H. Hargreaves (1967), Lacey (1970), and Lambart (1976, 1982) emerged.

Following the Manchester studies of the 1960s, there were groups of researchers using different approaches in London and several provincial centers. Edinburgh produced a generation of symbolic interactionists (see Atkinson,

1981a, 1984; Delamont, 1984a, 1984b; Hudson, 1977; Stubbs & Delamont, 1976; Wragg, 1975). A parallel group of symbolic interactionists flourished at the Open University (Hammersley & Woods, 1984, and A. Hargreaves & Woods, 1984, are edited collections from this group). At Birmingham a group of sociolinguists focused on classroom discourse (Coulthard & Montgomery, 1981, is a useful source for this school). Oxford produced research drawing on Harré and Secord's (1972) ethnogenics (see Harré, 1979; Marsh, Rosser, & Harré, 1978; Morgan, O'Neill, & Harré, 1979; Sluckin, 1981). Norwich's Centre for Applied Research in Education, and others, pioneered qualitative methods of evaluation and the idea of the reflective teacher researching her own classroom. (See Stenhouse, 1975; Hamilton *et al.*, 1977; Simons, 1987.) The London-based researchers blended symbolic interactionism, phenomenology, and Marxism into studies of social control and the curriculum (see Gorbutt, 1972; Sharp and Green, 1975; Young, 1971). [. . .]

TYPES OF QUALITATIVE RESEARCH

In this section we sketch seven approaches that have been used in British educational research: symbolic interactionism, anthropology, sociolinguistics, ethnomethodology, qualitative evaluation, neo-Marxist ethnography, and feminism. [. . .] Much British qualitative research combines elements of different types.

Symbolic interactionism

This approach has not enjoyed quite the same status as a school of thought in its own right in Britain as in America, and few British scholars would profess to be symbolic interactionists in any pure sense. Nonetheless, a very great deal of the qualitative research on education in Britain has been influenced by it. Although the Manchester school were not originally working in the symbolic interactionist tradition, D. H. Hargreaves's (1967) empirical research and his theoretical/methodological reflections increasingly incorporated interactionist ideas (Hargreaves, 1972; Hargreaves, Hestor & Mellors, 1975). Indeed, Hargreaves became an articulate advocate of interactionisms's claims, against some of the uninformed criticisms leveled against it in Britain (Hargreaves, 1978). Lacey's work too came to take on a more overtly interactionist stance (Lacey, 1977). Some members of the Edinburgh group moved to adopt a more consistently and explicitly symbolic interactionist set of perspectives (Delamont, 1983; Stubbs & Delamont, 1976). This group carried out fieldwork in a variety of educational settings: in an elite girls' school (Delamont, 1984a), among medical students (Atkinson, 1981a; Reid, 1982), in a working-class secondary school (Torode, 1976, 1984), on transfer from primary to secondary school (Nash, 1973), on secondary science teaching (Hamilton, 1976), among law students (Miller & Parlett, 1976), and among engineering students (Sheldrake & Berry, 1975).

The Open University (1971, 1977) provided another institutional base where symbolic interactionist thought was developed and disseminated. Hammersley (1974, 1976, 1977, 1980b, 1983, 1984, 1987) brought perspectives developed in the Manchester department, whereas Woods (1979, 1980a, 1980b, 1983, 1985) became one of the most single-minded of symbolic interactionists in Britain. The research focused on teachers' classroom strategies (Scarth, 1987) and pupils' adaptations to school (Woods, 1979), on patterns of classroom interaction (Hammersley, 1974, 1976, 1977), on pupils' perspectives and classroom behavior (Hammersley & Turner, 1980; Turner, 1983), on transfer between schools (Measor & Woods, 1984), on teachers' life histories (Sikes, Measor & Woods, 1985), and on the impact of public examinations on classroom teaching (Hammersley, Scarth & Webb, 1985; Scarth & Hammersley, 1988). A. Hargreaves (1978, 1979, 1980, 1986), working in a similar vein, has written on teachers' coping strategies using data drawn from middle schools. And Pollard (1979, 1980, 1982; Pollard & Woods, 1988) sought to develop the work on teacher and pupil strategies into an integrated model.

At Sussex, Ball (1981) followed Hargreaves, Lacey, and Lambart in an investigation of school organization and the genesis of pupil subcultures. Ball began with an explicit awareness of interactionist sociology and also contributed to its general methodological and theoretical perspectives (see Ball, 1987).

The backgrounds of symbolic interactionism and social anthropology which informed many of the early studies of schools and classrooms in Britain made for a high degree of explicit reflection and sophistication concerning methodology. Two of the most successful textbooks on ethnographic fieldwork published in Britain are by authors whose empirical research includes educational settings (Burgess, 1984a; Hammersley & Atkinson, 1983). Burgess has done much to document qualitative research methods in British studies of educational processes. The reader is referred to the series of autobiographical accounts by leading researchers under the editorship of Burgess (1984b, 1985a, 1985b, 1985c) and to his other collection of methodological papers (Burgess, 1982).

There is a characteristically British flavor imparted to the North American style of interactionism. First, studies of everyday life in schools and classrooms have consistently treated the teacher as a 'worker' faced with repeated problems of 'coping' and 'surviving' under trying circumstances. This represents a subtle but significant difference from much American writing, which has placed greater emphasis on the role of the teacher as representative of 'mainstream' culture, contrasted with local, regional or ethnic subcultures of student groups. British interactionists have thus frequently portrayed the classroom as a site of actual or potential conflict, in which the participants engage in strategic interaction. Teachers and pupils are locked in a competitive struggle for legitimacy and control. Classic interactionist concepts such as 'the definition of the situation', 'perspectives', and the like are deployed to depict situations of conflict and their resolution (or otherwise). Although accused by some critics of failing to do so, many British scholars who draw on interactionist theory and imagery have located their work in the context of broader social divisions within British society. It is entirely in keeping with respective sets of national preoccupations that North American scholars should more frequently represent a situation of cultural pluralism, while their British counterparts represent local manifestations of class conflict.[2]

Anthropology

Jacob (1987) discusses two American traditions – called holistic ethnography and cognitive anthropology – whose adherents (such as Spradley, 1979; Wolcott, 1967) are contrasted in her account. Both types of anthropologists, however, are grounded in American cultural anthropology. British social anthropology is rather different from American cultural anthropology, as the semiautobiographical essay by Leach (1984) makes clear. Landman (1978) has demonstrated that one difference is Britain's lack of applied anthropology. The US has a strong society for applied anthropology (the SfAA) and the Council on Anthropology and Education, who publish *Anthropology and Education Quarterly*. Britain has a tiny interest group (Group for Anthropology in Policy and Practice) and no journal. Although some British educational researchers have degrees in anthropology, there are very few studies that actually deploy anthropological concepts in the study of schools. Maryon McDonald (1987), who has studied education in Brittany, is a notable exception to this generalization. For a range of reasons (discussed in Atkinson & Delamont, 1980), the theoretical and analytic concerns of British social anthropology have rarely been deployed on UK society (but see Cohen, 1982, 1986) and have been utilized even more rarely to focus on educational processes. Not only have the theories and methods of anthropology not been applied to British education, but the substantive issues that have preoccupied American anthropology of education have also been neglected in Britain. It is particularly striking that, although Britain is a multilingual, multiracial, and multicultural society, this has not been noticeable in the anthropological research literature.

Little anthropological work has explicitly addressed the educational experiences and 'problems' of Britain's minority linguistic and/or ethnic groups. There are few ethnographies of Welsh- or Gaelic-speaking pupils or of British Cypriot, Maltese, Afro-Caribbean, African, Indian, or Bangladeshi children in schools. A few studies do exist (Driver, 1979; Fuller, 1980; Furlong, 1984; Wright, 1986) but nothing to parallel the American focus on its minority cultures, as revealed in the extensive bibliography by Wilcox (1982). Also, there has been no significant British ethnography of rural schooling, which, in the American style (e.g., Messerschmidt, 1982; Peshkin, 1978), might investigate the school in the context of its 'community' setting. Nash (1977) is the only British ethnography of Welsh village schools, and Hamilton (1974) of Scottish ones. American educational anthropology has always included studies of

Amerindians, Inuit, and other ethnic and linguistic minorities – often in remote areas – and emphasizes the culture clash between the home and the teacher.

Jacob's (1987) discussion of holistic ethnography completely misses the central uniting theme of American applied anthropology in the school: the 'culture clash'. Although the data have been collected in a range of apparently diverse settings, from the school in a remote Kwakiutl village on the northwest Pacific coast (Wolcott, 1967) to one catering to Puerto Rican adolescents in Chicago (Burnett, 1973), what unites so much of the apparently diverse research is a consistent preoccupation with issues of cultural variation and culture clash. This theme of much American educational writing predominates in the analyses of the role of the teacher. The American ethnographies have common features: they serve to document one of two things. Either they celebrate the cultural uniqueness of the researcher's chosen setting or they go on to stress the 'clash' between the pupils' culture(s) and that of the school, that is, a culture representative of white, urban, middle-class America. The school, therefore, is portrayed (implicitly or explicitly) as an arena where the diverse cultural backgrounds and assumptions of teachers and taught, of school and community, impinge on one another and conflict (e.g., Grobsmith, 1981; Kleinfeld, 1979). The British research is very different. Clashes between teacher and pupil are typically seen in class terms, and the teacher is often portrayed as a worker coping rather than an agent of cultural imperialism. What Jacob (1987) terms 'holistic ethnography' and cognitive anthropology have no direct counterparts in British educational research. [. . .]

Sociolinguistics

This type of research has contributed, in a variety of ways, to the qualitative analysis of educational processes in Britain. Jacob (1987) includes 'ethnography of communication' as one of her traditions. The British work closest to the studies she cites is generally termed sociolinguistic. Early work was conducted at Birmingham by discourse analysts and scholars in English, and in recent years the analysis of classroom discourse has been of major importance. Stubbs (1983), an early figure in the field, argued for systematic descriptive research on spoken interaction in classroom life. Since then, a substantial literature, most recently reviewed by Edwards and Westgate (1987), has been produced. There are many affinities with North American work, although the theoretical background (including Halliday's linguistic theories) and the evaluative implications have distinctively British emphases.

Sinclair and Coulthard (1975) sought to develop a systemic analysis of discourse in school classrooms, and in other settings such as meetings and medical consultations. The choice of classrooms derived from a desire to identify social occasions where communicative roles were clearly defined and differentiated. Their 'coding' of classroom talk was aimed at an exhaustive description of discursive functions; the model was derived from Halliday's linguistics and was couched in terms of inclusive 'ranks' comprising 'acts', 'moves', 'exchanges', and 'transactions' within the lesson. The emphasis on the intrinsic organization of discourse was a considerable advance over the ad hoc treatment of language advocated and practiced by 'interaction analysts' (for examples, see Burton, 1976; Coulthard, 1974; Coulthard & Ashby, 1976; Sinclair & Coulthard, 1975).

The Birmingham group's interest in educational linguistics was strengthened when Stubbs joined them from Edinburgh, but their overall program continued to have a broader empirical scope (see, e.g., Burton, 1980; Coulthard & Montgomery, 1981). Stubbs (1986) has continued to develop the approach within an educational context. The complexities of rules of discourse among children in the early years of schooling are documented by Willes (1981a, 1981b, 1983), who stresses the fact that young pupils are not explicitly introduced to those rules. Burton (1976) also applies the discourse-analysis model to primary school classrooms in England.

Other, usually less formal, studies of classroom talk were undertaken by observers whose background was in English teaching. They combined interests in improving pedagogy with an insightful, if at times rather impressionistic, evaluation of classroom language. They were among the first in Britain to draw attention to the control and transmission of knowledge implicit in teaching talk (Barnes, 1976; Barnes, Britton, & Rosen, 1969). And Barnes and his collaborators developed a systematic analytic framework (e.g., Barnes & Todd, 1977, 1981), based on types of 'frame' analysis, in an attempt to capture the multiple functions of utterances. Their work includes research on spoken interaction in small groups of pupils (Barnes & Barnes, 1984).

Wells and his research team at Bristol developed a highly detailed analysis of children's talk in the home and in the classroom (e.g., Wells, 1977, 1978, 1979, 1981a, 1981b, 1985; Wells & Montgomery, 1981; Wells & Wells, 1984). The data consist of taped, naturally occurring interactions. The data base and its linguistic analysis are superior to most North American studies: it contrasts, for example, with Heath's (1984) generalized ethnographic accounts of black and white language uses, another example of American concern with culture clash/ethnicity. Wells's work concentrates on the role of children as conversationalists and stresses the extent to which talk between teachers and pupils is limited and impoverished in comparison with talk in the home. The research seriously questions any model that proposes the school as an enriching environment contrasted with 'deficient' home settings. Many of the discourse analysts share a view that the restricted routines of classroom talk embody and enact unduly rigid pedagogy and control of classroom knowledge.

Ethnomethodology

There is a close affinity between the approach of discourse analysis and that of the ethnomethodologists. Ethnomethodology in general has found a small but significant number of practitioners in Britain, and educational settings have figured in their empirical investigations. British observers have used conversation-analytic insights to model classrooms as speech-exchange systems. They were among the first to embrace ethnomethodological inspirations – sometimes in the context of ethnomethodologically informed ethnographies and sometimes in more 'purist' forms. The British use of conversation analysis reflects a greater commitment to apply it to sociologically 'interesting' cases than was embraced by early ethnomethodologists in North America (see Atkinson, 1988, for a more detailed discussion of ethnomethodological theories, methods, and products).

Manchester has been a center for ethnomethodology in Britain. Payne (1976) emphasized the extent to which a classroom lesson is the accomplishment of its participants, with special reference to the management of its commencement and its subsequent stepwise, turn-by-turn achievement. Payne and Hustler (1980) commented on how teachers deploy the conventions of classroom talk to manage 'the class' as a cohort or collectivity, whereas Payne (1982) wrote about the incorporation of class members into the cohort. The ethnomethodologically informed approach, in common with discourse analysis, stresses the asymmetry in classroom speech exchanges, and views the characteristic pattern of events as the enactment of 'control' in the setting (cf. Atkinson, 1981b). Payne and Cuff (1982) and their contributors recommend the ethnomethodological approach to facilitate teachers' own analysis of their classroom practices and so contribute to the 'teacher as researcher' trend in qualitative research.

The analysis of turns at talk in school classrooms displays the elementary structural significance of interrogatory teacher-pupil exchanges. Further, it has drawn attention to the degree to which pupils have to work at the interpretation of teachers' questions if acceptable and appropriate answers are to be produced (Edwards & Mercer, 1987; French & MacLure, 1979, 1981; Hammersley, 1977; D. H. Hargreaves, 1984; MacLure & French, 1980; Mercer & Edwards, 1981). Conversation analytic and complementary perspectives again stress the interactional management of classroom knowledge.

Illuminative, democratic and other forms of evaluation

One of the earliest strands in the development of new approaches to the study of education came from the emerging discipline of curriculum evaluation. In the 1960s, the US tradition of quantitative evaluation, characterized for example by the work of Ralph Tyler (1949), had been imported into Britain to meet the increasing demands for evaluations arising from new curricular initiatives. By the end of the 1960s, however, this approach was being subjected to sharp critique, and qualitative alternatives were being developed. A significant event here was the publication of Parlett and Hamilton's proposal for illuminative evaluation, drawing on the ethnographic methods characteristic of social anthropology (Parlett and Hamilton, 1972). Also important was work carried out at the Center for Applied Research in Education at the University of East Anglia. This too showed a preference for qualitative method and, indeed, a willingness to explore a variety of such techniques. Early in their careers, Walker and Adelman (1976) had used stop-frame cinematography and slides accompanied by audiorecordings; later there was use of informant accounts to develop a taxonomy of teaching styles and the use of fictional accounts to highlight key aspects of teachers' experience (Walker, 1983). Throughout, the aim has been to provide teachers with images of their work and its context that will allow them to generate reflections on, and thereby develop, their own practice. In effect, it was the teacher who was to be as much the researcher as the evaluator; and the notion of 'teacher as researcher' has been at the heart of more recent developments at CARE and elsewhere (Stenhouse, 1975; Payne and Cuff, 1982; Hustler, Cassidy, & Cuff, 1986). Many came to the conclusion that the improvement of education would arise not from the introduction of better curriculum schemes but rather from teachers' own development of their craft knowledge, through reflection on their practices. And qualitative methods were chosen because they were believed to be best suited to facilitate this process.[3] A parallel development was democratic evaluation, pursued most notably by MacDonald and Simons (MacDonald, 1974; Simons, 1987: see also Norris, 1991; Elliott, 1986). Here too there was a primary reliance on qualitative methods, but the role of the external evaluator was retained; although it was conceptualized differently to the model implicit in older forms of evaluation. The aim of democratic evaluation is to supply information responsive to the needs of all those involved in what is being evaluated. Open access to information about policies and their implementation is seen as essential to a democratic society.

Neo-Marxist ethnography

One of the main institutional locations for the development of qualitative research in the early 1970s, as we noted earlier, was the London Institute of Education. *Knowledge and Control*, edited by M.F.D. Young (1971), was the first published product of the new movement and was very influential throughout Britain and abroad. Implicit in the Institute approach was a commitment to radical schooling, not just to progressivism but to forms of schooling that would incarnate a new form of society in which human freedom would be realized. In this way they shared much in common with contemporary radical movements among teachers and pupils. The link was also clear with forms of neo-Marxism that emphasized the writings of the young Marx on alienation and voluntarism (see, e.g., Sarup, 1978). The writings of the Institute members were eclectic, however, drawing on a wide range of sources.

One of the most widely cited articles coming from the London Institute was a study by Keddie (1971) of the perspectives and practices of progressive humanities teachers in a large secondary school. She argued that despite their commitment to treating pupils in individualized terms and their opposition to ability grouping, these teachers nonetheless judged pupils in terms of an academic ideal and according to their membership of different ability groups. Furthermore, their classroom teaching was transmission oriented so that in order to 'learn' pupils had to adopt the perspective of the teacher. It was the top band pupils who conformed in this way and who were regarded by the teachers as closest to their conception of the ideal pupil. The lower band pupils challenged the teachers' perspectives, and were accordingly declared unintelligent.

In the early period, the Institute researchers tended to stress voluntarism, though the presence of constraints was recognized. Later, much more emphasis came to be placed on the constraints operating on teachers that prevented them from adopting radical practices. Sharp and Green (1975) examined the work of teachers in a progressive primary school and came to focus on the way in which a variety of material and ideological constraints prevented teaching in this setting taking a radical form. Indeed, it was suggested that in some ways progressivism served the interests of capitalism even more effectively than more traditional forms of education, an argument also to be found in Bernstein (1974; see also Atkinson, 1985). A parallel piece of research focused on the attempts of secondary school teachers to get radical examination proposals through examination boards and on how the latter effectively served to pre-serve the continuation of traditional practices at the secondary level (Bowe & Whitty, 1983; Whitty, 1974, 1976).

By the mid-1970s, the influence of the Institute had spread throughout Britain, and studies of a similar kind, inspired by that influence and deriving from similar developments in other areas of sociology, began to appear. Most notable here was Willis's *Learning to Labour* (1977) about 12 'lads' in a secondary modern. Willis argued that these pupils developed a counterculture to the school that was founded on the working-class culture experienced by their fathers on the factory floor. This school counterculture was not, however, a simple derivation from shop-floor culture; it was a creative response by the 'lads' to their experiences at school. Willis argued that, whereas in some respects this counterculture 'pene-trated' to the reality of British capitalist society, in others it was distorted by ideology. Moreover, its effect was, ironically, to prepare the lads for factory work rather than to lead them to challenge society. Willis did not believe this to be a necessary effect of the counterculture, however, and proposed that radical pedagogy should be concerned with developing the insights implicit in the coun-terculture into a radical challenge to capitalism. (For a more recent study in much the same vein, focusing on male and female students in college, see Ag-gleton, 1987, and Aggleton & Whitty, 1985.)

Feminist research

There is a 'tradition' of British studies using qualitative methods that draw their inspiration from feminism, rather than any social scientific discipline or method. There are two positions adopted by extreme exponents of this approach: that qualitative research is better done by women because of their socialization as empathetic, sympathetic 'good listeners' (Oakley, 1981) and/or that quantitative methods and the ideal of objective, value-free social science are part of patriarchal dominance and must therefore be 'resisted' by female researchers and women under investigation (Roberts, 1981). Many researchers reject both of these exaggerated claims, but there has been a clearly defined group of women researchers influenced by feminism using qualitative methods to study girls and women and concerned to allow their respondents to 'speak for themselves'.

A commitment to hearing women's voices fits neatly with a research approach that explores and presents the actors' perspectives and strategies in their own terms. Arguments of this kind can be found in Roberts (1981) and in Bowles and Duelli-Klein (1983)-edited collections of papers on feminist research including educational studies – and Stanley and Wise (1983). Clarricoates (1980, 1987) examines gender divisions in elementary schools in the North of England showing that schools with working-class pupils enforced different gender roles from those with middle-class intakes. Several researchers have focused on adolescent girls, including McRobbie and Garber (1976), Fuller (1980), Stanworth (1983), Davies (1984), Griffin (1985), and Lees (1986).

CONCLUSION

In this paper, we have explored the diverse origins and development of British qualitative research on education. In our view this research cannot usefully be portrayed in terms of distinct, internally correct traditions, in the way that Jacob (1978 and 1988) presents American qualitative work. However, we identified seven different types of approach associated with particular groups of researchers. All of these persist today, though there continues to be much cross-fertilization and internal innovation.

NOTES

1. Hammersley (1980a, 1982), Woods (1983, 1985), Burgess (1985), Delamont (1981, 1983), Delamont and Galton (1986), and Delamont and Hamilton (1984).
2. An unfortunate consequence in the British context is that, with some specific exceptions, the study of ethnic differences has not figured prominently in the British literature. Certainly, it is sparse in comparison with the American corpus.
3. For a critique, see Atkinson and Delamont (1985).

REFERENCES

Aggleton, P. (1987). *Rebels without a cause*. London: Falmer.
Aggleton, P., & Whitty, G. (1985). Rebels without a cause? Socialisation and subcultural style among the children of the new middle class. *Sociology of Education* 58(1), 60–72.

Atkinson, P. (1981a). *The clinical experience.* Aldershot, England: Gower.

Atkinson, P. A. (1981b). Inspecting classroom talk. In C. Adelman (Ed.), *Uttering, muttering* (pp. 98–113). London: Grant McIntyre.

Atkinson, P. A. (1984). Wards and deeds. In R. G. Burgess (Ed.), *The research process in educational settings* (pp. 163–186). London: Falmer.

Atkinson, P. A. (1985). *Language, structure and reproduction.* London: Methuen.

Atkinson, P. A. (1988). Ethnomethodology: A critical review. *Annual Review of Sociology, 14,* 441–465.

Atkinson, P. A., & Delamont, S. (1980). The two traditions in educational ethnography. *British Journal of Sociology of Education, 1*(2), 139–152.

Atkinson, P. A., & Delamont, S. (1985). Bread and dreams or bread and circuses? A critique of 'case study' research in education. In M. Shipman (Ed.), *Educational research* (pp. 26–45). London: Falmer. (Reprinted in M. Hammersley (Ed.), *Controversies in classroom research* (pp. 238–255). Milton Keynes, England: Open University Press, 1986).

Ball, S. (1981). *Beachside comprehensive.* Cambridge, England: Cambridge University Press.

Ball, S. (1987). *The micropolitics of the school.* London: Methuen.

Barnes, D. (1976). *From communication to curriculum.* Harmondsworth, England: Penguin.

Barnes, D., & Barnes, D. (1984). *Versions of English.* London: Heinemann.

Barnes, D., Britton, J., & Rosen, H. (1969). *Language, the learner and the school.* Harmondsworth, England: Penguin.

Barnes, D., & Todd, F. (1977). *Communication and learning in small groups.* London: Routledge and Kegan Paul.

Barnes, D., & Todd, F. (1981). Talk in small learning groups. In C. Adelman (Ed.), *Uttering, muttering* (pp. 69–77). London: Grant McIntyre.

Bernstein, B. (1974). *Class, codes and control* (Vol. 3). London: Routledge and Kegan Paul.

Bowe, R., & Whitty, G. (1983). A question of content and control: recent conflicts over the nature of school examinations at 16+. In M. Hammersley & A. Hargreaves (Eds.), *Curriculum practice: some sociological case studies* (pp. 229–250). London: Falmer.

Bowles, G., & Duelli-Klein, R. (Ed.) (1983). *Theories of women's studies.* London: Routledge and Kegan Paul.

Burgess, R. G. (Ed.) (1982). *Field research: a sourcebook and a field manual.* London: Allen and Unwin.

Burgess, R. G. (1984a). *In the field.* London: Allen and Unwin.

Burgess, R. G. (Ed.) (1984b). *The research process in educational settings: ten case studies.* London: Falmer.

Burgess, R. G. (Ed.) (1985a). *Field methods in the study of education.* London: Falmer.

Burgess, R. G. (Ed.) (1985b). *Strategies of educational research.* London: Falmer.

Burgess, R. G. (Ed.) (1985c). *Issues in educational research.* London: Falmer.

Burgess, R. G. (1985). *Sociology, schools and education.* London: Batsford.

Burnett, J. H. (1973). Event description and analysis in the microethnography of urban classrooms. In F.A.J. Ianni & E. Storey (Eds.), *Cultural relevance and educational issues* (pp. 288–298). Boston: Little, Brown.

Burton, D. (1976). I think they know that. *Nottingham Linguistics Circular, 5*(1), 22–34.

Burton, D. (1980). *Dialogue and discourse.* London: Routledge and Kegan Paul.

Clarricoates, K. (1980). The importance of being Ernest, Emma, Tom, Jane. In R. Deem (Ed.), *Schooling for women's work* (pp. 26–41). London: Routledge and Kegan Paul.

Clarricoates, K. (1987). Child culture at school: a clash between gendered worlds? In A. Pollard (Ed.), *Children and their primary schools* (pp. 188–206). London: Falmer.

Cohen, A. P. (1982). *Belonging: identity and social organisation in British rural cultures*. Manchester, England: Manchester University Press.

Cohen, A. P. (1986). *Symbolising boundaries: identity and diversity in British cultures*. Manchester, England: Manchester University Press.

Coulthard, M. (1974). Approaches to the analysis of classroom interaction. *Educational Review, 22* (1), 38–50.

Coulthard, M., & Ashby, M. (1976). A linguistic description of doctor-patient interviews. In M. Wadsworth & D. Robinson (Eds.), *Studies in everyday medical life* (pp. 69–88). London: Martin Robertson.

Coulthard, M., & Montgomery, M. (Eds.) (1981). *Studies in discourse analysis*. London: Routledge and Kegan Paul.

Davies, L. (1984). *Pupil power: deviance and gender in school*. London and Philadelphia: Falmer.

Delamont, S. (1981). All too familiar? A decade of classroom research. *Educational Analysis, 3*(1), 69–83.

Delamont, S. (1983). *Interaction in the classroom* (2nd ed.). London: Methuen.

Delamont, S. (1984a). The old girl network. In R. G. Burgess (Ed.), *The research process in educational settings* (pp. 15–38). London: Falmer.

Delamont, S. (1984b). Lessons from St Luke's. In W. B. Dockrell (Ed.), *An attitude of mind* (pp. 30–41). Edinburgh: Scottish Council for Research in Education.

Delamont, S., & Galton, M. (1986). *Inside the secondary classroom*. London: Routledge and Kegan Paul.

Delamont, S., & Hamilton, D. (1984). Revisiting classroom research. In S. Delamont (Ed.), *Readings on interaction in the classroom* (pp. 3–38). London: Methuen.

Driver, G. (1979). Classroom stress and achievement. In V. S. Khan (Ed.), *Minority families in Britain* (pp. 131–146). London: Macmillan.

Edwards, D., & Mercer, N. (1987). *Common knowledge: the development of understanding in the classroom*. London: Methuen.

Edwards, A. D., & Westgate, D. (1987). *Investigating classroom talk*. London: Falmer.

Elliott, J. (1986). Democratic evaluation as social criticism: or putting the judgement back into evaluation. In M. Hammersley (Ed.), *Controversies in classroom research* (pp. 228–237). Milton Keynes, England: Open University Press. (First edition).

French, P., & MacLure, M. (1979). Getting the right answer and getting the answer right. *Research in Education, 22*(1), 1–23.

French, P., & MacLure, M. (Eds.) (1981). *Adult-child conversation*. London: Croom Helm.

Fuller, M. (1980). Black girls in a London comprehensive. In R. Deem (Ed.), *Schooling for women's work* (pp. 52–65) London: Routledge.

Furlong, V. J. (1984). Black resistance in the liberal comprehensive. In S. Delamont (Ed.), *Readings on interaction in the classroom* (pp. 212–236). London: Methuen.

Gorbutt, D. (1972). The new sociology of education. *Education for Teaching, 8/9*, 3–11.

Griffin, C. (1985). *Typical girls?* London: Routledge and Kegan Paul.

Grobsmith, E. (1981). *Lakota of the Rosebud*. New York: Holt, Rinehart and Winston.

Hamilton, D. (1974). *The fieldwork: Project PHI reports*. Glasgow, Scotland: University of Glasgow, Education Department.

Hamilton, D. (1976). The advent of curriculum integration. In M. Stubbs & S. Delamont (Eds.), *Explorations in classroom research* (pp. 195–213). Chichester, England: Wiley.

Hamilton, D., Jenkins, D., King, C., MacDonald, B., & Parlett, M. (Eds.) (1977). *Beyond the numbers game*. London: Macmillan.

Hammersley, M. (1974). The organization of pupil participation. *Sociological Review, 22*(3), 355–68.

Hammersley, M. (1976). The mobilisation of pupil attention. In M. Hammersley & P. Woods (Eds.), *The process of schooling* (pp. 104–115). London: Routledge and Kegan Paul.

Hammersley, M. (1977). School learning: The cultural resources required to answer a teacher's question. In P. Woods & M. Hammersley (Eds.), *School experience* (pp. 58–86). London: Croom Helm.

Hammersley, M. (1980a). Classroom ethnography. *Educational Analysis, 2*(2), 47–74.

Hammersley, M. (1980b). On interactionist empiricism. In P. Woods (Ed.), *Pupil strategies* (pp. 198–213). London: Croom Helm.

Hammersley, M. (1982). The sociology of classrooms. In A. Hartnett (Ed.), *The social sciences in educational studies* (pp. 227–242). London: Heinemann.

Hammersley, M. (1983). *The ethnography of schooling*. Driffield, England: Nafferton.

Hammersley, M. (1984). The paradigmatic mentality: a diagnosis. In L. Barton & S. Walker (Eds.), *Social crisis and educational research* (pp. 230–255). London: Croom Helm.

Hammersley, M. (1987). Heap & Delamont on transmission and British ethnography of schooling. *Curriculum Inquiry, 17*(2), 235–237.

Hammersley, M., & Atkinson, P. (1983). *Ethnography: principles in practice*. London: Tavistock.

Hammersley, M., Scarth, J., & Webb, S. (1985). Developing and testing theory. In R. G. Burgess (Ed.), *Issues in classroom research* (pp. 48–66). London: Falmer.

Hammersley, M., & Turner, G. (1980). Conformist pupils? In P. Woods (Ed.), *Pupil strategies* (pp. 29–49). London: Croom Helm.

Hammersley, M., & Woods, P. (Eds.) (1976). *The process of schooling*. London: Routledge.

Hammersley, M., & Woods, P. (Eds.) (1984). *Life in school*. Milton Keynes, England: Open University Press.

Hargreaves, A. (1978). Towards a theory of classroom coping strategies. In L. Barton & R. Meighan (Eds.), *Sociological interpretations of schooling and classrooms* (pp. 73–100). Driffield, England: Nafferton.

Hargreaves, A. (1979). Strategies, decisions and control. In S. J. Eggleston (Ed.), *Teacher decision-making in the classroom* (pp. 134–169). London: Routledge.

Hargreaves, A. (1980). Synthesis and the study of strategies. In P. Woods (Ed.), *Pupil strategies* (pp. 162–197). London: Croom Helm.

Hargreaves, A. (1986). *Two cultures of schooling*. London: Falmer.

Hargreaves, A., & Woods, P. (Eds.) (1984). *Classrooms and staffrooms*. Milton Keynes, England: Open University Press.

Hargreaves, D. H. (1967). *Social relations in a secondary school*. London: Routledge and Kegan Paul.

Hargreaves, D. H. (1972). *Interpersonal relations and education*. London: Routledge.

Hargreaves, D. H. (1978). Whatever happened to symbolic interactionism? In L. Barton & R. Meighan (Eds.), *Sociological interpretations of schooling and classrooms* (pp. 7–22). Driffield, England: Nafferton.

Hargreaves, D. H. (1984). Teachers' questions: open, closed and half-open. *Educational Research, 26*(1), 46–52.

Hargreaves, D. H., Hester, S., & Mellor, S. (1975). *Deviance in classrooms*. London: Routledge.

Harré, R. (1979). *Social being*. Oxford, England: Blackwell.

Harré, R., & Secord, P. (1972). *The explanation of social behaviour*. Oxford, England: Blackwell.

Heath, S. B. (1984). *Ways with words*. Cambridge, England: Cambridge University Press.

Hudson, L. (1977). Picking winners: a case study of the recruitment of research students. *New Universities Quarterly, 32*(1), 88–106.

Hustler, D., Cassidy, T., & Cuff, T. (Eds.) (1986). *Action research in classrooms and schools*. London: Allen and Unwin.

Jacob, E. (1987). Qualitative research traditions: a review. *Review of Educational Research, 57*(1), 1–50.

Jacob, E. (1988). Clarifying qualitative research. A focus on traditions. *Educational Researcher, 17*(1), 16–24.

Keddie, N. (1971). Classroom knowledge. In M.F.D. Young (Ed.), *Knowledge and control* (pp. 133–160). London: Collier-Macmillan.

Kleinfeld, J. S. (1979). *Eskimo school on the Andreafsky.* New York: Praeger.

Lacey, C. (1970). *Hightown Grammar.* Manchester, England: Manchester University Press.

Lacey, C. (1977). *The socialisation of teachers.* London: Methuen.

Lambart, A. (1976). The sisterhood. In M. Hammersley & P. Woods (Eds.), *The process of schooling* (pp. 152–159). London: Routledge and Kegan Paul.

Lambart, A. (1982). Expulsion in context. In R. Frankenberg (Ed.), *Custom and conflict in British society* (pp. 188–208). Manchester, England: Manchester University Press.

Landman, R. H. (1978). Applied anthropology in post-colonial Britain. *Human Organization, 37*(3), 323–327.

Leach, E. R. (1984). Glimpses of the unmentionable in the history of British social anthropology. In *Annual review of anthropology* (pp. 1–23). Palo Alto, CA: Annual Reviews.

Lees, S. (1986). *Losing out.* London: Hutchinson.

MacDonald, B. (1974). Education and the control of education. In B. MacDonald & R. Walker (Eds.), *Innovation, Evaluation, Research and the Problem of Control.* Centre for Applied Research in Education: University of East Anglia.

MacLure, M., & French, P. (1980). Routes to right answers. In P. Woods (Ed.), *Pupil strategies* (pp. 74–93). London: Croom Helm.

Marsh, P., Rosser, E., & Harré, R. (1978). *The rules of disorder.* London: Routledge and Kegan Paul.

McDonald, M. (1987). The politics of fieldwork in Brittany. In A. Jackson (Ed.), *Anthropology at home* (pp. 120–138). London: Tavistock.

McRobbie, A., & Garber, J. (1976). Girls and subcultures. In S. Hall & T. Jefferson (Eds.), *Resistance through rituals* (pp. 209–222). London: Routledge and Kegan Paul.

Measor, L., & Woods, P. (1984). *Changing schools.* Milton Keynes, England: Open University Press.

Mercer, N., & Edwards, D. (1981). Ground rules for mutual understanding. In N. Mercer (Ed.), *Language in school and community* (pp. 34–46). London: Edward Arnold.

Messerschmidt, D. (Ed.) (1982). *Anthropologists at home in North America.* Cambridge, England: Cambridge University Press.

Miller, C., & Parlett, M. (1976). Cue-consciousness. In M. Hammersley & P. Woods (Eds.), *The process of schooling* (pp. 143–150). London: Routledge and Kegan Paul.

Morgan, J., O'Neill, C., & Harré, R. (1979). *Nicknames: their origins and social consequences.* London: Routledge and Kegan Paul.

Nash, R. (1973). *Classrooms observed.* London: Routledge and Kegan Paul.

Nash, R. (1973). *Schooling in rural societies.* London: Methuen.

Norris, N. (1991). *Understanding educational evaluation.* London: Kogan Page.

Oakley, A. (1981). Interviewing women. In H. Roberts (Ed.), *Doing feminist research* (pp. 30–61). London: Routledge.

Open University. (1971). *E282: school and society.* Milton Keynes, England: Open University Press.

Open University. (1977). *E202: schooling and society.* Milton Keynes, England: Open University Press.

Parlett, M., & Hamilton, D. (1972). Evaluation as illumination (Occasional Paper No. 9). Edinburgh, Scotland: University of Edinburgh, Centre for Research in Educational Sciences. Reprinted in D. Tawney (Ed.), *Curriculum evaluation today* (pp. 84–100). London: Macmillan.

Payne, G. (1976). Making a lesson happen. In M. Hammersley & P. Woods (Eds.), *The process of schooling* (pp. 33–40). London: Routledge and Kegan Paul.

Payne, G. (1982). Dealing with a late-comer. In G. Payne & E. Cuff (Eds.), *Doing teaching* (pp. 90–103). London: Batsford.

Payne, G., & Cuff, E. (Eds.) (1982). *Doing teaching*. London: Batsford.

Payne, G., & Hustler, D. (1980). Teaching the class. *British Journal of the Sociology of Education, 1*(1), 49–66.

Peshkin, A. (1978). *Growing up American*. Chicago: Chicago University Press.

Pollard, A. (1979). Negotiation, deviance and 'getting done' in primary school class-rooms. In L. Barton & R. Meighan (Eds.), *School, pupils and deviance* (pp. 75–94). Driffield, England: Nafferton.

Pollard, A. (1980). Teacher interests and changing situations of survival threat in prim-ary school classrooms. In P. Woods (Ed.), *Teacher strategies* (pp. 34–60). London: Croom Helm.

Pollard, A. (1982). A model of classroom coping strategies. *British Journal of Sociology of Education, 3*(1), 19–38.

Pollard, A., & Woods, P. (Eds.) (1988). *Sociology and teaching*. London: Croom Helm.

Reid, M. (1982). Marginal man: the identity dilemma of the academic general practi-tioner. *Symbolic Interaction, 5*(2), 325–342.

Roberts, H. (Ed.) (1981). *Doing feminist research*. London: Routledge and Kegan Paul.

Sarup, M. (1978). *Marxism and education*. London: Routledge and Kegan Paul.

Scarth, J. (1987). Teacher strategies: a review and a critique. *British Journal of Sociol-ogy of Education, 8*(3), 245–262.

Scarth, J., & Hammersley, M. (1988). Examinations and teaching: an exploratory study. *British Educational Research Journal, 14*(3), 231–249.

Sharp, R., & Green, A. (1975). *Education and social control*. London: Routledge and Kegan Paul.

Sheldrake, P., & Berry, S. (1975). *Looking at innovation*. Windsor, England: National Foundation for Educational Research.

Sikes, P., Measor, L., & Woods, P. (1985). *Teacher careers: crises and continuities*. London: Falmer.

Simons, H. (1987). *Getting to know schools in a democracy*. London: Falmer.

Sinclair, J., & Coulthard, M. (1975). *Towards an analysis of discourse*. London: Ox-ford University Press.

Sluckin, A. (1981). *Growing up in the playground*. London: Routledge and Kegan Paul.

Spradley, J. (1979). *Participant observation*. New York: Wiley.

Stanley, L., & Wise, S. (1983). *Breaking out*. London: Routledge and Kegan Paul.

Stanworth, M. (1983). *Gender and schooling*. London: Hutchinson.

Stenhouse, L. (1975). *An introduction to curriculum research and development*. Lon-don: Heinemann.

Stubbs, M. (1983). *Language, schools and classrooms* (2nd ed.). London: Methuen.

Stubbs, M. (1986). *Educational linguistics*. Oxford: Blackwell.

Stubbs, M., & Delamont, S. (Eds.) (1976). *Explorations in classroom observation*. Chichester, England: Wiley.

Torode, B. (1976). Teachers' talk. In M. Stubbs & S. Delamont (Eds.), *Explorations in classroom observation* (pp. 173–194). Chichester, England: Wiley.

Torode, B. (1984). *The extra-ordinary in ordinary language: social order in the talk of teachers* (Konteksten 5). Amsterdam: University of Amsterdam, Institut Preventieve en Sociale Psychiatrie.

Turner, G. (1983). *The social world of the comprehensive school*. London: Croom Helm.

Tyler, R. W. (1949). *Basic principles of curriculum and instruction*. Chicago: University of Chicago Press.

Walker, R. (1983). The use of case studies in applied research and evaluation. In A. Hartnett (Ed.), *The social sciences and educational studies* (pp. 190–204). London: Heinemann.

Walker, R., & Adelman, C. (1976). Strawberries. In M. Stubbs & S. Delamont (Eds.), *Explorations in classroom observation* (pp. 133–150). Chichester, England: Wiley.

Wells, G. (1977). Language use and educational success. *Research in Education, 18*, 9–34.

Wells, G. (1978). Talking with children. *English in Education, 12*, 15–38.

Wells, G. (1979). Describing children's linguistic development at home and at school. *British Educational Research Journal, 5*(1), 75–89.

Wells, G. (Ed.) (1981a). *Learning through interaction.* Cambridge, England: Cambridge University Press.

Wells, G. (1981b). Some antecedents of early educational attainment. *British Journal of Sociology of Education, 2*(2), 181–200.

Wells, G. (1985). *Language, learning and education.* Slough, England: NFER-Nelson.

Wells, G., & Montgomery, M. (1981). Adult-child interaction at home and at school. In P. French and M. MacLure (Eds.), *Adult-child conversation* (pp. 210–243). London: Croom Helm.

Wells, G., & Wells, J. (1984). Learning to talk and talking to learn. *Theory into Practice, 23*(3), 190–197.

Whitty, G. (1974). Sociology and the problem of radical educational change. In M. Flude & J. Ahier (Eds.), *Educability, schools and ideology* (pp. 112–137). London: Croom Helm.

Whitty, G. (1976). Teachers and examiners. In G. Whitty & M. Young (Eds.), *Explorations in the politics of school knowledge* (pp. 212–222). Driffield, England: Nafferton.

Wilcox, K. (1982). Ethnography as a method and its applications to the study of schooling: a review. In G. Spindler (Ed.), *Doing the ethnography of schooling* (pp. 456–488). New York: Holt.

Willes, M. (1981a). Learning to take part in classroom interaction. In P. French & M. MacLure (Eds.), *Adult-child conversation* (pp. 73–90). London: Croom Helm.

Willes, M. (1981b). Children becoming pupils. In C. Adelman (Eds.), *Uttering, muttering* (pp. 51–68). London: Grant McIntyre.

Willes, M. (1983). *Children into pupils.* London: Routledge and Kegan Paul.

Willis, P. (1977). *Learning to labour.* Farnborough, England: Saxon House.

Wolcott, H. F. (1967). *A Kwakiutl village and school.* New York: Holt, Rinehart and Winston.

Woods, P. (1979). *The divided school.* London: Routledge and Kegan Paul.

Woods, P. (Ed.) (1980a). *Teacher strategies.* London: Croom Helm.

Woods, P. (Ed.) (1980b). *Pupil strategies.* London: Croom Helm.

Woods, P. (1983). *Sociology and the school.* London: Routledge and Kegan Paul.

Woods, P. (1985). Sociology, ethnography and teacher practice. *Teaching and Teacher Education, 1*(1), 51–62.

Wragg, E. C. (1975). The first generation of interaction analysis studies in Britain. In G. Chanan & S. Delamont (Eds.), *Frontiers of classroom research* (pp. 13–24). Windsor, England: National Foundation for Educational Research.

Wright, C. (1986). School processes: an ethnographic study. In J. Eggleston, D. Dunn, & M. Anjali (Eds.), *Education for some* (pp. 127–180). Stoke-on-Trent, England: Trentham.

Young, M.F.D. (Ed.) (1971). *Knowledge and control.* London: Collier-Macmillan.

3

SELF-DOUBT AND SOFT DATA: SOCIAL AND TECHNICAL TRAJECTORIES IN ETHNOGRAPHIC FIELDWORK

S. J. Ball

For the student ethnographer, the decision to choose fieldwork as the primary method for research is typically a plunge into the unknown. Participant observation in natural settings is probably the least well understood, most feared, and most abused of all the contemporary methods of educational research. Crucially – and this is often ignored or underplayed by methods texts and in methods courses – the choice of ethnography carries with it implications about theory, epistemology, and ontology. Ethnography not only implies engagement of the researcher in the world under study; it also implies a commitment to a search for meaning, a suspension of preconceptions, and an orientation to discovery. In other words, ethnography involves risk, uncertainty, and discomfort.

For some novitiate researchers, the entire enterprise of ethnography looks from the outset like a combination of *Star Trek* and *Mission Impossible*. But added to the uncertainty and the ever present possibility of failure, there is yet another cruel rub. Not only do researchers have to go into unknown territory, they must go unarmed, with no questionnaires, interview schedules, or observation protocols to stand between them and the cold winds of the raw real. They stand alone with their individual *selves*. They themselves are the primary research tool with which they must find, identify, and collect the data. They must charm the respondents into cooperation. They must learn to blend or pass in the research setting, put up with the boredom and the horrors of the empty notebook, cringe in the face of *faux pas* made in front of those whose cooperation they need, and engage in the small deceptions and solve the various ethical dilemmas which crop up in most ethnographies. No wonder that many students confronted for the first time with the possibility of their own research think first about designing a questionnaire. That skill can be picked up from textbooks and learned in seminars.

Ethnography is not like that. Indeed, it probably is unteachable. The prime ethnographic skills cannot be communicated or learned in the seminar room or out of the textbook. Students can be prepared, forewarned, or educated in ethnography, but the only way to learn it is to do it. The only way to get better at it is to do more of it. My point is that ethnographic fieldwork relies primarily on the engagement of the self, and that engagement can only be learned enactively.

The self is critical in the conduct and understanding of ethnography in a twofold sense – in both practical and methodological terms (in the strict use of that term). First, the engagement of the self is basic to the conduct of fieldwork inasmuch as the ethnographer must 'get by' in the research setting, and must establish 'rapport' with respondents. Maintaining the research self is a deliberate process quite unlike most social interactions. It requires careful planning and sensitive and reflective involvement with actors in the field. It requires a studied presentation of self (or selves) and the adaptation of the research self to the requirements of the field. It is much more like going on a blind date than going to work. First, second, and third impressions all count. The research role must be constructed responsively and appropriately in relation to the setting under study. The researcher must achieve a compromise between an ideal self-as-researcher and an acceptable and possible self in the field setting.

Secondly, self-awareness provides the mechanism for analysis of data within the fieldwork process and the evaluation of the adequacy of data outside of the immediacies of fieldwork. What I have in mind is a model of the process which George Herbert Mead calls the 'internal conversation', or a kind of self-interaction defined by Blumer (1969),

> With the mechanism of self-interaction the human being ceases to be a responding organism whose behavior is a product of what plays upon him from the outside, the inside or both. Instead he acts toward his world, interpreting what confronts him and organizing his action on the basis of that interpretation. (Blumer, 1969, p. 63)

This kind of self-conscious engagement with the world is what defines the process of ethnography. In microcosm, such engagement allows the researcher to connect the processes of data analysis and data collection. It also provides the possibility of technical rigour in the ethnographic process. The basis of this rigour is the conscious and deliberate linking of the social process of engagement in the field with the technical processes of data collection and the decisions that that linking involves. I call that linking *reflexivity* [. . .].

In this paper I consider how reflexivity connects dialectically the social and technical trajectories of fieldwork. The trajectories and the reflexive relation between them are portrayed in Figure 1. I will illustrate these trajectories with some of the issues that typically arise in the fieldwork process. I will limit the discussion to the *social* trajectory, although, as I indicate in Figure 1, that trajectory is related dynamically to the technical trajectory as well.

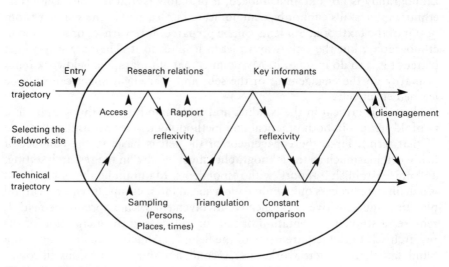

Figure 1   Heuristic representation of the ethnographic research process

ENTRY

The negotiation of entry to educational settings usually is conducted through formal channels. It is normal to accept the routes into school laid down in organizational procedures. The superintendent or principal is approached for permission, which, if granted, provides us *entry*, but perhaps not *access*. Permission from the principal does not always guarantee the cooperation of teachers or students. The researcher actually may be 'tainted' by the entry process and become identified with the formal authorities in the system. Certain forms of entry actually may inhibit the possibilities of access. Realistically, in any fieldwork setting we are confronted with multiple negotiations of micro-access. Legitimacy frequently has to be won and renewed repeatedly rather than simply being officially granted. The title 'university teacher' can be a handicap in some situations.

The point is that means of access actually may constrain the sorts of data and the research relationships available to the fieldworker in the early days in the field (Geer, 1964). Respondents will act and react according to the initial designation of the researcher as *arriviste*. The failure to appreciate how you are perceived and identified may inhibit, distort, or channel your perception of events. The researcher never can be the invisible fly on the wall, as sometimes is claimed, but is always and inevitably a part of the scene. Thus, the claim that non-participant observation has been achieved in ethnographic fieldwork always is suspect. Is it possible to have no account at all taken of oneself? Is it possible to be in but not of social life?

King (1984) indicates some of the problems he faced in trying to become a taken-for-granted in an English infant school:

> My routine became to spend a short first visit to a new classroom, making no notes, to be observed by the children rather than to observe. This was to allow the teacher and the children to get over any unease or curiosity. I politely refused requests for help, referring the child to the teacher, and met requests for approval only with smiles. To begin with I kept my standing so that physical height maintained social distance. Most importantly, I avoided eye contact; if you do not look, you will not be seen. These measures led to my being, for the most part, ignored by the children in my later visits (although I did sometimes talk to individual children). I tested this by moving from one observation spot to another, and then noting some children looking at where I had been, before finding me in the new position. I found it helped to sit down at this later stage, often using furniture or even the unoccupied Wendy House [playhouse] as a convenient 'hide'. (King, 1984, p. 123)

King's account points out the distinction between entry and access and demonstrates his awareness of the perceptions that the teacher and students held of him. In order to satisfy the former, he had to go through an elaborate process of frustrating the latter's attempts to colonize him as a teacher. The problem that remains is what the children actually made of King's attempts at social distancing, what did they think this tall man was doing hiding in the Wendy House? The example also raises the question of how far a researcher may fail to respond to actors' role expectations and still collect worthwhile data.

Actors' responses will reflect the researcher's attempt to take or make a research role. Clearly, some educational researchers when faced with this dilemma have sought comfort in taking on a teacher, counsellor, or other official role. Other researchers have tried to construct new, idiosyncratic roles that stand outside the available organizational identities. I suggest that the role, whatever it is, will influence the kinds of data elicited in the research setting. The taking of a ready-made role may leave the setting relatively undisturbed, and thus much may remain unsaid. The making of a recognizable research role may create disturbance, but in so doing it may make the taken-for-granted more obvious. There are advantages and disadvantages in each case; one is not necessarily better than the other. Let me use another example to demonstrate the point.

Hammersley (1984) reports his observation in a school staffroom (faculty lounge):

> Beside the operation of . . . selectivity in perception and data recording, and the biases that may have been involved, there is also the question of the effects of my presence on what occurred in the staffroom. While one of the reasons for collecting data on staffroom talk rather than relying on interviews with teachers was to minimize the effects of the researcher on the data, such effects may still have been present. These are presumably likely to have been greatest where I was talking to a teacher on his own.

The effect was quite noticeable in the case of one of the teachers, Webster, where what he said to me contrasted sharply with what he said in the presence of his colleagues. This is not necessarily to imply that what he said to me was invalid, simply that this represents a different kind of data from more typical staffroom exchanges. (Hammersley, 1984, p. 54)

Here Hammersley uses the possibility of different types of data, one set against the other, to consider the limitations of his research relationship. Data are considered and evaluated in the context of his research relationship. Casually observed data is set against, rather than alongside, the deliberately elicited. The researcher's role, the respondents' perceptions, the methods of data collection, and the analysis are closely bound together in this view.

In all these respects there are possibilities of choice about how data is to be collected, what research role is to be sought, and what kind of social relationships are to be aimed for. But choices are real only when we are aware of alternatives. Too many fieldworkers are almost oblivious to the impressions they create and the effects those impressions have in the field. Such researchers lack the kind of reflexivity I am arguing for here. Their data and their analyses are likely to be inadequate as a result. The nature, limitations, and possibilities of data can be fully appreciated only when we begin to know how the actors' perceptions of the researcher have influenced what they have and have not said and done. Naive claims about blending into the scene are not enough to convince an informed reader that the problem of the research role has been solved.

SOCIAL RELATIONS IN THE FIELD

One controversial aspect of the relational dependency of data is the influence of categorical identities on the possibilities of data collection. By that I refer primarily to the effects of gender and ethnicity. Hardline categoricalists (there are plenty of them about) argue that men cannot effectively research women and whites cannot effectively research blacks. In some cases, any research formulated in these terms is taken by definition to be inadequate and distorted. For obvious reasons, the reverse position is less often taken. In other words, the history and immediacy of power relations and ideological assumptions built into male–female and white–black research are insurmountable obstacles and make it impossible to establish workable, equitable research relations. But power relations in the research process also can work the other way. Both Scott (1974) and Porter (1984) report difficulties in operating as young female researchers researching older, professional men.

Often the indications of limitations built into cross-category research come from the accounts of intra-category encounters. Thus, Finch (1984), reporting on her research on the wives of clergymen, suggests,

It seems to me that there are grounds for expecting that where a woman researcher is interviewing other women, this is a situation with special characteristics conducive to the easy flow of information. (Finch, 1984, p. 74)

The implication is that a male–female interview would make the flow of information more difficult and more inhibited. In part at least, Finch sees the issue in terms of sexual politics:

> However effective a male interviewer might be at getting women interviewees to talk, there is still necessarily an additional dimension when the interviewer is also a woman, because both parties have a subordinate structural position by virtue of their gender. (Finch, 1984, p. 76)

However, there also may be occasions when cross-category relations in the field can be exploited in the quest for good data.

Dingwall (1980) has noted that it is conventional wisdom that women make more empathetic interviewers than men.

> It is quite clear that certain sets of data are made more readily available to personable young women . . . much as we may regret this on ideological grounds, it is always a temptation to engage such a person, particularly in studies of older men. (Dingwall, 1980, p. 881)

Elsewhere, Wax (1971) has warned the interviewer to 'remember that a coquette is in a much better position to learn about men than a nun' (quoted in Scott, 1984, p. 169). This kind of thinking about data elicitation raises other possibilities and choices for the research encounter. Gender relations could become a planned-for part of the researcher's role-making in the field.

Social relations refer not only to the way in which data are collected, but also to the status attributed to the data and to interpretation of the data in the light of the ways in which data are collected. Thus, Scott (1984) adds,

> Understandings of the place of women in sociological research overlook an important factor, and that is the experience of the woman researcher herself, how she and *her research* [italics added] are affected by gender assumptions, and how these assumptions cross cut dimensions of status and hierarchy. (Scott, 1984, p. 169)

Scott suggests that not only may research on women be different, but that women's research generally may be different. Gherardi and Turner (1987) argue that women are different sorts of researchers, more at home in the soft-data paradigm and its interpersonal methods.

NATURALISTIC SAMPLING

Returning to the social trajectory of fieldwork indicated in Figure 1, in the language of qualitative research, 'sampling' normally is a dirty word. And yet, in educational research, especially research in complex educational organizations, sampling is inevitable and necessary, but too often is ignored by fieldworkers. Few published ethnographies in education seem to deal with the implications of naturalistic sampling for the reading of the research. A great deal is left to be taken on trust. I use the term 'naturalistic sampling' in a simple and straightforward sense to refer to the dispersal of the researcher's time and energy in the organization by *places*, *persons*, and *times*.

Places

If we accept the imperatives of symbolic interactionism, then we must expect that settings affect and influence social action. Social actors will 'present' themselves differently in different settings. There are a multiplicity of settings in schools, although some ethnographies are written as if schools were 'setless'. Some of these sets should be obvious. Teacher behaviour within the formalities of the classroom often contrasts sharply with backstage life in the faculty lounge or staffrooms. Woods (1979) graphically has portrayed life in the staffrooms of English schools as a setting within which teacher's 'private selves' come to the fore and in which humour plays a key role. But clearly, students also show different selves in different settings. Their school lives are not of a piece. They are not necessarily conformist, or rebellious, or apathetic in all subjects, or with all their teachers. They are not one-dimensional characters as some ethnographies suggest. Measor and Woods (1984), for example, give a fascinating account of the 'knife-edge strategies' indulged in by otherwise academically successful and conformist students when in non-academic subject lessons.

Students have their own backstage arenas. School life does not cease at the classroom door, but goes on in the corridors, changing rooms, and what is referred to in England as 'behind the bicycle sheds'. Again, the emphasis in most schools ethnographies is almost entirely on classroom life. There is much that researchers do not know about the lives of those they study, but too often accounts fail to alert readers to the limits within which the portrayal and analysis should be read. Understandably, researchers celebrate the achievements of knowing and are loath to display their ignorance. Implicitly or explicitly, ethnographers claim too often to have produced definitive accounts of the settings they have studied.

Times

Time is probably the most neglected dimension in ethnographic research. Except for a few classic works – such as Roth's (1963) account of a TB sanatorium, Bullivant's (1978) yearly cycle of activities in a Jewish school, Smith and Geoffrey's (1968) microethnography of an urban classroom, and Strauss, Schatzman, Bucher, Ehrlich, and Sabshin's (1964) portrayal of day and night shifts in psychiatric institutions – time rarely appears in ethnographic reports. And yet, in all educational establishments time is a complex, often overbearing, and frequently referred to fact of life. But time is not just a matter of data in its own right; it also bears on the interpretation of other data. I have written elsewhere about the implications of time and timing for the interpretation of data (Ball, 1983; Ball, Hull, Skelton & Tudor, 1984). Two points are worth reiterating.

First, in the peculiar nature of classrooms, early-year encounters between teacher and new students are of special significance. Unusual, unrepeated, and important things happen in these initial encounters. They become part of a rarely referred to, but critical, history for ongoing interactions. Much of the order of classroom life rests upon conflicts and negotiations which take place in the first few weeks of the new school year. Beynon (1985) has written brilliantly about this process. But it is often the case that teachers are reluctant to have observers present for these initial encounters; most researchers are used to teachers asking them to stay out of their classes until 'things settle down'.

Secondly, the weekly and yearly cycles of school life also have contextual and situational effects on joint action. For most teachers, Monday mornings and Friday afternoons affect what is possible in the classroom, and teachers must make decisions accordingly. The end of semester, the run up to Christmas, and other times in the yearly cycle of schools also affect the course of events. But how often are fieldworkers really aware of when they collect their data and the special or limited significance which that timing gives to their data? How often do readers see in articles and books the times of day or the days of the week attached to the ethnographic observations?

Persons

In some ways this category is the most complex aspect of naturalistic sampling in fieldwork and is more directly related to the researchers' social-relations skills. Complex organizations are riddled and divided by intricate social networks. In educational settings these networks, as far as teachers are concerned, form around subject specializations, age, ethnicity, gender, shared social interests, religious affiliations, and seniority. The problems of entry and access adumbrated above often involve penetration of these various networks. The researcher may have to satisfy very different kinds of expectations and be a very different kind of person to get by in some or all of them. It is easy to stay where life is most comfortable, with people you like and get along with. But it is difficult to recognize the ways in which your view of the organization is coloured and constrained by the network you inhabit. The young student researcher may feel more comfortable at the bottom looking up. As long as that perspective is made clear in the analysis and report, there is no problem. But problems exist if claims are made about what 'the teachers' generally think, believe, or do. (The sampling of persons may be complicated further by the gender and ethnic issues referred to above.) Furthermore, researchers should be aware that the membership of any network changes over time and in different situations. The researcher may be 'in' a group, but yet can be a 'peripheral, active, or complete' member (Adler & Adler, 1987). And the membership role may shift subtly or dramatically over time. Research roles seldom are fixed. As an interpersonal process, research is, indeed normally must be, socially dynamic.

Becker, Geer, Hughes, and Strauss' (1961) attempts at the numerical analysis of data representation and coverage can be a useful tool in assessing the adequacy of generalized claims. This is something I have tried in my own work (Ball, 1981, p. 304). The technique can be adapted infinitely to check the representativeness of data across groups and contexts and forms of elicitation. In this way it can be used as a tool of reflexivity that requires the researcher to face up to the partiality of data coverage or to an over reliance on data from some people, places, or times.

Another aspect of the making of social relationships in the field, which is crucial to data collection, is the discovery and cultivation of key informants. Anthropologists have been forthcoming about their key informants, but educational researchers less so (see Ball, 1984; Burgess, 1985). Burgess (1985) suggests four main role possibilities for key informants in schools; they may act as guide, assistant, interpreter, or historian. However, Burgess also makes the point that 'it is essential that researchers make some critical appraisal of the extent to which informants provide only partial guidance to the institutions in which they are located' (Burgess, 1985, p. 92). We are back to reflexivity again, back to self-doubt and distrust, that is, the distrust of data. The key informant offers a perspective; it is not the only perspective. It embodies its own distortions and partiality. The accounts of events, or history, or people to whom the researcher has no direct access sponsored by key informants will be biased and limited by the roles and commitments the informants hold. Those accounts are not neutral or necessarily accurate. Informants have their own concerns and purposes for being helpful. They may gain attention, status, or dubious pleasures from being associated with the researcher. On occasions the researcher actually may be negatively perceived in the field as a result of being associated with an informant. Thus, the interpretation of data is not merely a theoretical exercise; it also is a contextual exercise. The theoretical may help us with questions about the meaning or import of data. The contextual may help us with questions about its adequacy, partiality, or reliability.

Again, what is crucial is choice and, therefore, the degree of control that researchers have over their research. Sampling involves careful and sometimes difficult decisions about how to use time, whom to spend time with, and whom to seek out. The important thing is that deliberate choices are made and that researchers consider the implications of their choices for the claims that can be made about the data collected and the kind of analysis that can be offered as a result. If there is no reflexivity, there will be no possibility of choice. The rigour of any ethnography rests firmly upon the researcher's awareness of what it is possible to say given the nature of the data that was and was not collected. In each case, the choices made involve the specific deployment of the researcher in terms of where to be, when, and with whom.

	Pre-school	Lunch-time	After hours
Times	17	504	125

	Formal meetings	Faculty lounge	Corridors & offices
Places	631	84	188

	Teaching faculty	Administration	Support staff
People	206	842	81

Figure 2 Naturalistic sampling and the representation of data (Taking a hypothetical example of a study of school administration, this breakdown might suggest that the researchers should get up earlier in the morning, spend more time talking with teachers in the faculty lounge, and seek out more of the support staff to talk to)

As a simple way of checking and monitoring data collection, 'slices of data' actually can be quantified in terms of their distribution across times, places, or people (see Figure 2). Poor representation in any one field category may indicate limitations to the sorts of interpersonal claims which the researcher can or should make.

The issue of naturalistic sampling takes us only part way in understanding the processes of sampling in ethnographic fieldwork. The naturalistic often shades over into the theoretical. Theoretical sampling shifts the issue from one of adequate coverage and representation to one of analysis and conceptual development. Theoretical sampling involves the use of analytical insights derived from data collected up to a particular point in time in order to make decisions about the collection of further data (Strauss, 1988, p. 16–21, 274–279). That is to say, either natural or conceptual categories emerge from the ongoing analysis of data as especially significant or problematic. Data collection, then, actually may be organized around these emergent categories. This may be part of a secondary process of 'progressive focussing' whereby other sorts of data are no longer being collected. Again, choices are involved. It is unlikely in the course of fieldwork that theoretical sampling decisions will be clearcut. Hunches, third-party suggestions, or pragmatism all play their part in orienting the researcher to one area of pursuit rather than another. Choice indicates control and reflexivity. What is required is the ability or skill to stand back from the field, to review data, and to make selective decisions about future strategies in the field. Such decision-making is not in itself technical or mechanical; it is, rather, specifically tied to the amount, nature, and quality of data collected and to the possibilities of data collection in particular settings.

THE SKILFUL SELF

As I have indicated, the conduct of ethnographic fieldwork relies fundamentally on the social relations skills of the researcher. The researcher's task is to make themselves acceptable to all parties in the field, if possible, to take on a research role that allows maximum flexibility in forms of social relations and social interaction. The more complex the setting under study, the more difficult it becomes to arrive at a workable role and *persona*. In educational research, this issue becomes particularly acute when fieldwork involves relations both with teachers and administrators and students. Researchers will go to inordinate lengths to avoid situations or roles that invest their relations with students with any kind of authority. And yet, the avoidance of authority in some circumstances can damage credibility with teachers. Ethnographers seek to be all things to all people and to sublimate their own personalities, commitments, and beliefs as far as is humanly and ethically possible. But some people find that the adoption of this kind of minimal and malleable self can be uncomfortable on occasions.

Peshkin (1984) describes his awareness of and difficulty with aspects of this matter in his experience of being a Jewish ethnographer in a Christian fundamentalist high school, Bethany.

> Because I feared losing access at Bethany, I was more conscious of my behaviour there than anywhere else I had been. Feeling alien, I was unusually aware of the persona I created to be an effective (i.e., data-collecting) presence at Bethany and of the resulting discrepancy between my research and my human selves. This awareness was the basis for eventually understanding how consistently and meaningfully I manipulated my behaviour, blending in chameleon-like when invisibility was in order, and appearing in this or that posture when I needed to produce a particular effect. In time, I realized that I had couched my trust-building demeanour within the general role of an as-if Christian, a part that required accommodations of appearance – short hair, no beard, suit and tie; language – no minced oaths ('gee whiz', 'gosh', etc.) or profanity; and behaviour – regular attendance at all church activities expected of Bethany members. (Peshkin, 1984, p. 259)

Peshkin's problem and his message are both complex. He clearly is aware that he is engaged in constant small acts of deception, and he also writes of the sense of guilt that this produced (a guilt that was probably exaggerated by the peculiar nature of the setting under study), but he expresses the way in which his ability to collect 'good' data was dependent on his ability to maintain 'good' behaviour. Part of the time he found himself trading on a role as a 'fictive Christian', and given the nature of the setting, he was faced constantly with the pressure and expectation of 'going native'. As Peshkin explains, 'Our interviewer's role, most empathetically that of the dumb stranger or outsider, elicited a new response from Bethanyites to us: proselytizing' (Peshkin, 1984, p. 260). At Bethany, as in most other social settings, there is no special role set apart for researchers. Being a researcher does not exclude other *personas*, roles, and typifications from the process of interaction in the field, and data arises in the nexus of possibilities and constraints embedded in the research relationships thus created. Peshkin's learning about Bethany was not a simple, one-way process. Part of his 'understanding', his sub-text of knowledge about the place as a participant in it, was derived directly from the Bethanyites' responses to him as an outsider and as a 'fictive Christian'. The presentation of self he employed did not neutralize the effect of his presence; rather, it stimulated particular responses which Peshkin could then analyse and make sense of. All of this, as I have tried to show, needs to be grasped reflexively in the fieldwork process, even at times on a minute-by-minute basis.

The ethnographer can be considered to be involved in any fieldwork interaction on at least three levels. First, in terms of 'normal' interaction, fieldworkers must strain to keep their everyday 'good' researcher *persona* in place. Second, as data gatherers, fieldworkers must shift and select 'data' from what is going on. This includes what should be said and done next, if appropriate, in order to elicit more data. Third, as reflexive analyst, the fieldworker must weigh the impact and effects of their presence, their *personae* and the respondents' perception of them, for the status, usefulness, and limitations of the data recorded. Data does not exist in a vacuum, or it does so only rarely.

SOFT DATA AND THE SKILFUL SELF

All of this leads to another more important question about the degree of 'softness' of qualitative data. It is the question that cynical researchers, or more often cynical nonresearchers, love to ask. That is, 'If someone else did the fieldwork, would the ethnography have turned out differently?' The answer to that must be 'yes'. But it is a qualified yes. I believe that the differences between my analysis and yours typically would be small rather than large. The differences would be matters of emphasis and orientation, rather than in the story to be told. The complexity and the 'becomingness' of social life belies the possibility of a single, exhaustive, or definitive account. And both as an analytical decision-making process and as a social process, we should expect different researchers to pick their way through fieldwork differently.

Decisions about whom to talk to, where to be, and when to be there partially will determine what data is and is not collected. Decisions made in the field about sampling, the roles adopted and relationships established, and the events and encounters participated in all will contribute to the construction of a particular fieldwork trajectory and a limited set of possibilities for interpretation. 'In qualitative research, the researcher is the instrument. There are no reliability and validity co-efficients for the researcher who is observing and interviewing participants in the natural setting' (Brown, 1988, p. 95). The presence, the effect, and the biases and selections of the researcher cannot be removed from qualitative research. Qualitative research cannot be made 'researcher-proof'. Clearly, it is possible to point to a few cases where restudies have produced major discrepancies in findings. The Redfield (1930)–Lewis (1951) and Mead (1928)–Freeman (1983) examples are best known, but others perhaps are more intriguing because they highlight differences in the fieldwork processes as well as in the analysis and interpretation.

One example is the work of Gartrell (1979) and Slater (1976), who have studied the Nyiha people of southwestern Tanzania. Slater described the Nyiha as hostile, withdrawn, apathetic, suspicious, and as exhibiting little individuality. In contrast, Gartrell portrays them as friendly, vital, warm, and welcoming. Their accounts differ in other important ways. Interestingly, the starting point for these differences is the social responses of the Nyiha to outsiders. Both Gartrell and Slater describe how the Nyiha reacted to them as anthropologists. Gartrell's critique of Slater's work points to a number of differences in their respective research roles and research relationships. Both are women, but Slater was a lone researcher in the field, while Gartrell was accompanied by her husband, a geologist; Slater travelled by Land Rover, but Gartrell did not. Slater, I am suggesting, transgressed the Nyiha established views about women's behaviour (they should be submissive and dominated by men). Additionally, Slater employed as an interpreter and informant a highly educated but arrogant man whose manner may have inhibited and alienated the Nyiha.

Now, I can say nothing about the adequacies or inadequacies of either of these studies. The significant thing is that part of the explanation of the differences between the accounts is found in the nature of the interactions between the researchers and the researched and the researched's perceptions of the researchers. Gartrell seemed to operate reflexively in making sense of the research process as the product of social interaction and mutual interpretation, and also seemed to be aware of the nature of her personal impact in the field. But also, to some extent, she had the advantage of being able to set her experiences against those reported by Slater. Two sets of data, rather than one, always are more likely to generate insights.

ART OR SCIENCE

When students are introduced in methods courses to the techniques of fieldwork, the tendency is to emphasize the technical aspects of data collection and analysis. The stresses and tensions of the fieldwork process get much less attention. Yet, as I have indicated, fieldwork involves a personal confrontation with the unknown and requires the aspirant to come to grips with the use of theory and method in the context of a confused, murky, contradictory, and emergent reality. In many respects it is a rite of passage. This all is very different from the systematic and pristine research reports that most ethnographers eventually produce. Wax (1952) describes the situation in anthropology, where young anthropologists often embarked on a first field trip in a spirit not unlike that of adolescent primitives facing initiation into the tribe. In solitary agony, supported only by the wise sayings of their anthropological ancestors, they met their crucial and mysterious ideal. (Wax, 1952, p. 34)

Educational ethnography may not be all that different. In a simple sense, many accounts of the ethnographic experience make it sound easy. The boredom and tiredness, the gaffs and false trails, and the participant observation syndrome that wherever you are the action is going on somewhere else, all are glossed over and coded out. Take, for example, a recently published account of data gathering in qualitative research. The processes I have tried to capture in this paper are compressed into two short, research-made-simple, paragraphs:

> Data collection begins as soon as the researcher has identified a research-able problem and goes into the field. Once the setting has been chosen for study, the researcher immerses himself in the social milieu. Initial observations allow the researcher to describe the social structure, observe patterns of behaviour, and begin to understand the environment.
>
> Since grounded research requires interpersonal interaction, the researcher must observe his own behaviour as well as the behaviour of his subjects. Only by being aware of his own 'mind-set' and 'bracketing' his own values can the researcher begin to search out and understand the world of others. (Hutchinson, 1988, p. 130)

If only the business of grounded research was so simple! I have two complaints about this view. First, complex and difficult processes involved in the selection of a case, gaining entry, being accepted, establishing rapport, and beginning to be able to record, let alone understand, data are reduced to mere technicalities. Second, by a technical sleight of hand, the researcher as social being is exorcised from the research process, thence to be cast as a soulless and socialless data-gathering and analysing machine. Do we do justice to the research experience and are we being fair to our students or our readers when we peddle these neatly packaged methodological prescriptions? [. . .]

One of the failings of much ethnography that is based on interactionist theory is the non-application of theory reflexively to the process of research. We hide behind technicalities and absent presences in the field of study and except ourselves from the analysis we apply to others. Being like the fly on the wall, immersion, passing, and acceptance are used as sleights of hand to avoid consideration of the ways in which data are arrived at in doing field-work. Presumably, ethnographers are not, after all, 'closet positivists' and do not regard data as simply being 'there', waiting to be gathered, to be observed, by any researcher who happens along. Data are a social construct of the research process itself, not just of the 'natives' under study. Data are a product of the skills and imagination of the researcher and of the interface between the researcher and the researched. The choices, omissions, problems, and successes of the fieldwork will shape the process of the research in particular ways, as I have indicated. Indeed, what counts as data, what is seen and unnoticed, what is and is not recorded, will depend on the interests, questions, and relationships that are brought to bear in a particular scene. The research process will generate meaning as part of the social life it aims to describe and to analyse.

The problems of conceptualizing qualitative research increase when data, and the analysis and interpretation of data, are separated from the social process which generated them. In one respect, the solution is a simple one. It is the requirement for methodological rigour that every ethnography be accompanied by a *research biography*, that is, a reflexive account of the conduct of the research which, by drawing on fieldnotes and reflections, recounts the processes, problems, choices, and errors which describe the fieldwork upon which the substantive account is based.

In the same way that we would not expect to read a quantitative research report without some idea of the instruments employed to collect data, we should not expect to read qualitative research without some idea of the instrument employed – the researcher herself or himself. To be clear, I am not trying to trivialize ethnographic research; neither am I suggesting that ethnographic research inevitably lacks rigour. Quite the opposite. There are a range of theoretically appropriate techniques available to test and ensure rigour. But rigour and pseudo-objectivity are not the same thing. The first is a demonstrable set of procedures, including the presentation of a research biography. The second is a stance, a matter of style and form in the writing up of research. As such, it is merely a claim, an appeal, a facade, behind which researchers hide themselves. Rather like the child on the bicycle who shouts 'look no hands', this is the 'researcher-as-immaterial' position.

It is perverse that a tradition committed to the search for subjectivity, that is based upon and relies upon achieving inter-subjectivity, should attempt to cloak itself in the mysteries of 'objectivity'. As Goetz (1988) notes, this pseudo-objectivity 'is highlighted by investigators' use of the third person as "the researcher" and other fashions of science writing' (Goetz, 1988, p. 292). My preference always is to use 'I' in the writing of qualitative research; that is the 'researcher-as-instrument' position. To write the researcher out of the report is to deny the dependency of the data on the researcher's presence.

Part of the process of educating new ethnographers involves being able to encourage them to read ethnographic materials, and yet so much ethnographic writing is presented in a sanitized scientific style. The form of presentation of data belies the means employed to collect it. The possibilities of the reflexivity available to the author are denied to the reader. The organic link between data collection and data analysis, and between theory and method, is broken. Presumably we should attempt to relate social theory to research method, substantive theory to epistemology, and presentation and style to ontology.

REFERENCES

Adler, P. & Adler, P. (1987). *Membership roles in the field*. Beverly Hills, CA: Sage.
Ball, S. J. (1981). *Beachside comprehensive*. Cambridge: Cambridge University Press.
Ball, S. J. (1983). Case study research in education: some notes and problems. In M. Hammersley (Ed.), *The ethnography of schooling* (pp. 77–104). Driffield: Nafferton.
Ball, S. J. (1984). Beachside reconsidered: reflections on a methodological apprenticeship. In R. Burgess (Ed.), *Strategies of educational research* (pp. 69–96). Lewes: Falmer.
Ball, S. J., Hull, R., Skelton, M. & Tudor, R. (1984). The tyranny of the 'devil's mill': time and task at school. In S. Delamont (Ed.), *Readings on interaction in the classroom*. London: Methuen.
Becker, H., Geer, B., Hughes, E. C. & Strauss, A. (1961). *Boys in white*. Chicago: Chicago University Press.
Beynon, J. (1985). *Initial encounters in the secondary school*. Lewes: Falmer.
Blumer, H. (1969). *Symbolic interactionism: perspective and method*. Englewood Cliffs, NJ: Prentice-Hall.
Brown, M. McG. (1988). Reconstruction of which reality? Qualitative data analysis. In J. P. Goetz & J. Allen (Eds), *Qualitative research in education: substance, methods, experience* (pp. 91–103). Athens: University of Georgia, College of Education.
Bullivant, B. M. (1978). *The way of tradition*. Victoria: Australian Council for Educational Research.
Burgess, R. (Ed.) (1984). *The research process in educational settings: ten case studies*. Lewes: Falmer.
Burgess, R. (1985). In the company of teachers: key informants and the study of a comprehensive school. In R. Burgess (Ed.), *Strategies of educational research* (pp. 79–100). Lewes: Falmer.
Dingwall, R. (1980). Ethics and ethnography. *Sociological Review, 28*(24), 871–891.
Finch, J. (1984). It's great to have someone to talk to: the ethics of interviewing women. In C. Bell and H. Roberts (Eds), *Social researching*. London: Routledge & Kegan Paul.
Freeman, D. (1983). *Margaret Mead and Samoa: the making and unmaking of an anthropological myth*. Cambridge, MA: Harvard University Press.
Gartrell, B. (1979). Is ethnography possible? A critique of *African odyssey*. *Journal of Anthropological Research, 35*(4), 426–446.
Geer, B. (1964). First days in the field. In P. Hammond (Ed.), *Sociologists at work*. New York: Basic Books.
Gherardi, S. & Turner, B. (1987). *Real men don't collect soft data* (Quaderno 13). Trento: Universita di Trento, Dipartimento do Politica Sociale.
Goetz, J. (1988) [Review of *Membership roles in field research*]. *The International Journal of Qualitative Studies in Education, 1*(3), 291–294.
King, R. (1984). The man in the Wendy House: researching infants' schools. In R. Burgess (Ed.), *The research process in educational settings: ten case studies* (pp. 117–138). Lewes: Falmer.
Hammersley, M. (1984). The researcher exposed: a natural history. In R. Burgess (Ed.), *The research process in educational settings: ten case studies* (pp. 39–68). Lewes: Falmer.
Hutchinson, S. (1988). Education and grounded theory In R. Sherman & R. Webb (Eds), *Qualitative research in education: focus and methods* (pp. 123–140). Lewes: Falmer.
Lewis, O. (1951). *Life in a Mexican village: Tepoztlan restudied*. Urbana: University of Illinois Press.
Mead, M. (1928). *Coming of age in Samoa*. New York: William Morrow.

Measor, L. & Woods, P. (1984). *Changing schools*. Milton Keynes: Open University Press.

Peshkin, A. (1984). Odd man out: the participant observer in an absolutist setting. *Sociology of Education, 57*, 254–264.

Porter, M. (1984). The modification of method in researching postgraduate education. In R. Burgess (Ed.), *Strategies of educational research* (pp. 139–162). Lewes: Falmer Press.

Redfield, R. (1930). *Tepoztlan: a Mexican village*. Chicago: University of Chicago Press.

Roth, J. (1963). *Timetables*. New York: Bobbs-Merrill.

Scott, S. (1984). The personable and the powerful: gender and status in sociological research. In C. Bell & H. Roberts (Eds), *Social researching* (pp. 165–178). London: Routledge & Kegan Paul.

Slater, M. K. (1976). *African odyssey: an anthropological adventure*. Garden City, NY: Anchor.

Smith, L. & Geoffrey, W. (1968). *Complexities of an urban classroom*. New York: Holt, Rinehart and Winston.

Strauss, A. (1988). *Qualitative analysis for social scientists*. Chicago: Cambridge University Press.

Strauss, A., Schatzman, L., Bucher, R., Ehrlich, D. & Sabshin, M. (1964). *Psychiatric ideologies and institutions*. London: Collier-Macmillan.

Wax, R. (1952). Reciprocity in fieldwork. *Human Organization, 11*(3), 34–41.

Wax, R. (1971). *Doing fieldwork*. Chicago: University of Chicago Press.

Woods, P. (1979). *The divided school*. London: Routledge & Kegan Paul.

4

OBJECTIVITY IN EDUCATIONAL RESEARCH*

E. Eisner

Objectivity is one of the most cherished ideals of the educational research community. In fact, it is so important that if our work is accused of being subjective, its status as a source of knowledge sinks slowly into the horizon like a setting sun. Yet, though we use the term *objective* with ease in our conversations and in our literature, its meaning is not particularly clear, nor, I will argue, are the consequences of the tacit, almost unexamined assumptions upon which it rests. When we speak of being objective, just what do we mean? One thing, apparently, is that we have taken pains to try to diminish or eliminate bias. To be objective or to do an objective study is to be or do something that is not primarily about ourselves, but about the world itself. Objectivity means in some contexts being fair, open to all sides of the argument. In other contexts, objectivity refers to a method or procedure through which we acquire information; an objective test is an example of such a procedure. In common discourse, to be objective or to have an objective view is to see things the way they are.

When we conceptualize objectivity, we ineluctably imply its opposite, subjectivity, and between the two there is no doubt about which one comes out on top. We want to be objective in our views, objective in our methods, and above all, to have objective knowledge. To use the vernacular, we want to see and to tell it like it is.

I know that in talking about objectivity as a condition through which the world can be accurately seen, described, and interpreted, I will be accused of creating a 'straw person'. No one, I will be told, believes that *complete* objectivity is possible, but that we ought to be as objective as we can. But just what

* The major ideas in this paper are derived from a chapter in *The Enlightened Eye: Qualitative Inquiry and the Enhancement of Educational Practice*, by Elliott Eisner. New York: Macmillan and Company, 1991.

do we mean by 'being as objective as we can'? Do we mean that we can get to know only a part of the world as it really is? Do we mean that we should try to neutralize ourselves from our work? Is either possible? Some think so. After all, we do say that we discover the facts; we do not create them. We discover the laws that govern the universe; we do not make them. The truth *is*; it is not a fabrication. The distinctions we make between the inner and the outer, between object and subject, abound in our vocabulary. In fact, we take pains to depersonalize our language in order to create the illusion that we ourselves have had no hand in our own work. We refer to 'the author', we use the imperial 'we', we talk about 'subjects' or use the even more depersonalized 'S'. We formalize our talk because what we want is the truth of the matter and the best way to undermine truth is to accuse someone of being subjective. Objectivity, like democracy and virtue, are things we believe we should strive for. Furthermore, if we give up objectivity as an ideal, what do we replace it with? If we give up objectivity, don't we fall into the bottomless pit of solipsism? Then what?

My comments address these questions. My analysis will be built upon a distinction between what Newell (1986) calls ontological and procedural objectivity. I hope to persuade readers that ontological objectivity cannot, in principle, provide what we hope for, and that procedural objectivity offers less than we think. I will then present a conception that I believe provides a more reasonable and useful way of thinking about the status of our empirical beliefs.

When we say we have an ontologically objective view of things, we mean that we see things the way they are. We see them in a way that reveals their actual features. To see things the way they are is to experience or know them in their ontological state. Veridicality is what we call such a state. What we seek, in the best of all worlds, is veridicality in both perception and understanding. What we wish to see and know is not some subjective, make-believe world create through fantasy, ideology, or desire, but what is really out there.

Those familiar with epistemology will know that veridicality as an ideal is predicated upon a correspondence theory of truth. The aim of epistemology, as the Greeks conceived of it, was to achieve true and certain knowledge. Such an achievement was what differentiated knowledge from belief. Knowledge was *episteme*, belief was *doxa*. Thus, whatever we *knew* was, by definition, true. If it wasn't true, we could not know it. We could *believe* it to be true, but belief and knowledge were regarded then and today as different states of being.

It should also be noted that as an ideal, correspondence between the world and the inquirer not only refers to what the inquirer perceives and understands but to what he or she has to say about the world. In other words, correspondence is to occur not only in perception and understanding but in representation as well. At its best, such representation provides, as Rorty (1979) chided, a mirror to nature. Ontological objectivity gives us an undistorted view of reality.

Procedural objectivity, the second type of objectivity, is achieved by using a method that eliminates, or aspires to eliminate, the scope for personal judgment. One of the most common examples of such a method is the objectively scored achievement test. Once the test has been constructed, identifying a correct or incorrect response does not require interpretation. Although there are interpretive issues at stake at the level of test construction, at the level of scoring, the optical scanner will do. Since no judgment is needed in scoring, the procedure is procedurally objective – hence, we say that we have an objective test or an objective method for scoring responses.

Operational definitions are also procedurally objective. When we define a concept or a skill by what it is that we do to measure it, we mean that we employ a set of procedures that others can also use. Furthermore, we fully expect that when such procedures are used, they will yield identical or nearly identical results as long as the procedures are followed and as long as the phenomenon that was measured does not itself change. When we design tests or use procedures that yield responses whose evaluation depends upon personal judgment, we refer to them as subjective, and as most of us have been taught, subjective judgements cannot be trusted. Traditionally, the aim of the research enterprise, from a methodological perspective, is to use a procedurally objective set of methods in order to gain an ontologically objective understanding of the events and objects we study.

The problems with ontological objectivity and procedural objectivity are important, not only because they lead to certain practical problems in the conduct of empirical research (we often tend, for example, to avoid studying what we cannot measure), but also because they reinforce a view of knowledge that is itself problematic. Consider, for example, the correspondence theory of truth upon which ontological objectivity rests.

How can we ever know if our views of reality match or correspond to it? To know that we have a correspondence between our views of reality and reality itself, we would need to know two things. We would need to know reality, as well as our views of it. But if we knew reality as it really is, we would not need to have a view of it. Conversely, since we cannot have knowledge of reality as it is, we cannot know if our view corresponds to it.

Some argue that a 'true' view of reality allows us to predict or control events. When we are able to do this, our view of reality may be said to correspond with reality itself. But our ability to predict or control events does not entitle us to conclude that the views we hold about the world correspond to the world as it really is. Witch doctors have for years used currare to treat pain and have beliefs about why it works. The fact that given their beliefs it works does not mean that their views are true, or that our views are. Using prediction and control as criteria for verifying belief is an instance of affirming the consequent, a procedure that is not logically justified, as Popper (1959) and others have pointed out. Indeed, Popper's view is that we can never verify the truth of a claim, we can only refute it; and even refutation, Popper claims, cannot be certain. Popper is a fallibilist, not a verificationist.

Related to the impossibility of knowing that we know the world in its pristine state – a kind of immaculate perception – is the framework-dependent character of perception. Perception of the world is perception influenced by skill, point of view, focus, language, and framework. The eye, after all, is not only a part of the brain, it is a part of tradition. How shall teaching be perceived? It depends upon what I think counts. Am I interested in 'wait time'? If I am, then I will look for it. The clarity of language, the teacher's relationship and rapport with students, the significance of the ideas presented, the teacher's personal style, warmth, and enthusiasm are all candidates for attention. Which to choose depends upon framework. To paraphrase Kant, percepts without frameworks are empty, and frameworks without percepts are blind. We secure frameworks through socialization, professional and otherwise. What we come to see depends upon what we seek, and what we seek depends upon what we know how to say. Artists, Gombrich reminds us, do not paint what they can see, they see what they are able to paint. An empty mind sees nothing.

There is, of course, a further complication regarding ontological objectivity. That complication deals with the limitations inherent in representation. Any report of the world has to take some form and be carried by some symbol system (Goodman, 1976). Some systems, such as language, describe. Others, such as visual art, depict. Some languages describe literally, others metaphorically. Some visual systems depict visually but appeal basically to our gut – expressionism, for example. Others depict visually but appeal to our imagination – surrealism. Still others depict visually but appeal to our optical experience – the work of Josef Albers and color field painting come to mind. The same holds true for narrative structures. No single genre can say everything. What one sees is that even within a single symbol system there are unique constraints and unique possibilities. Because any symbol system both reveals and conceals, its use provides, of necessity, a partial view of the reality it is intended to describe or depict. In fact, the form of representation we choose to use is constitutive of the understanding we acquire: the medium is a part of the message.

To complicate matters still further, the particular schemata we use also structure perception. These schemata may be thought of as 'structures of appropriation' (Eisner, 1991). They define the contours through which our perception and comprehension of the world is created. In this sense, Goodman's (1978) point about the world-making nature of symbol systems becomes especially cogent: To pro-life proponents, a fertilized egg is a child and its destruction is murder. To the pro-choice population, it is an unviable protoplasm that has not yet achieved the status of a person. Each group creates its own world through the image of the human it embraces. Which view is the objective one?

Given these considerations, the prospects for achieving ontological objectivity – the pristine, unmediated grasp of the world as it is – seem to fade. For many, I suspect, the absence of what Goodman has called 'something stolid underneath' creates a troublesome psychological problem. Without an anchor how can we maintain our stability? The need for such an anchor creates the motivation to find it, to assure ourselves that it is there, and that with adequate effort and ingenuity, it will be found. The quest, as Dewey (1929) lamented, is a quest for certainty.

As for procedural objectivity, the creation of procedures that eliminate judgment is certainly possible. Hermetically sealed, plastic-wrapped achievement tests, whose questions are to be answered by filling in blanks with graphite so that they can be scored by machines untouched by human hands, provide ample testimony to the attractiveness of such procedures. Such tests are not only politically safer than exercising judgment – exercising judgment on high-stake tests can be dangerous – they are also very efficient. Yet consensus achieved through procedural objectivity provides no purchase on reality. It merely demonstrates that people can agree: we hope for good reasons, but what constitutes good reasons as contrasted with poor ones is itself a matter of consensus. That might be all we can ever have, but we ought to recognize it for what it is.

Why the need for objectivity? Part of the reason, I believe, has to do with our intellectual traditions. The distinctions between knowledge and belief, biased and unbiased perception, truth and falsity are directly related to familiar dichotomies between inner and outer, mind and body, subject and object. The legacy of the Enlightenment and the effort to create a tidy, intellectually orderly world contributes further to beliefs with which we have become so comfortable. Indeed, it is very difficult to alter the naive realism that pervades our culture. When Sergeant Friday says he wants 'the facts, just the facts', he is not only making a request, but expressing a philosophy of mind. Take away the prospects for a neatly defined, objectively knowable world, and we have lost our bearings.

As understandable as such needs may be, there are, to make a pun, more constructive ways to look to our relationship to the world. The ways I will describe are rooted in the work of Dewey, Piaget, Cassirer, Langer, Goodman, and Arnheim. They participate in Rorty's philosophy and in the ideas of poststructuralism.

If the ideal of ontological objectivity is rejected, must we therefore be thrust into a solipsistic subjectivism? Once we give up our hope for knowing the world as it really is – the kind of immaculate perception I mentioned earlier – do we fall into a personal abyss from which there is no escape and no possibility of communication with others? I think not. We need not embrace a solipsistic subjectivism by recognizing that ontological objectivity is impossible. With Dewey, Piaget, Goodman, and others, I believe we are better served by recognizing that whatever it is we think we know is a function of a *transaction* between the qualities of the world we cannot know in their pure, non-mediated form, and the frames of reference, personal skills, and individual histories we bring to them. These histories are, of course, a contribution of the culture in which we live, both the social culture and our more narrowly defined personal culture. What we see and understand is not *given* by what Dewey (1938) called 'objective conditions'; they are *taken* by us. What we are able to take depends upon both the features of the world-out-there, a world we cannot directly know, and what we bring to it. It is in the transaction between objective conditions and personal frames of reference that we *make* sense. The sense we make is what constitutes experience.

Experience thus conceived is a form of human achievement; it is not simply had, it is made. The features of this construction depend upon the frameworks we are able to employ and our skill in their use. What can be made with any particular framework is not makable with any other. Each provides a special value. Indeed, acculturation and education can be considered the psychosocial processes used to provide frameworks to the young so that the worlds they make for themselves will have some commonality with those of others. It is this commonality, this *communis*, that makes communication possible. When people do not share frameworks, there is no common ground; they cannot understand each other.

The argument that I have made for a framework-dependent view of cognition and the importance of regarding knowledge as the result of transaction is sometimes misunderstood by some as a form of mindless relativism. My views are both relativistic and pluralistic, but I hope not mindless. The relativity of my views pertains to the belief that knowledge is always constructed relative to a framework, to a form of representation, to a cultural code, and to a personal biography.

My pluralism relates to the belief that there is no single, legitimate way to make sense of the world. Different ways of seeing give us different worlds. Different ways of saying allow us to represent different worlds. Helping people participate in a plurality of worlds made, I believe, is what education ought to try to achieve. The ability to participate in a variety of worlds need not lead to a Tower of Babel. And the specter of everyone marching to the same drummer or forced to speak an official social science Esperanto thrills me not. We need multiple voices and we need people who can understand them.

If we relinquish the search for an ontological objectivity, do we give up the ideal of Truth? Not necessarily. We can retain truth as a regulative ideal as long as we understand that what we regard it to be depends upon shared frameworks for perception and understanding, and that truth, in the literal sense, is relevant only to literal statements. Insofar as our understanding of the world is of our own making, what we consider true is also the product of our own making. The history of science provides ample evidence that what we regard as true changes. It will, undoubtedly, continue to change as we are persuaded that other paradigms or frameworks are more attractive or more useful.

Furthermore, we ought not to limit inquiry only to those forms for which a literal conception of truth is a relevant criterion. A novel as well as a statistical mean can enlarge human understanding. Fields like history, anthropology, sociology, and political science, fields that depend upon interpretation and imagination, are themselves literally fictions – things made (Geertz, 1973). They are the results of a framework-defined world transacting with a framework-dependent mind. The facts never speak for themselves. What they say depends upon the questions we ask.

The upshot of my message is to urge that we recognize objectivity for what it is: a concept built upon a faulty epistemology that leads to an unrealizable ideal in its ontological state and a matter of consensus (we hope for good reasons) in its procedural state. I also urge that we accept the idea that all experience is transactive; hence all we can know is the result of a transaction between our sentient and intelligent selves and a world we cannot know in its pristine state.

The world has changed since Copernicus told us how it worked. The world has changed since Tycho Brae provided a picture of the heavens. The world has changed since Newton, Einstein, and Bohr gave us their versions of how it is. I suspect it will continue to change. It seems to me high time that we recognized the creative dimensions of human rationality and accepted the notion that a view of the world from God's knee is unlikely, at least for most of us. Therefore, is the hope for an objective view useful? Can we ever know the world as it really is? How could we know if we had? Do we need another ideal? I think we do. Recognizing and accepting the inevitable transaction between self and world seems to me more realistic and more useful. This recognition would underscore the constructed, tentative, and framework-dependent character of perception and knowledge. It would contribute to a more pluralistic and tentative conception of knowledge, one more dynamic and less dogmatic, one with a human face. It would recognize that *doxa*, not *episteme*, is all we can have.

I close with a quotation from one of the world's leading philosophers of science, Stephen Toulmin. Writing about the relationship of belief to knowledge, he says,

> All of our scientific explanations and critical readings start from, embody, and imply some interpretive standpoint, conceptual framework, or theoretical perspective. The relevance and adequacy of our explanations can never be demonstrated with Platonic rigor or geometrical necessity. (Not to mince matters, *episteme* was always too much to ask.) Instead, the operative question is, Which of our positions are rationally warranted, reasonable, or defensible – that is, well-founded rather than groundless opinions, sound *doxai* rather than shaky ones? (1982, 115)

What Toulmin has to teach us is that belief, supported by good reasons, is a reasonable and realistic aim for inquiry. The reasons Toulmin alludes to are judged good not by a correspondence we cannot determine, but by the exercise of reason. What we believe, in the end, is what we ourselves create. With such a vision, the scope for method in research can be widened and the criteria for assessment made more generous. Such a prospect when put into practice will not only make possible the use of a more diversified array of talent, but it may also help us better understand and improve educational practice.

REFERENCES

Dewey, J. (1929). *The question for certainty*. New York: Minton, Balch.
Dewey, J. (1938). *Experience and education*. New York: Macmillan.

Eisner, E. W. (1991). *The enlightened eye: qualitative inquiry and the enhancement of educational practice.* New York: Macmillan.

Geertz, C. (1973). *The interpretation of cultures.* New York: Basic Books.

Goodman, N. (1976). *The languages of art.* Indianapolis: Hackett.

Goodman, N. (1978). *Ways of worldmaking.* Indianapolis: Hackett.

Newell, R. W. (1986). *Objectivity, empiricism, and truth.* London: Routledge and Kegan Paul.

Popper, K. (1959). *The logic of scientific discovery.* New York: Basic Books.

Rorty, R. (1979). *Philosophy and the mirror of nature.* Princeton, NJ: Princeton University Press.

Toulmin, S. (1982). The construal of reality: criticism in modern and post modern science. In W.J.T. Mitchell (Ed.), *The politics of interpretation* (pp. 99–118). Chicago: University of Chicago Press.

5

SUBJECTIVITY AND OBJECTIVITY: AN OBJECTIVE INQUIRY

D. C. Phillips

A person does not have to read very widely in the contemporary methodological or theoretical literature pertaining to research in the social sciences and related applied areas, such as education, in order to discover that objectivity is dead. When the term happens to be used, it is likely to be set in scare-marks – 'objectivity' – to bring out the point that a dodolike entity is being discussed. Or 'there is no such thing', authors confidently state, unmindful of the fact that if they are right, then the reader does not have to break into a sweat – because if there is no such thing as objectivity, then the view that there is no such thing is itself not objective. But, then, if this view is the subjective judgment of a particular author, readers are entitled to prefer their own subjective viewpoint – which, of course, might be that objectivity is *not* dead!

A couple of illustrations should suffice to set the stage. The first is from Gunnar Myrdal (1969):

> The ethos of social science is the search for 'objective' truth. The faith of the student is his conviction that truth is wholesome and that illusions are damaging, especially opportunistic ones. He seeks 'realism', a term which in one of its meanings denotes an 'objective' view of reality . . . How can a biased view be avoided? (p. 3)

After an interesting discussion of the deep-seated sources of bias and opportunism in belief, Myrdal suggests that some techniques exist to help achieve at least a degree of objectivity.

A second example comes from Elliot Eisner; unlike Myrdal, he does not try to soften the blow but boldly sets out to face a future in which the demise of objectivity is not mourned:

> What I have even more quarrel with is the view that a scientifically acceptable research method is 'objective' or value-free, that it harbors no

particular point of view. All methods and all forms of representation are partial. (1986, p. 15)

Or, from a different work, 'What is meant by objective? Does objective mean that one has discovered reality in its raw, unadulterated form? If so, this conception of objectivity is naive' (1979, p. 214).

It is not intended that the present chapter will develop into a paradoxical discussion of the self-referential puzzles generated by such remarks. But it is the intent, at the outset of the inquiry, to point out the oddity of trying to write an essay for a learned symposium – a paradigm case of an exercise in the marshaling of objective considerations – if, indeed, there is no escape from subjectivity. It would be too quixotic; and it would be better to take the bull by the horns and proceed by using rhetoric (much as is being done now), or special pleading, or appeals to the readers' baser motives.

Believing the task *not* to be quixotic, the present author is inspired to inquire why objectivity has sunk into such disrepute and to investigate whether it deserves the fate that has befallen it. Because the issues concerning objectivity and subjectivity transcend disciplinary and methodological boundaries, the discussion will have to be far-ranging, but it will keep returning to the specific issues raised by qualitative research.

The issues, then, are these: Why is it doubted that qualitative research – or, indeed, any research – can be objective, and are these doubts reasonable? What notion of objectivity is involved here? Is Eisner correct in suggesting that the traditional notion of objectivity is naive? If all views are subjective, are they all on a par, or are some more subjective than others? (And does the notion of degrees of subjectivity make sense?)

One further point remains to be made in this prelude. It is clear that in normal parlance the term *objective* is commendatory, while *subjective* carries negative connotations. After all, it is not a good thing for a judge, a physicist, an anthropologist, or a professor to be subjective. It is even worse to be biased – this latter term being sometimes used to mark the contrast with objectivity.[1] (Such negative evaluations are likely to change, of course, if it turns out that objectivity is dead, and that there is no option but to be subjective.) In what follows, the discussion will attempt to avoid using the terms in a judgmental way – at least until it has been established, objectively, that either term can justifiably be so used.

THE INTELLECTUAL ROOTS OF THE ATTACK ON OBJECTIVITY

The fields of philosophy of science and epistemology have undergone something of a revolution in recent decades. The traditional foundationalist or justificationist approach to epistemology has largely been abandoned in favor of a nonfoundationalist approach; in philosophy of science, the work of

Popper, closely followed by that of Kuhn, Hanson, Feyerabend, and Lakatos, has been the center of much debate. Acting under these influences, some individuals have moved in the direction of relativism (although this is not what had been intended by most of the individuals just mentioned). But the very same forces – supplemented by one or two others – have also given rise to the strong attack on objectivity. It will be as well to discuss the major influences in turn.

Nonfoundationalist epistemology

Traditional epistemologies, whether of rationalist or empiricist persuasion, were foundationalist or justificationist in the sense that they regarded knowledge as being built upon (or justified in terms of) some solid and unchallengeable foundation. It was the presence of this solid foundation that served as the justification for the knowledge claims that were made. Where the traditional schools of epistemology fell out with each other was over the issue of what, precisely, constituted this foundation. Empiricists (such as Locke, Berkeley, and Hume) saw the foundation as being human experience – sense impressions or some such item. Rationalists (like Descartes) claimed it was human reason; the starting place for the construction of knowledge was to be those beliefs that appeared indubitable after scrutiny in the light of reason.

In the twentieth century there has been a steady erosion of foundationalism of both varieties. It is now recognized that there is no absolutely secure starting point for knowledge; nothing is known with such certainty that all possibility of future revision is removed. All knowledge is tentative. Karl Popper (1968) is probably the best-known advocate of this newer perspective, but he is not, by far, a solitary figure. In his words:

> The question about the sources of our knowledge . . . has always been asked in the spirit of: 'What are the best sources of our knowledge – the most reliable ones, those which will not lead us into error, and those to which we can and must turn, in case of doubt, as the last court of appeal?' I propose to assume, instead, that no such ideal sources exist – no more than ideal rulers – and that *all* 'sources' are liable to lead us into error at times. And I propose to replace, therefore, the question of the sources of our knowledge by the entirely different question: '*How can we hope to detect and eliminate error?*' (p. 25; emphasis in original)

It is important to note that abandonment of the notion that knowledge is built on an unshakable foundation does not mean that the traditional notion of truth has been abandoned. Popper constantly reminds his readers that truth is an essential regulative ideal. He offers this nice image:

> The status of truth in the objective sense, as correspondence to the facts, and its role as a regulative principle, may be compared to that of a mountain peak which is permanently, or almost permanently, wrapped in clouds. The climber may not merely have difficulties in getting there –

he may not know when he gets there, because he may be unable to distinguish, in the clouds, between the main summit and some subsidiary peak. Yet this does not affect the objective existence of the summit . . . The very idea of error, or of doubt . . . implies the idea of an objective truth which we may fail to reach. (p. 226)

It makes little sense to search for a summit if you do not believe that a summit exists; and it makes little sense to try to understand some situation if you believe that *any* story about that situation is as good as any other. In this latter case, to inquire is to waste one's energy – one might as well have just invented any old story. But if some stories are regarded as being better than others, then this belief, upon unpacking, will be found to presuppose the notion of truth as a regulative ideal.

The crucial point for the present discussion is that it does not follow from any of the recent developments in epistemology outlined above that the notion of objectivity has been undermined. This would only follow were objectivity equated with certainty. This is to say that the following argument is a *non sequitur*, at least until some further premise is added to link the antecedent to the consequent: If no knowledge is certain, then there is no possibility for any viewpoint to be objective. It might be objected here that Popper himself referred to the real existence of his cloud-covered mountain top and that he said it might never be possible to know one had reached it – showing that attainment of 'objective truth' might not be possible. But it is crucial to note that here he was not discussing objectivity, he was discussing truth. When we abandon foundationalism, we abandon the assurance that we can know when we have reached the truth; but, as Popper's story also illustrates, we do not have to abandon the *notion* of truth, and we do not have to abandon the view that some types of inquiries are better than others.

Leaving the notion of truth, and returning to the issue of the objectivity of inquiries, there is good reason to hold that certainty and objectivity should not be linked. For if they were, all human knowledge would thereby become subjective (for no knowledge is certain), and this would have the effect of washing out a vital distinction. Consider two observers of a classroom in which a science teacher has been conducting a lesson on a difficult topic. One observer claims to have noticed that the students did not understand the material, but the only evidence she gives is that 'I did not understand the material myself'; the other observer also claims that the students did not learn, but offers by way of evidence the test scores of the students, a videotape of the classroom showing the puzzled demeanor of the students, and interview protocols where a random sample of the students seemed rather confused about the topic. The new epistemology would have us recognize that neither of these two views is absolutely certain, but it is not the consequence of the new epistemology that we would have to judge both views as being equally subjective. For it is evident that one of the observers was greatly influenced by her own personal reactions to the lesson, and this unduly affected how she perceived the classroom; whereas the other observer had taken pains to marshal relevant evidence (even if that evidence was not absolutely incorrigible). In a straightforward and nontroublesome sense, the second observer's opinion would be regarded by all normal language users as being more objective (even if the opinion later turned out to be wrong).

This example suggests the following hypothesis: 'Objective' seems to be a label that we apply to inquiries that meet certain procedural standards, but objectivity does not *guarantee* that the results of inquiries have any certainty. (It implies that the inquiries so labeled are free of gross defects, and this should be of some comfort – just as a consumer prefers to buy an item that has met rigorous inspection standards, although this does not absolutely insure that it will not break down.) The other side of the coin is that a biased, bigoted person who jumps to some subjective conclusion about, say, a political candidate who happens to be of different ethnicity may not always be wrong. His or her biased judgment may turn out to be true. Thus the narrow-minded black Democrat who had no time for Richard Nixon, and who claimed he would be a dishonest president, nevertheless turned out to be right. (Just as a consumer who purchases a shoddy piece of merchandise occasionally 'lucks out' and never has any trouble with it.) Or, to use a less loaded example but one that is historically accurate, in its heyday Newtonian physics was supported by a wealth of objective evidence, that is, evidence that was free from personal contamination and that was, in large part, accepted by an international community whose members had subjected it to critical scrutiny and cross-check. Nevertheless, in our day evidence has accumulated that makes it hard to believe that the Newtonian framework is anything but a reasonably good approximation of the truth (but not as good, for example, as the Einsteinian framework, which itself is probably not absolutely true). Thus those scientists of earlier times who rejected Newton for their own personal (subjective) reasons turned out to have been right in doing so (although, of course, whatever positive views they did hold may well have been defective also).

To put the point pithily, neither subjectivity nor objectivity has an exclusive stranglehold on truth. But why, then, should objectivity be preferred if it is not guaranteed to lead to the truth? The answer is implied in the discussion above: At any one time, the viewpoint that is the most objective is the one that currently is the most warranted or rational – to deny this is to deny that there is any significant difference between the warrants for the views of the two class-room observers in the earlier example. If we give this up, if we hold that a biased or personally loaded viewpoint is as good as a viewpoint supported by carefully gathered evidence, we are undermining the very point of human inquiry. If a shoddy inquiry is to be trusted as much as a careful one, then it is pointless to inquire carefully. The philosopher Ernest Nagel (1979) put it well:

> Those attacks on the notion that scientific inquiry can be objective are tantamount to an endorsement of the view that the grounds on which conclusions in the sciences are accepted are at bottom no better than are the grounds on which superstitious beliefs are adopted. Those attacks

may therefore . . . justify almost any doctrine, no matter how unwarranted it may be. (p. 85)

In light of these remarks, it would seem that Elliot Eisner (1979) was both right and wrong when he stated that 'to hold that our conceptions of reality are true or objective to the extent that they are isomorphic with reality is to embrace a hopeless correspondence theory of truth' (p. 214). He was right to criticize the identification of objectivity as 'isomorphic with reality'; however, he was wrong to treat 'objective' and 'true' as synonyms, and he was wrong to suggest that nonfoundationalism leads to the rejection of the correspondence theory of truth. It is worth commenting here, to forestall a philosophical misunderstanding, that the correspondence theory of truth is firmly entrenched in contemporary philosophy, and it is supported by weighty – but not by absolutely conclusive – considerations. Eisner runs together two issues that philosophers keep separate, for good reasons: The first is the issue of what account best clarifies the *meaning* of the term 'truth', and it is here that the correspondence theory is alive and well, as Popper's story of the cloudy mountain illustrates. The second is the issue of what *test* or *criterion* we can rely on in order to judge if a theory actually *is* isomorphic with reality. On this second matter, nonfoundationalists would answer that there is no such test or criterion, as once again Popper's allegory illustrates. Eisner has reasoned back, invalidly, from the negative response to the second, to a negative judgment about the first.[2]

Hansonism

It is now widely accepted that observation is always theory-laden. Due largely to the work of N. R. Hanson (although Wittgenstein and Popper could claim priority), researchers are aware that when they make observations they cannot argue that these are objective in the sense of being 'pure', free from the influence of background theories or hypotheses or personal hopes and desires.[3] Qualitative researcher John Ratcliffe (1983) was reflecting this view when he wrote that 'most research methodologists are now aware that *all* data are theory-, method-, and measurement-dependent' (p. 148; emphasis in original). And he continued on to turn this point into a thinly veiled attack on objectivity: 'That is, "facts" are determined by the theories and methods that generate their collection; indeed, theories and methods *create* the facts' (p. 148; emphasis in original). If the observer's prior theoretical commitments do, indeed, determine what he or she sees as being the facts of a situation, then subjectivity would seem to reign supreme.

It is here that the distinction between low-level and high-level observation becomes relevant. The distinction is similar to the one that research psychologists have in mind when they speak of 'high-inference' and 'low-inference' variables. While observation is never theory-free, it does not follow that many (or most) observations are such that people from a wide variety of quite different theoretical frames will be in total disagreement about the facts of the case. There are many situations where all frameworks are likely to lead to the same results – they overlap, as it were. This is particularly so in cases of low-level observations, such as 'there is a patch of red', or 'the object on the left is heavier'. Even people who do not share the same language can agree on such matters, for the only problem they face is the relatively trivial one of translation. (Thus my Korean students might not understand when I speak of 'a patch of red', but with the help of a bilingual dictionary they can quickly come to comprehend – and to agree with me!) To put it in a nutshell, relatively speaking, low-level observation is high in objectivity, in the sense that the reports of my observations transcend the merely personal or subjective. My observations are open for cross-check, testing, and criticism by other inquirers, and there is nothing in Hanson to suggest that people with beliefs that differ from my own are *bound* to disagree with me about such observations. Contrary to what some radical Hansonists claim, there is no evidence that people with markedly different theoretical frames – for example, Freudians and behaviorists – actually see different things at the basic or low-inference level being discussed here. They might notice – or fail to notice – different things, but when these are brought to their attention they agree about what they have seen. Of course, they might still disagree about the significance of what they have observed, but this is not a point under contention in the present context.

Even Hanson's (1965) famous claim that the astronomers Tycho Brahe and Johannes Kepler would see different things while watching the dawn is a claim that can be recast to support the point being made here.[4] Both scientists would agree that the sun was moving higher in the sky relative to the horizon – a point Hanson acknowledges; but of course Brahe would interpret this as the sun's moving, while Kepler would regard it as a case of the earth's rotating away from the sun. Their disagreement is spectacular, and Hansonists get good mileage from it, but what gets obscured is the agreement of the two men at the 'low-inference' level. Ernest Nagel (1979) has made a similar point, using a different example:

> It is simply not true that every theory has its own observation terms, none of which is also an observation term belonging to any other theory. For example, at least some of the terms employed in recording the observations that may be made to test Newton's corpuscular theory of light (such terms as 'prism', 'color', and 'shadow'), underwent no recognizable changes in meaning when they came to be used to describe observations made in testing Fresnel's wave theory of light. But if this is so, the observation statements used to test a theory are not necessarily biased antecedently in favor of or against a theory; and in consequence, a decision between two competing theories need not express only our 'subjective wishes', but may be made in the light of the available evidence. (p. 93)

If, however, the results of observation are couched in abstract theoretical terms – in 'high-inference' terms – then there might well be disagreement or misunderstanding. Consider the following example: Most people, whether Freudians or behaviorists, Republicans or Democrats, Americans or Australians or Koreans, deists or atheists, astrologers, or astronomers, would agree upon a visit to a classroom that they saw a teacher working with a particular number of pupils. They also probably would agree with the low-inference observation that at a certain stage in the lesson the teacher asked one pupil a series of questions. They might not all agree, however, with the high-inference observation that at this point the teacher was forcing the pupil to do some high-order cognitive task involving Piagetian abstract reasoning. For all the observers to agree with *this* observation and, more to the point, to be able to discuss, to criticize, and to evaluate warrants, they would all have to share the same theoretical framework as well as speak the same language (and this is what Hanson seemed to have in mind when he wrote of 'theory-laden perception'). And it is worth noting, in passing, that even if they all did have the same framework, it is not certain that they would necessarily agree – for some might judge that the Piagetian categorization of the pupil's task was erroneous. Similarity of framework is, at best, a guarantee of communication, but not of much else.

The moral of the example is this: Just because, on some accounts, the more abstract description is 'less objective' in the sense that it is less 'pure' and more 'contaminated' by theory, it does not follow that there is no hope for observers to enter into mutual and fruitful discussion, criticism, and evaluation. At a lower level of abstraction there might well be full overlap of categories and terminology (and thus the possibility of a higher degree of objectivity), and this more objective, low-inference observation would serve both as a constraint on the nature of the abstract accounts that could be put forward and as a springboard for critical evaluation.

Israel Scheffler (1967) seems to have had something like this in mind when he stated that the fact that none of the statements we assert

> can be *guaranteed* to be an absolutely reliable link to reality does not mean that we are free to assert any statements at will, provided only that they cohere. That the statement 'There's a horse' cannot be rendered theoretically certain does not permit me to call anything a horse. (p. 119; emphasis in original)

Scheffler points out that language offers constraints on what is to count as a horse (just as, in the earlier examples, it provided constraints on what is to count as a patch of red and what is to count as a pupil answering a question), and 'such constraints generate credibility claims which enter my reckoning critically as I survey my system of beliefs' (p. 119). In short, then, Hanson has pointed to a problem that ought to be in the forefront of the minds of observers; but in pointing out the theory-laden nature of high-inference observations he has not offered grounds for abandoning the notion of objectivity.

There is a further consideration that strengthens this optimistic conclusion. In the earlier discussion the point was made that the term *objective* is used more or less as a seal of approval, marking the fact that an inquiry or conclusion meets certain quality standards. There are poor inquiries, infected with personal biases, and there are more worthy inquiries, where the warrants that are offered are pertinent and have been subjected to critical scrutiny. The same situation exists with respect to observations. There are certain well-documented factors that influence observers and that can make their work less credible. (In social science terminology, they can be spoken of as 'threats to the validity' of observational or qualitative work.) For example, it is known that observers are prone to misjudge frequencies of occurrence of events they are watching, unless they use some quantitative scoring; and they are prone to be over-influenced by positive instances and underinfluenced by negative instances. (For a discussion of the significance of these factors, see Phillips, 1987b.) Thus the conclusions reached by a shoddy observer who has not controlled these factors would be properly judged by the research community as being less objective than the conclusions reached by a more careful person. Once again, objectivity is seen to be a vital notion, and its abandonment would be fatal for the integrity of the research endeavor.

The myth of 'the more the merrier'

In an influential essay, Michael Scriven (1972) points out that sometimes objectivity is thought about in terms of the number of inquirers or observers – data that only one person has been able to collect are regarded as subjective and dubious, but there is usually a more favorable judgment when a number of people have been involved.[5] Scriven argues, however, that quality and number of investigators do not always go together. Thus he distinguishes between qualitative objectivity, where the data are of high quality (no matter how many observers or inquirers were involved), and quantitative objectivity, where more than one person has replicated the findings (which does not guarantee veracity). Scriven writes of the two types of objectivity:

> Now it would certainly be delightful if these two senses coincided, so that all reports of personal experience, for example, were less reliable than all reports of events witnessed by a large number of people. But as one thinks of the reliability of reports about felt pain or perceived size, on the one hand, and reports about the achievements of stage magicians and mentalists on the other, one would not find this coincidence impressive. (pp. 95–96)

Scriven's points are crucial; he has shown that it is untenable to give an account of objectivity solely in terms of group consensus – qualitative objectivity is not reducible to quantitative. Thus the audience consensus that a magician has made a woman levitate freely in the air and the group consensus that the world is flat are objective views in the quantitative sense only, that is, those things are what the groups concerned are agreed upon. But the consensus is *only* that: and the agreement does not mean that the views concerned are correct, or warranted, or that they have been reached in a way that has avoided sources of bias and distortion. And yet the number of observers remains a crucial factor in many influential accounts of objectivity. Fred Kerlinger (1973), for example, in his widely used textbook on behavioral research, refers to an 'objective procedure' as 'one in which agreement among observers is at a maximum' (p. 491). Kerlinger neglected to point out that what is crucial is *how* the agreement was brought about!

Something more is needed to account for the qualitative sense of 'objectivity' – some account has to be given of what makes a viewpoint objective in the sense of having a respectable warrant and being free from bias. Alternatively, one could follow Elliot Eisner's lead; in effect he denies that there is any such thing as qualitative objectivity, and thus there is *only* group consensus or quantitative objectivity. The problem here – apart from the issue of whether he is right about the null status of qualitative objectivity – is that quantitative objectivity is not worth very much. Indeed, it is not worthy of the label 'objectivity' at all; a more appropriate term is simply 'consensus'. And the problem, of course, is that consensus about an incorrect or untrustworthy or substandard position is hardly worth writing home about. Eisner's (1979) view has the same defect as Kerlinger's: 'What so-called objectivity means is that we believe in what we believe and that others share our beliefs as well. This process is called consensual validation' (p. 214). It is important to realize, along with Scriven, that 'consensual' and 'validation' are uncomfortable bedfellows. Scriven makes it clear that 'validity' is a term that belongs with 'qualitative objectivity', not with 'quantitative' or 'consensus'. Nevertheless, Eisner's and Kerlinger's concern with the role of the community of believers is not entirely misplaced, as will soon be seen.

The missing ingredient, the element that is required to produce objectivity in the qualitative sense, is nothing mysterious – but it has nothing to do with consensus. Gunnar Myrdal, Karl Popper, and Israel Scheffler have put their fingers on it: It is acceptance of the *critical tradition*. A view that is objective is one that has been opened up to scrutiny, to vigorous examination, to challenge. It is a view that has been teased out, analyzed, criticized, debated – in general, it is a view that has been forced to face the demands of reason and of evidence. When this has happened, we have some assurance (though never absolute assurance) that the view does not reflect the whim or bias of some individual or group; it is a view that has respectable warrant. Myrdal (1969) states:

> The method of detecting biases is simple although somewhat laborious. When the unstated value premises of research are kept hidden and for the most part vague, the results presented contain logical flaws. When inferences are confronted with premises, there is found to be a *non sequitur*

concealed, leaving the reasoning open to invasion by uncontrolled influences . . . This element of inconclusiveness can be established by critical analysis. (pp. 53–54)

Popper (1976) expresses a similar point in a manner that makes even clearer that a community of inquirers can only hope to be qualitatively objective when conditions allow them to subscribe to – and actually apply in practice – the critical spirit:

> What may be described as scientific objectivity is based solely upon a critical tradition which, despite resistance, often makes it possible to criticize a dominant dogma. To put it another way, the objectivity of science is not a matter of the individual scientists but rather the social result of their mutual criticism, of the friendly-hostile division of labour among scientists, of their co-operation and also of their competition. For this reason, it depends, in part, upon a number of social and political circumstances which make criticism possible. (p. 95)

Thus Eisner and Kerlinger need to do two things to strengthen their accounts. In the first place, they have to stress that the community of inquirers must be a critical community, where dissent and reasoned disputation (and sustained efforts to overthrow even the most favored of viewpoints) are welcomed as being central to the process of inquiry. Second, they must abandon their references to agreement or consensus. A critical community might never reach agreement over, say, two viable alternative views, but if both of these views have been subjected to critical scrutiny, then both would have to be regarded as objective. (Once again, the term *objective* does not mean true.) And even if agreement is reached, it can still happen that the objective view reached within such a community will turn out to be wrong – this is the cross that all of us living in the new nonfoundationalist age have to learn to bear!

Kuhnism

Thomas S. Kuhn popularized the notion that inquirers always work within the context of a paradigm – a framework that determines the concepts that are used and that also contains exemplars, or model inquiries, which direct attention toward some problems as being key and away from other problems or issues regarded (from that perspective) as somewhat trivial. Many scholars have interpreted Kuhn as supporting a relativistic position whereby it does not make sense to ask which one of various competing paradigms is the correct one; since such judgments can only be made from within a paradigm, inquirers are not able to step outside to examine their paradigms etically. In a sense, then, all inquirers are trapped within their own paradigms; they will judge certain things as being true (for them) that other inquirers in other paradigms will judge as being false (for them). To those who have taken such relativism seriously, there has seemed to be little place in the Kuhnian universe for objectivity.

Thus, sometimes when the possibility of achieving objectivity is being questioned, the focus of attention is the framework within which inquiry is being pursued. For example, Freudians use a particular theoretical frame – they are guided by distinctive concepts and hypotheses – and, of course, for a dedicated worker in this psychoanalytic tradition, the possibility of using some quite different framework does not arise as a practicable alternative. The same situation exists, it has been argued, even if the inquirer does not subscribe to some well-known paradigm; for even here, the inquirer must be working with *some* concepts and hypotheses that serve as bedrock for the endeavor. Thus, to repeat Ratcliffe (1983):

> Most research methodologists are now aware that *all* data are theory-, method-, and measurement-dependent. That is, 'facts' are determined by the theories and methods that generate their collection; indeed, theories and methods *create* the facts. And theories, in turn, are grounded in and derived from the basic philosophical assumptions their formulators hold regarding the nature of and functional relationship between the individual, society, and science. (p. 148; emphasis in origianl)

Gunnar Myrdal, Elliot Eisner, and the 'anarchist' philosopher of science Paul Feyerabend (1978) are among those making similar points.

It is a somewhat controversial point whether choice of a framework or paradigm can be made objectively; but it is clear that the tide of philosophical debate has been running steadily against Kuhn (and relativism) and hence in favor of the view that it *is* possible to judge as better or worse the considerations that are advanced in support of any particular paradigm. (For a summary of the relevant arguments, see Newton-Smith, 1981; Siegel, 1987). More to the point, the following is also very clear: *Within* any particular framework inquirers can go about their work with more or less facility. Not all Freudians are equally adept; some are bunglers, some are misogynists or suffer from homophobia, and some may even be anti-Republican or anti-Democrat in orientation, and their work as Freudians might be indelibly stamped by these predilections. So sometimes when objectivity is being discussed, the focus of interest is whether it is possible to escape from bias while working or making judgements inside one's framework. Myrdal (1969) seems to have had this focus when he wrote:

> Biases are thus not confined to the practical and political conclusions drawn from research. They are much more deeply seated than that. They are the unfortunate results of concealed valuations that insinuate themselves into research at all stages, from its planning to its final presentation. As a result of their concealment, they are not properly sorted out and thus can be kept undefined and vague. (p. 52)

The point, of course, is that the two foci – choice between paradigms, and choices and work within a particular paradigm – must not be confused. An argument that establishes that at one of these levels objectivity is impossible to achieve (accepting, for the moment, that such an argument could be mounted) does not address the issue of whether the other type of objectivity lies out of reach. There are, however, grounds for believing that this confusion does exist. Eisner, for example, argues strongly that it is naive to believe in framework objectivity, but his published advice on the methodology of qualitative research does not stress the dangers of bias in judgment within frameworks, and he does not discuss in any detail the steps that can be taken to avoid it. As was seen earlier, with one broad stroke he does away with objectivity in all its senses, replacing it with consensual validation. (For a further discussion of these issues, see Phillips, 1987b.)

Can objectivity of judgment within a framework or paradigm be achieved? It seems clear that the answer is in the affirmative. Consider a group of qualitative researchers who are working on similar problems, using the same intellectual framework to shape their approaches. What property must their judgments have in order to be regarded as objective? As was shown earlier, it will not suffice for these inquirers merely to *agree* in their judgments. Instead, they would have to show that their own personal biases and valuations had been exposed to critical examination, and the role that these predilections played in their investigations would need to have been rigorously examined. Furthermore, as already mentioned, qualitative research (no less than quantitative research) is subject to a variety of threats to its validity – qualitative researchers are liable to misjudge the frequency rate of certain behaviors that are of interest, they are likely to be unduly influenced by positive instances and not so sensitive to the significance of negative instances, they are likely to be unduly influenced or 'anchored' by experiences undergone early in the research, and so on (Sadler, 1982). To achieve objectivity within a paradigm, then, the researcher has to ensure that his or her work is free from these problems, and again the presence of a critical tradition is the best safeguard. When work is sent to blind peer review, when researchers are forced to answer their critics, when researchers are supposed to be acquainted with the methodological and substantive literature (and when others can point out when they are not), and when researchers try honestly to refute their own dearly held beliefs, then bias and the other obvious shortcomings are likely to be eliminated, and the judgment (or judgments) reached by the community of scholars should be objective in the relevant sense.

The conflation of the contexts of discovery and justification

The philosopher of science Hans Reichenbach (1953) drew what is now a well-known distinction between the context of discovery in science and the context of justification. In recent years some have argued that the distinction between these is blurry at best, and a few seminal writers seem to have ignored the distinction altogether – though with arguably disastrous results.[6] Nevertheless, for heuristic purposes Reichenbach's distinction turns out to be a very fruitful one.

The relevant point in the present context is this: processes involved in, and even central to, the *making* of discoveries during the pursuit of a research program may not be involved – and might be counterproductive if allowed to intrude – when the discoveries are *checked* and *tested* and *critically evaluated*. Both Israel Scheffler (1967) and Karl Popper (1976) see this distinction as crucial for understanding objectivity in research. Thus Popper, having in mind the context of discovery, writes that

> We cannot rob the scientist of his partisanship without also robbing him of his humanity, and we cannot suppress or destroy his value judgments without destroying him as a human being *and as a scientist*. Our motives and even our purely scientific ideals . . . are deeply anchored in extra-scientific and, in part, in religious valuations. Thus the 'objective' or the 'value-free' scientist is hardly the ideal scientist. (p. 97; emphasis in original)

Objectivity in research is not, for Popper, a property of the individual researcher: 'It is a mistake to assume that the objectivity of a science depends upon the objectivity of the scientist' (p. 96). Objectivity, in this view, is a property of the context of justification; as we have seen in the earlier discussion it is in a sense a social matter, for it depends upon communal acceptance of the critical spirit.

CONCLUSION

Before bringing this discussion to a close, a penultimate point must be made. It may have been noted that, throughout, nothing has been made of the distinction between quantitative and qualitative inquiry. For many authors, of course, the distinction is crucial, and qualitative inquiry can only be objective insofar as it approximates to quantitative inquiry. Fred Kerlinger (1973) seems to be representative of this stance:

> Objective methods of observation are those in which anyone following the prescribed rules will assign the same numerals to objects and sets of objects as anyone else. An objective procedure is one in which agreement among observers is at a maximum. In variance terms, observer variance is at a minimum. This means that judgmental variance, the variance due to differences in judges' assignment of numerals to objects, is zero. (p. 491)

He acknowledges that all methods of observation are inferential but sees procedures that assign numbers as 'more objective'.

From the point of view of the new nonfoundationalist epistemology, there is little difference between qualitative and quantitative inquiry. Bad work of either kind is equally to be deplored; and good work of either kind is still – at best – only tentative. But the good work in both cases will be objective, in the sense that it has been opened up to criticism, and the reasons and evidence offered in both cases will have withstood serious scrutiny. The works will have faced potential refutation, and insofar as they have survived, they will be regarded as worthy of further investigation.

Another way of putting this is that in all types of inquiry, insofar as the goal is to reach credible conclusions, there is an underlying epistemological similarity. Even in hermeneutics – a mode of qualitative inquiry that at first sight seems far from the 'objective' science of physics – there is appeal to evidence, there is testing and criticism of hypotheses (Follesdal, 1979).

It turns out, then, that what is crucial for the objectivity of any inquiry – whether it is qualitative or quantitative – is the critical spirit in which it has been carried out. And, of course, this suggests that there can be *degrees*; for the pursuit of criticism and refutation obviously can be carried out more or less seriously. 'Objectivity' is the label – the 'stamp of approval' – that is used for inquiries that are at one end of the continuum; they are inquiries that are prized because of the great care and responsiveness to criticism with which they have been carried out. Inquiries at the other end of the continuum are stamped as 'subjective' in that they have not been sufficiently opened to the light of reason and criticism. Most human inquiries are probably located somewhere near the middle, but the aim should be to move in the direction that will earn a full stamp of approval!

ACKNOWLEDGEMENTS

I wish to thank the members of the California Association for Philosophy of Education, and especially Harvey Siegel, for the comments and criticisms that have helped to make this paper more objective.

NOTES

1. Myrdal seems to use 'bias' in this way throughout his book.
2. A similar confusion bedeviled critics of William James's work; see Phillips (1984).
3. Hanson's work and its general impact – and the ways in which it has been misinterpreted – is discussed in Phillips (1987a).
4. See particularly the concession Hanson (1965) makes at the bottom of p. 23.
5. Ernest House (1980) discusses Scriven's essay admiringly and in some depth.
6. See, for example, the mischief this causes in some of Piaget's work, as discussed by Phillips (1982).

REFERENCES

Eisner, E. (1979). *The educational imagination.* New York: Macmillan.
Eisner, E. (1986, September). The primacy of experience and the politics of method. Lecture delivered at the University of Oslo, Norway.
Feyerabend, P. (1978). *Against method.* London: Verso.

Follesdal, D. (1979). Hermeneutics and the hypothetico-deductive method. *Dialectica,* *33*(3–4), 319–336.

Hanson, N. R. (1965). *Patterns of discovery.* Cambridge: Cambridge University Press.

House, E. (1980). *Evaluating with validity.* Beverly Hills, CA: Sage.

Kerlinger, F. (1973). *Foundations of behavioral research* (2nd ed.). New York: Holt, Rinehart & Winston.

Myrdal, G. (1969). *Objectivity in social research.* New York: Pantheon.

Nagel, E. (1979). *Teleology revisited.* New York: Columbia University Press.

Newton-Smith, W. (1981). *The rationality of science.* London: Routledge.

Phillips, D. C. (1982). Perspectives on Piaget as philosopher. In S. & C. Modgil (Eds), *Jean Piaget: consensus and controversy* (pp. 13–29). London: Holt, Rinehart & Winston.

Phillips, D. C. (1984). Was William James telling the truth after all? *The Monist, 67*(3), 419–434.

Phillips, D. C. (1987a). *Philosophy, science, and social inquiry.* Oxford, UK: Pergamon.

Phillips, D. C. (1987b). Validity in qualitative research. *Education and Urban Society,* *20*(1), 9–24.

Popper, K. (1968). *Conjectures and refutations.* New York: Harper.

Popper, K. (1976). The logic of the social sciences. In T. Adorno et al. (Eds), *The positivist dispute in German sociology* (pp. 87–104). New York: Harper.

Ratcliffe, J. (1983). Notions of validity in qualitative research methodology. *Knowledge Creation, Diffusion, Utilization, 5*(2), 147–167.

Reichenbach, H. (1953). *The rise of scientific philosophy.* Berkeley & Los Angeles: University of California Press.

Sadler, D. (1982). Intuitive data processing as a potential source of bias in naturalistic evaluations. In E. House et al. (Eds), *Evaluation Studies Review Annual* (Vol. 7, pp. 199–205). Beverly Hills, CA: Sage.

Scheffler, I. (1967). *Science and subjectivity.* Indianapolis: Bobbs-Merrill.

Scriven, M. (1972). Objectivity and subjectivity in educational research. In L. Thomas (Ed.), *Philosophical redirection of educational research* (71st Yearbook of the NSSE; pp. 94–142). Chicago: National Society for the Study of Education.

Siegel, H. (1987). *Relativism refuted.* Dordrecht, The Netherlands: Reidel.

PART 2:

Doing educational research

6

HOW TO THINK ABOUT CAUSALITY

J. Hage and B. F. Meeker

[. . .]

Time and asymmetry: irreversibility and entropy

One of the few features of causality that is generally agreed upon is that a causal process goes in one direction only, and that the action of the cause comes first in time. (Recall that teleology, the idea that a cause is the end state toward which an event is heading, is not acceptable scientifically.) If we know the sequence in which events occur, we must take that into account in establishing which causes what; the one that occurs second can never be the cause of the one that occurred first.

For example, if we know that a high school student's parents finished their education before the student entered high school, we might be able to attribute the student's success in school to the parents' education, but we could not attribute the parents' education to the student's success in high school. In an individual case, of course, we might find that a parent had dropped out of school, and then later in life returned to finish a degree after seeing his or her own children through high school. If in fact the parent's graduation follows the son's or daughter's in time sequence, we would not be able to attribute the child's success to the parent's eventual degree; we would have to attribute it to something existing at the time the child was in high school.

But suppose, you might say, the child was highly motivated to do well because the parent had not finished and kept telling the child he would go back to school and finish as soon as the child's education was complete? Could we not attribute some of the child's behavior to the parent's future education? No, not at all; but we could possibly attribute the child's educational behavior to the parent's goals and advice, which did exist prior to the child's success in school.

In the physical sciences, time is itself one of the fundamental concepts out of which theory and observation is built. One of the basic laws of physics, the Second Law of Thermodynamics, tells us that physical systems tend to greater disorder over time. In other words, a physical system cannot be put back in exactly the same state it was in previously without expenditure of additional energy. This is one reason that causality must work in one direction (cause first, effect later in time); changes that occur over time cannot be reversed.

We may apply this to social systems also. A person, group, organization, set of beliefs and so on is never exactly the same at two different points in time. For construction of causal theories, this means several things. First, we should always look for time sequences. We may not always be able to find them empirically, nor may we be able to propose them theoretically. We may not have enough knowledge to hypothesize which of two events came first, or we may have only cross-sectional data to look at. We should, however, always ask the question.

Secondly, we must take time sequences into account when we know them. Having asked the question which of two events occurred first, or which might theoretically have occurred first, if there is an answer we must use that sequence in our theory. This will affect the way we conceptualize and measure variables, because we will be deliberately looking for states or events that may be seen as part of a sequence, and that are located at a particular point in time. The time at which something occurs becomes an integral part of observation or measurement.

If we do know a time sequence, however, we must avoid the error of assuming that a time sequence somehow proves causality. This is one of the classic errors in reasoning (it even has a Latin name: *post hoc ergo propter hoc* – following the fact therefore caused by the fact), and is the same kind of error as assuming that correlation proves causality. Just because I did my laundry on Tuesday morning and had an automobile accident on Tuesday afternoon does not mean doing my laundry caused me to have an accident. I might be able to figure out a causal link, of course; for example, having laundry baskets in my car obstructed my vision so I did not see an on-coming car and hence ran into it. If I do this, I am thinking of a causal mechanism, a process or chain of events by which the laundry creates the conditions under which the accident occurs. This is what I should do, to use causal reasoning properly and also to avoid future accidents. If I cannot construct a theory about a mechanism, I should not assume a causal link between two events that occur in a time sequence.

The idea that nothing is exactly the same at two different time points has another implication. This is that when things appear not to be changing, we need to seek causal explanations just as much as when we do observe change. The stability of an organization, or the lack of change in an individual's behavior or attitudes, requires explanation in the same way that observed changes require explanation; some 'energy' must have been expended to keep them that way. If we consider, for example, a 'traditional' society, in which there is a strong emphasis on continuity, on doing things the 'way the ancestors did', we will notice that a great deal of effort goes into maintaining the tradition. Socialization of children, ritual, social activities, authority patterns, art and so on are required to keep the society from changing. In the case of a physical organism, energy in the form of food, shelter and exercise is necessary to keep the organism from deterioration.

It is less obvious, and perhaps more controversial, to assert that ideas, beliefs, and attitudes of individuals are also different at different time points (even if they register the same value on some measure), and that some causal process goes into maintenance as well as change of ideas and attitudes. This point is recognized by [those who have argued] that the past is always being re-created by individuals and groups in light of the present. A memory of a past event is recalled differently because the person recalling it has new experiences, ideas, and beliefs to form the context for the memory. Likewise, an attitude may be stable ('I've never liked turnips, and I still don't') but that is because the information and experiences the person has in the meantime support the attitude, or at least do not contradict it. People engage in behavior and seek out experiences that support their existing attitudes, and avoid those that do not. These processes provide a causal mechanism for explaining both change and persistence of cognitions and attitudes.

What if we observe a social system, a set of beliefs or customs, that appears to change and then later to return to an earlier state? According to the principle of time asymmetry, there is no such thing as something 'automatically' returning to a previous state. Something else must happen to cause a return to a previous state, and that something else is a different causal process. A process that creates a change cannot be reversed. When it appears that a situation has been reversed, we must assume that another causal process is operating, creating change that leads to a state that looks like a previous state, although it is never exactly the same. For example, many programs designed to 'rehabilitate' persons such as criminals or drug abusers have a high rate of recidivism. People enter the program, change in some ways, and then apparently return to their previous state. The return to a previous state requires a causal explanation just as much as does the change induced by the program. Usually, such an explanation is in terms of a failure of the program to deal with the 'underlying causes' of the problem. That is, processes that were creating the behavior in the first place have resumed their action.

Reciprocal causation, equilibrium, and disequilibrium

The crucial role of time in causality raises another important issue: asymmetry and the question of reciprocal causality. In trying to decide which event is the cause and which the effect, we must assume that the cause creates the effect but that the effect does *not* create the cause. For example, the height of an athlete may affect his or her skill at playing basketball, but the athlete's skill at basketball does not affect height. In our previous example, we have noted that the parents' education affected the children's but the children's education did not affect the parents'. We may want to note that time sequence is important to establishing this asymmetry; a person's height is primarily affected by genetic features that are present at birth, and parents generally finish their education long before their children do. The other point we can make about asymmetry is that we can think of a mechanism or mechanisms whereby height creates basketball playing and parents' education creates children's. The tall youth may be encouraged to play, the short one discouraged, for example; the college-educated parent may begin saving for a child's college education when the child is quite young while the high school dropout parent may not have the financial resources to do so. On the other hand, it is difficult to think of a mechanism whereby differences in basketball playing experience can create differences in height. It is also difficult, although not impossible, to think of a mechanism whereby differences in children's education can create differences in parents' education.

In many cases, however, it is quite possible to think of mechanisms whereby one event creates another at one time, and the reverse causal process occurs at a different time. We can think of such a relationship between coordination and basketball playing, for example; the better coordinated athlete will be encouraged to play more, and the more frequent player will become better coordinated. Similarly, in a few cases the experience of sending a child to college may create in the parent a desire to attend himself. In the case of attitudes and behavior, the causal process can work in both directions; people seek experiences consistent with their attitudes, and having engaged in certain behavior may change or reinforce an existing attitude. In organizations, having to replace a key person may create conditions that make it difficult for the successor, and hence increase rates of turnover. Such two-way causal processes are called reciprocal or mutual causal processes.

Do reciprocal causal processes violate the principles of time sequence and asymmetry? No, because we do not assume that they occur simultaneously. In each case, the process must be assumed to work in successive time periods, or with different populations. For example, the effect of parents' education on children's occurs at one time, and the effect of children's on parents' (if it occurs) happens later. It may also happen in the two directions at the same time but with different people: parents who are college educated are saving and planning for their children's college, encouraging the children to think about it, providing high school advantages that will help with college, exposing the children to friends who intend to go to college, and so on. At the same time, a population of non-college parents may be having the experience of seeing their own children apply for and attend college (or possibly drop out of school) and change their own aspirations and behavior as a result. In this case, there are two processes operating quite differently for different populations. In empirical research, we would observe individuals moving in both directions (children being influenced by parents, and parents by children) but not the same individuals in the same time period. If more children are influenced by parents than vice versa, we will on average observe more movement in one direction than in the other.

One of the most familiar examples of a process of reciprocal causation is a *feedback* mechanism, which keeps a system in a state of equilibrium. For example, a thermostat on a furnace works this way. One causal process works through the burning of fuel in the furnace, which creates an increase in temperature. At a certain temperature, the switch on the thermostat expands and shuts off the furnace. With the furnace off, the temperature drops, the material in the thermostat contracts until the switch is turned on, and the furnace starts again. The result (when the system is working properly) is a house maintained at a temperature within a specified range. Many social systems have feedback processes. The classic market is one example: when prices of a product are low, many people buy the product. The increase in demand makes the product scarcer, and enables the producer to raise the price. A higher price discourages buyers, which then encourages sellers to lower a price in order to complete for buyers. The result (when the process works) is to maintain prices and quantity of sales within a stable range. The reciprocal effect is called a feedback, because it feeds the result of one stage back into the cause for the next stage.

A system in which a feedback process keeps a state (such as the temperature of the house or the price of candy bars) within a limited range is said to be in equilibrium; the average state of the system does not change over time. As we have suggested, any system that appears not to change over time is probably being maintained by some causal processes. Feedback mechanisms are something to look for in such a case. Or, to take another example, beliefs and behavior may each affect the other to create what on average looks like no relationship between the two (this example is adapted from Chen and Land, 1986). If people who believe they are susceptible to tooth decay are more likely to see a dentist (their belief causes their behavior by mobilizing their fear and desire to prevent dental problems), and if people who see a dentist often are less likely to believe they are susceptible to tooth decay (their behavior has caused their beliefs, through reassuring them that their teeth are in good condition and well cared for), and if the two processes have approximately equal effects, we will observe no overall correlation between belief about one's susceptibility to tooth decay and behavior of seeing a dentist.

There are also growth processes that are in equilibrium. The most typical is the growth of the economy. If it grows too fast, then it is said to be overheating, there is a risk of inflation, and the state may step in and attempt to slow down the growth rate. Conversely, if growth rates become too low, say below 2 per cent, then there is concern about rising unemployment, and the state will attempt to stimulate the economy in various ways. Nor is economic growth the only factor that is monitored. The cost of health care, the quality of education, the production of scientists and engineers, the level of infant mortality, and many other macro societal performances are monitored and attempts are made to increase or decrease the rate of change. The people who are trying to monitor these rates of change and make things work, whether they are teachers in a school, social workers in a community, politicians in a legislature, or bureaucrats in government, use causal thinking. An intervention requires causal thinking of some sort.

Not all reciprocal causal processes produce equilibrium, however. Some may lead to an ever-increasing rate of change or some form of disequilibrium. The self-fulfilling prophecy involved in a run on a bank is an example; the rumor of the bank's failure causes people to withdraw funds, which in turn causes the bank's solvency to decrease, which in turn causes more fear of the bank's failure and more withdrawals, and so on until (unless the cycle is stopped) the bank does fail. Escalation of conflicts whether between individuals or nations may have this type of reciprocal causation also. An initial act of hostility causes the injured party to retaliate, which in turn causes the original actor to become more angry, fearful, or hostile and to engage in more hostile behavior.

Sometimes reciprocal causation can result in a system moving to a totally different state over time. The example we have been using of parents and children influencing each other's education can be pursued to its ultimate conclusion, which would be that all adults would have a college education. This is because once a person has a college education, he or she does not move back into the state of not having one; all the movement is in one direction. Thus, if many parents influence their children and a few children influence their parents, as long as there are any children of non-college parents who do attend college, over the course of many generations the system will change to one in which all people have attended college. (See Coleman, 1964, for examples of a number of types of equilibrium processes and the mathematics that can be used to describe them.)

We can summarize by saying that there are at least three different kinds of causal feedback processes found in social systems. The first and most commonly mentioned is the cybernetic control described above in the example of the thermostat. Conflict rates, crime rates, and various kinds of performances that are closely monitored are all examples. The second kind is the growth processes described in the discussion of the economy, and the third is those feedback processes that produce disequilibrium.

State variables and process variables

In thinking about causal relationships, we find it useful to make a distinction between *state* and *process* variables. In a causal process, a state variable is a condition that we can observe, which is stable enough for us to measure, and which is either the beginning or end of a causal process.

For example, we observe and can measure parents' education and son's or daughter's education, or organizational size and structural differentiation, or capital formation and economic growth. Much more difficult to observe are the social processes and their causal mechanisms that connect parents' education with their children's education, size with structural differentiation, and capital formation with economic growth. We may name a pair of variables, but the causal linkages are multiple and operate under a whole series of conditions that affect the way they work. A process variable is a condition that changes as a causal process unfolds, making it difficult to capture or measure, but necessary to hypothesize in order to answer the question 'How did this happen; how did A affect B?' Below we discuss status attainment processes as one extended example.

Most of the standard demographic variables are state variables: gender, race, education, size or region of place of residence, attitude and so on. State variables that apply to organizations include size, complexity, or centralization of authority. An example of process variables would be the processes we might propose as intervening between two state variables, if we think one 'causes' another. For example, if we believe that gender causes differences in income (males earn more than females), we need to specify what some of the processes are by which males' and females' incomes are created and why those processes differ. We might include type of occupation and processes of recruitment into occupation, overt and covert discrimination in hiring or promotion, gender-based differences in achievement motivation, or differences in the integration of work and family responsibilities for men and women. We do not assume that people simply show up at a pay window and line up for different-sized paychecks on the basis of gender; other intervening processes must be there.

We may not immediately be able to observe all the processes; some may be moving too fast for us to catch (for example, a particular employment decision) or others may be difficult to document (because people will not provide true answers to our questions, for example). However, we need to propose them in order to understand the causal process. We should also note that what constitutes a state variable in one causal theory may well be a process variable in another. For example, if we investigate discrimination in employment as a process we may use recruitment practices of a firm as a state variable; something observable, stable over time, and itself both a result of some causal processes and an instigator of others.

CAUSALITY AS A NETWORK

[. . .] Consideration of the complexity of real world events and processes leads us to look for a complex set of conditions in any causal situation, which set of conditions combined creates the effect. Within the set of conditions, however, we then look for a condition or event that is essential to the ability of that complex set of conditions to create the effect. [. . .] We need some way of presenting a theory that takes the complexity into account while still allowing for systematic analysis of relationships. A useful model for this is a *network*. A network consists of points (representing events or states) and lines connecting the points (representing relationships between the events or states).

A standard way of showing this kind of theory is a 'path model' [. . .]. A path model is a kind of graph, consisting of points and directed lines or arrows. When we want to hypothesize a causal relationship between one event and another, we draw an arrow pointing from one point to another, or from the cause to the effect. A line joining two points without an arrowhead can be used to indicate that we think the two events are related but do not know the causal direction (by convention in using this kind of graph, a noncausal relationship is drawn with a curved line, and causal arrows are straight lines). Two points that are not connected by an arrow have no direct causal connection (see Blalock, 1969).

For example, if we want to discuss the effects of a change in speed laws for automobile traffic, we may suggest that lowering the speed limit saves fuel, because cars run more efficiently at lower speeds, and that lowering the speed limit reduces death from accidents, because there are fewer accidents at lower speeds, and fatalities from the accidents that do occur are fewer. This could be expressed as shown in Figure 1.

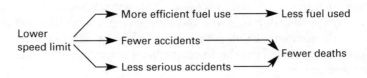

Figure 1

Links in the causal network: direct, indirect, spurious, and conditional

Direct causal effects

In the causal network in Figure 1, the arrows from lower speed limit to more efficient fuel use, to fewer accidents, and to less serious accidents represent a direct causal connection. We hypothesize that lowering the speed limit created conditions under which processes that produce efficient fuel use (properties of the internal combustion engine, for example) will operate. Likewise, lowering the speed limit will create conditions under which the processes that produce accidents (drivers losing control of their cars, for example) will operate less and hence produce fewer accidents. In turn, the arrow from more efficient fuel use to less fuel used is a direct causal connection. The amount of fuel used is controlled directly by how efficiently cars use their fuel. (Notice that we do not say that consumption of fuel by automobiles is the only factor that controls the amount of fuel used, just that it is a factor, and [. . .] if it is changed the amount of fuel consumed will change.) Finally, the number and seriousness of accidents exerts a causal control over the number of highway fatalities. (Once again, this may not be the only factor; for example, improvements in medical treatment of accident victims could also affect the number of highway fatalities.)

Spurious causal effects

If the effects of changing the speed limit are as pictured in Figure 1, a curious thing will happen; we will observe that the decline in fuel consumption and the decline in highway fatalities will occur at about the same time, and will be correlated statistically. They may even occur with an observable time sequence, since fuel is consumed at the moment the car is driven, while people may take a while to die from the effects of accidents. Does this mean that a decline in fuel use caused a decline in highway deaths? No; to suggest that would be to make two of the errors we have all been warned against, assuming that correlation or time sequence proves causality. We can think of no mechanism or process through which a decline in fuel consumption could create fewer deaths, nor one through which a decline in deaths could create less fuel consumption (if anything, this should work the other way, since there are now more people around to drive and use up fuel!) This illustrates nicely how causality is a theoretical statement, an argument about some mechanism of change. It is theory and only theory that lets us decide how to interpret the meaning of the statistical associations we find.

On the other hand, the decline in fuel consumption and the decline in highway fatalities are not completely unrelated. That is, they are not related only by chance. To say they are *un*related would be to say that there is in any given time period a probability that fuel consumption will go down, and also a probability that highway deaths will decline, and that it just happened that in the time period we are examining these two probabilities coincided. The correlation we observe is not due to chance; it is because the two events are *both* caused by the same event, the change in speed laws. This type of relationship, in which two events are associated because both are caused by the same prior event rather than because one causes the other, is called a *spurious* relationship. Since the word spurious means 'false' it is easy to assume that a spurious relationship is not causal at all, but it really means that two events are part of the same causal network although they have no causal effect on each other. A genuinely 'false' causal relationship would be one that relates two events only by chance.

Examples of spurious relationships abound; positive correlations have been found between such things as the number of storks and the birth rate (storks choose rural areas to live in, which also have higher birth rates) and the price of whiskey and the salaries of Baptist ministers (both caused by inflation or recession).

Spurious causal relationships are particularly important for applied social scientists to look for. This is because many of the unanticipated and unintended consequences of social intervention occur as events spuriously related to the event that was the intended consequence. In our example, the intended consequence of a change in speed laws may have been to reduce fuel consumption, and the reduction in traffic fatalities may have been entirely unexpected. In this case, the unanticipated consequence is also a desirable one, but it often happens that there are undesired consequences of social intervention.

Next we have the case of *indirect* causal relationships. [. . .] We assert that there will always be indirect links on the chain of causality between event A and event B, and that a large part of the effort of both theorists and methodologists must be to specify the links in the chain of indirect causality.

Indirect causal relationships

In the example above, the link between speed limit and fuel consumption is *indirect*; the lower speed limit affects something else, in this case the efficiency of the engines, which in turn affects the dependent variable, the rate of fuel consumption. The effect of lower speed limit on fatalities operates through two mechanisms: one is that fewer accidents occur at lower speeds and the other that accidents that occur at lower speeds are less severe. These in turn depend on other intermediate mechanisms, some social (for example, that people actually drive more slowly when the speed limit is lower), some physical (the actions of automobiles at different speeds), and some physiological (the response of the human body to crashes of different severity).

The 'cause' in our model above, the speed laws, may itself be caused by other events further back in the network; for example, a fuel shortage or a public outcry over highway deaths. We should also note that other mechanisms might produce the same effects; for example, manufacturing more fuel-efficient cars could lower fuel consumption, and increasing drivers' skills and safety consciousness could lower accident and fatality rates. The search backward for more ultimate causes, and forward for more intervening mechanisms between cause and effect, can be never-ending. In this sense, the construction of causal theory is always open-ended – we do not feel we have the final answer. Another way to look at this is to say that any particular study is one point only in a long causal sequence, examining in detail a few steps in the sequence.

Conditional causality

Another thing we may notice in our causal network above is that a failure of one of the indirect links could make the 'cause' ineffective; for example, if drivers do not obey the new speed laws none of the subsequent changes will occur. This consideration illustrates another type of causal relationship, one that occurs under some conditions but not under others. The process we have traced out will occur only if drivers are (somehow) motivated to obey the new speed laws. Under the condition that this does not happen, the rest of the processes will not occur either. In the United States, for example, drivers in the western part of the country are more likely to drive faster than the speed laws because there is less traffic and longer distances between towns. Another condition might be how much the governor of the state supports the speed laws and how much he/she is willing to spend to enforce the laws. The idea of countervailing causes (a causal process that causes another causal process not to work) is useful here. Looking for and trying to explain exceptions, cases where a generalization does not hold, or statistical outliers can help to identify conditions under which a cause is ineffective and why.

In many cases, we will find that a causal process works in opposite ways under different conditions. For example, students who have a high tolerance for ambiguity learn better under an unstructured teaching style, while students with a low tolerance for ambiguity learn better under a structured teaching style (see Pedhazur, 1982, for this and other examples from educational research). Teaching style has a causal link to learning through the mechanism of the students' processing of information, but this mechanism works in opposite ways for different types of students. This is a conditional causal relationship, and developing a picture of the causal network means specifying what the conditions are under which the mechanisms work differently (or, as in our first example, work under one condition but not under another).

SOME EXAMPLES OF CAUSAL THINKING

An example is in order. Suppose we walk into a room and perceive a person holding a smoking gun and another person lying on the floor. We observe two state variables and make a causal inference that the change in one variable, the firing of the gun, caused a change in another variable, the person lying on the floor. This is a relatively simple causal process because it is a physical one. But it illustrates what is very common in all the sciences: we observe two situations, which we will call state variables, that we assume are part of the same system. We do not observe the actual causal process that is the trajectory of the bullet or even the firing of the gun. However, we hypothesize a mechanism, a series of events, whereby the change in one variable has created a change in the other.

The example above illustrates a physical process. By social causality we mean a social process or mechanism that produces a change in some variable. The problem is similar to the smoking gun example; we observe two variables and try to infer a causal process.

A sociological example: peer influences on academic aspirations

An example of a 'causal model' that appeared first in 1968 and 1970, when path models were first becoming popular in sociological journals, is by

Duncan, Haller and Portes (1971). The authors are interested in developing theory about the causes of (or influences on) the aspirations of high school students: do they want to go on to college or not, and what kind of occupation do they aspire to? Results of surveys of high school boys showed that there was a strong correlation between the aspirations of those boys who named each other as 'best friends'. That is, if one of a pair of friends said he wanted to go to college, the other in the pair was very likely also to say he wanted to attend college. The same surveys also show that the social status of the boys' parents and their aspirations for their sons are correlated with the boys' aspirations (parents with prestigious jobs and college educations are likely to have sons who aspire to college, and boys who say their parents want them to go to college are likely also to say they want to attend college). The boys' own academic ability, as measured by intelligence tests, is also related; boys with higher intelligence scores are more likely to aspire to college.

What is the causal network for these variables, as proposed by Duncan *et al.*? There is the time sequence; in this sample of 17-year-old boys, the parents' occupation and income must be assumed to be established before the sons' ideas about college attendance have been formed. It is also assumed in this model that the boys' intelligence is established before their aspirations, and that we do not know the causal connection between parents' social status and sons' intelligence. (In another discussion of the problem, this causal connection might be a good link to pursue.) The interesting question in this study is the role of the best friend. Several types of causal relationships are plausible.

First, we could argue that the correlation between best friends' aspirations is totally spurious. This could be the situation if boys choose their best friends because the friend has a similar background to their own. Secondly, the level of aspiration of a boy and his choice of best friend are both caused by the status of his parents, so that the best friend has parents who are also influencing him to have aspirations that will turn out to be similar to the first boy's. A graph of this would be as shown in Figure 2. In this model, there are only two causal mechanisms: one on the arrow from parents' Socio-Economic Status (SES) to SES of parents of best friend (boys choose friends who have similar background, interest, tastes, etc.), and one on the arrow from SES of parents to son's aspiration (parents' SES somehow causes sons to aspire to a similar SES).

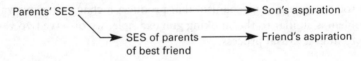

Figure 2

A second causal network would also suppose that some of the causal mechanisms work through the actions of the boys themselves in their relationships with their friends. That is, the friends influence each other directly.

If this is the case, we should assume that there is a reciprocal causal relationship; each boy influences the other. If we assume that there is also some causal influence of the boys' parents on his aspirations, this provides a picture as in Figure 3.

Figure 3

A third causal link might be from the characteristics of the boy's parents to the aspirations of his friend, and vice versa. It may be that having adults one knows well (such as the parents of one's best friend) who have attended college may make a high school boy want to attend college even if his own parents have not. (Or vice versa, having close contact with adults who did not attend college may make a high school student less likely to want to attend college even if his own parents did.) In other words, adults other than one's parents may also be role models, and it is likely that the parents of one's best friend are also role models. This path model would look like Figure 4.

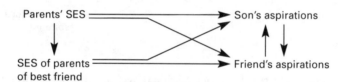

Figure 4

In the model presented by Duncan *et al.*, the variables of boys' intelligence and occupational as well as educational aspiration are also included. Does a boy's intelligence affect his friend's aspirations as well as his own? The assumption that Duncan *et al.* make is that this is not likely; it makes sense to think that a boy who is academically talented will feel more enthusiastic about pursuing higher education, but not that his talent will directly affect his friend's aspirations. There is no arrow from intelligence to friend's aspirations, although there is from the boy's own intelligence to his aspirations.

For the relationship between occupational and educational aspirations, there are once again several possibilities. We could argue that high school students first make up their minds what they want to be when they grow up, and then form their educational aspirations to meet the requirements of their chosen occupation. Thus, someone who wants to be a doctor or a teacher will assume he must attend college, while someone who wants to be a carpenter will assume he needs an apprenticeship rather than a college degree. The causal

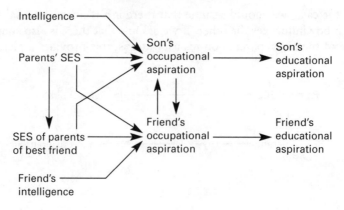

Figure 5

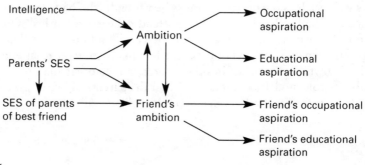

Figure 6

arrow would then run from occupational aspiration to educational aspiration. However, it is also possible that high school students do not have clear occupational goals but rather more vague 'ambitions' in which those who are more ambitious will want college degrees not only in order to get professional jobs but also for prestige in its own right. If this is the case, an unobservable general state of 'ambition' will cause both occupational and educational aspiration. The first model would be as in Figure 5, and the final model would be as in Figure 6. (This model is a simplified version of Duncan *et al.*'s final model; we have not included parents' aspirations for their sons separated from parents' SES.)

This is an example of the development of causal reasoning in sociological theory. Our critique of it is that it does not go far enough toward specifying the causal processes or mechanisms involved in the paths or arrows. How does the parents' SES influence the son's ambition? How does the SES of one's friends' parents influence one's own aspiration? How do the boys influence each other? A variety of processes are probably important. It is not possible to observe all of them, and the actual test of the model must include things that can be observed. It is also important, however, to think about the processes that may not be observable. (Duncan *et al.* actually do this when they introduce the concept of 'ambition' which is not directly observed in their study; they also introduce some statistical techniques for inferring it from observations.)

In filling in the causal processes, we can borrow from other areas of sociology. The key is to focus on sequences of events that are likely to influence a student's aspiration level. One kind of sequence can be explained by reference group theory, with the parents as a reference group imitated by the child; the more the parents read, the more the child reads. This influences scores on achievement tests as well as aspirations, and the test scores increase aspiration through a feedback process. Another sequence may be explained by social reinforcement. The parents value social status and use rewards and punishments as a way of reinforcing the child's aspirations and thus maintaining their own status. Still a third sequence comes from socialization processes. The parents teach the children about the advantages and disadvantages of going to college and how this can affect not only income and status but freedom of choice in later life.

The importance of knowing causal mechanisms and processes becomes more apparent if we move to a question of social intervention. If we want to raise the aspirations of schoolchildren, we are forced to recognize that we cannot alter the SES of the parents but we can try to change the characteristics of the friend. Evidence that schoolchildren learn from their peers was one of the factors behind the decisions of US courts in the 1970s to order local school districts to achieve racial integration of their schools. The mechanism for achieving racial balance that was tried at that time was 'busing', which means moving black children from all-black schools to predominately white schools (and vice versa) with school buses. In some instances children had to spend an hour to go just one way in the school bus. The operation of countervailing causes had not been anticipated; many white parents responded by removing their children from public schools and putting them in private schools. The consequence was that in some cities, the policy of busing produced greater racial imbalance even though its original intent was to achieve more balance.

Still another social policy in the United States designed to have an impact on school aspirations is the program called Headstart. The assumption in this program is that children's aspirations to achieve are already shaped before they arrive at school at age 5. Furthermore, performance in school will be affected by the amount of verbal stimulation received before age 5. Thus the idea of Headstart was to provide a pre-school program for children aged 3 to 5 in which more verbal stimulation and motivation would be provided. This program has proved to be enormously popular and does appear to have an impact on dropout rates over the long term.

Both busing and Headstart as social interventions have only understood part of the complex process by which aspirations are formed. The fact that one seems to have been more successful than the other illustrates how important it is to understand a whole network of causal processes. We should not be interpreted as being critical of these social experiments; we are not. Attempts to change society make us appreciate better what we do and do not know. [. . .]

CONCLUSION

[. . .] Causes occur in time prior to their effects and represent some mechanism or process which produces a change. These occur in a complex network of causal links. Types of causal link include direct, indirect, spurious, and conditional, and may also include reciprocal and feedback processes. Typically in sociology we focus on state variables such as sex, age, income, centrality, size, or complexity and do not explicate the causal mechanisms which relate the independent and dependent variables. The concept of social causality provides a useful service by calling attention to this neglected aspect of theory. Both theory development and empirical research will be enriched by considering questions of causality.

Another reason why causality is so important is the need to develop better and more effective social intervention strategies that focus on social processes. This will lead to more credibility for the social sciences as well as to more effective social policies.

REFERENCES

Blalock, H. (1969) *Theory Construction: from Verbal to Mathematical Formulations*, Prentice-Hall, Englewood Cliffs, NJ.

Chen, M. and Land, K. C. (1986) Testing the health belief model: LISREL analysis of alternative models of causal relationships between health beliefs, *Social Psychology Quarterly*, Vol. 49, pp. 45–60.

Coleman. J. S. (1964) *Introduction to Mathematical Sociology*, Free Press, New York, NY.

Duncan, O. D., Haller, A. O., and Portes, A. (1971) Peer influences on aspirations: a reinterpretation, in H. M. Blalock (Ed.) *Causal Models in the Social Sciences*, Aldine, Chicago, pp. 219–44.

Pedhazur, E. J. (1982) *Multiple Regression in Behavioral Research: Explanation and Prediction* (2nd edn), Holt, Rinehart & Winston, New York, NY.

7

INCREASING THE GENERALIZABILITY OF QUALITATIVE RESEARCH

J. W. Schofield

TRADITIONAL VIEWS OF GENERALIZABILITY

Campbell and Stanley (1963) laid the groundwork for much current thinking on the issue of generalizability just over twenty-five years ago in a groundbreaking chapter in the *Handbook of Research on Teaching*. They wrote, '*External validity* asks the question of *generalizability*: To what populations, settings, treatment variables, and measurement variables can the effect be generalized?' (1963: 175). They then went on to list four specific threats to external validity: the interaction of testing and the experimental treatment, the interaction of selection and treatment, reactive arrangements, and the interference of multiple treatments with one another. Although Campbell and Stanley specifically included populations, settings, treatments, and measurement variables as dimensions relevant to the concept of external validity, the aspect of external validity that has typically received the lion's share of attention in textbook and other treatments of the concept is generalizing to and across populations. This may well be due to the fact that, because of advances in sampling theory in survey research, it is possible to draw samples from even a very large and heterogeneous population and then to generalize to that population using the logic of probability statistics.

Campbell and Stanley (1963), as well as many others in the quantitative tradition, see the attempt to design research so that abstract generalizations can be drawn as a worthy effort, although issues connected with internal validity are typically given even higher priority. Thus researchers in the quantitative tradition have devoted considerable thought to the question of how the generalizability of experimental and quasi-experimental studies can be enhanced. Such efforts are consistent with the fact that many quantitatively oriented researchers would agree with Smith (1975: 88) that 'the goal of science is to be able to generalize findings to diverse populations and times'.

In contrast to the interest shown in external validity among quantitatively oriented researchers, the methodological literature on qualitative research has paid little attention to this issue, at least until quite recently. For example, Dobbert's (1982) text on qualitative research methods devotes an entire chapter to issues of validity and reliability but does no more than mention the issue of generalizability in passing on one or two pages. Two even more recent books, Kirk and Miller's *Reliability and Validity in Qualitative Research* (1986) and Berg's *Qualitative Research Methods for the Social Sciences* (1989), ignore the issue of external validity completely. The major factor contributing to the disregard of the issue of generalizability in the qualitative methodological literature appears to be a widely shared view that it is unimportant, unachievable, or both.

Many qualitative researchers actively reject generalizability as a goal. For example, Denzin writes:

> The interpretivist rejects generalization as a goal and never aims to draw randomly selected samples of human experience. For the interpretivist every instance of social interaction, if thickly described (Geertz, 1973), represents a slice from the life world that is the proper subject matter for interpretive inquiry . . . Every topic . . . must be seen as carrying its own logic, sense of order, structure, and meaning. (1983: 133–4)

Although not all researchers in the qualitative tradition reject generalization so strongly, many give it very low priority or see it as essentially irrelevant to their goals. One factor contributing to qualitative researchers' historical tendency to regard the issue of external validity as irrelevant and hence to disregard it is that this research tradition has been closely linked to cultural anthropology, with its emphasis on the study of exotic cultures. This work is often valued for its intrinsic interest, for showing the rich variety and possible range of human behavior, and for serving a historical function by describing traditional cultures before they change in an increasingly interconnected and homogeneous world. For researchers doing work of this sort, the goal is to describe a specific group in fine detail and to explain the patterns that exist, certainly not to discover general laws of human behavior.

Practically speaking, no matter what one's philosophical stance on the importance of generalizability, it is clear that numerous characteristics that typify the qualitative approach are not consistent with achieving external validity as it has generally been conceptualized. For example, the traditional focus on single-case studies in qualitative research is obviously inconsistent with the requirements of statistical sampling procedures, which are usually seen as fundamental to generalizing from the data gathered in a study to some larger population. This fact is often cited as a major weakness of the case study approach (Bolgar, 1965; Shaughnessy and Zechmeister, 1985).

However, the incompatibility between classical conceptions of external validity and fundamental aspects of the qualitative approach goes well beyond this. To give just one example, the experimental tradition emphasizes replicability of results, as is apparent in Krathwohl's statement: 'The heart of external validity is replicability. Would the results be reproducible in those target instances to which one intends to generalize – the population, situation, time, treatment form or format, measures, study designs and procedures?' (1985: 123). Yet at the heart of the qualitative approach is the assumption that a piece of qualitative research is very much influenced by the researcher's individual attributes and perspectives. The goal is *not* to produce a standardized set of results that any other careful researcher in the same situation or studying the same issues would have produced. Rather it is to produce a coherent and illuminating description of and perspective on a situation that is based on and consistent with detailed study of that situation. Qualitative researchers have to question seriously the *internal* validity of their work if other researchers reading their field notes feel the evidence does not support the way in which they have depicted the situation. However, they do not expect other researchers in a similar or even the same situation to replicate their findings in the sense of independently coming up with a precisely similar conceptualization. As long as the other researchers' conclusions are not inconsistent with the original account, differences in the reports would not generally raise serious questions related to validity or generalizability.

In fact, I would argue that, except perhaps in multisite qualitative studies, which will be discussed later in this paper, it is impractical to make precise replication a criterion of generalizability in qualitative work. Qualitative research is so arduous that it is unlikely that highly-quality researchers could be located to engage in the relatively unexciting task of conducting a study designed specifically to replicate a previous one. Yet studies not designed specifically for replication are unlikely to be conducted in a way that allows good assessment of the replicability issue. Of course it is possible, even likely, that specific ideas or conclusions from a piece of qualitative work can stimulate further research of a qualitative or quantitative nature that provides information on the replicability of that one aspect of a study. However, any piece of qualitative research is likely to contain so many individual descriptive and conceptual components that replicating it on a piece-by-piece basis would be a major undertaking.

THE INCREASING INTEREST IN GENERALIZABILITY IN THE QUALITATIVE TRADITION

In the past decade, interest in the issue of generalizability has increased markedly for qualitative researchers involved in the study of education. Books by Patton (1980), Guba and Lincoln (1981), and Noblit and Hare (1988), as well as papers by Stake (1978), Kennedy (1979), and others, have all dealt with this issue in more than a cursory fashion. Two factors seem to be important in accounting for this increase in attention to the issue of generalizability. First, the uses of qualitative research have shifted quite markedly in the past decade or two. In the area of education, qualitative research is not an approach used primarily to study exotic foreign or deviant local cultures. Rather it has become an approach used widely in both evaluation research and basic research on educational issues in our own society. The issue of generalizability assumes real importance in both kinds of work.

The shift in the uses of qualitative work that occurred during the 1970s was rapid and striking. The most obvious part of this shift was the inclusion of major qualitative components in large-scale evaluation research efforts, which had previously been almost exclusively quantitative in nature (Fetterman, 1982; Firestone and Herriott, 1984). The acceptance of qualitative research as a valid and potentially rich approach to evaluation progressed to the point that Wolcott wrote, with only some exaggeration, 'By the late 1970s the term "ethnography" . . . had become synonymous with "evaluation" in the minds of many educators' (1982: 82). Evaluations are expensive and time-consuming undertakings. Although formative evaluations are usually site-specific, the worth of a summative evaluation is greatly enhanced to the extent it can inform program and policy decisions relating to other sites. In fact, as Cronbach (1982) points out, when summative evaluations are reported, no more than a fraction of the audience is interested primarily in the specific program and setting that was the object of the study. Even at the study site itself, by the time the evaluation is completed, changes may well have occurred that have important consequences for program functioning and goal achievement. Thus the question of whether an evaluation's findings can usefully be generalized to a later point in time at the site at which the evaluation was conducted is an issue that, although often ignored, requires real consideration.

The issue of generalizability is also salient for more basic qualitative research on educational issues [. . .]. Funding agencies providing resources for qualitative studies of educational issues are presumably interested in shedding light on these issues generally, not just as they are experienced at one site. For example, I am currently directing a qualitative study of computer usage in an urban high school. It is clear that the impetus for the funding of this study by the Office of Naval Research derived from concerns about the Navy's own computer-based education and training efforts, not from concerns about the public schools. Quite apart from the goals of funding agencies, many qualitative researchers themselves hope to accomplish more than describing the culture of the specific school or classroom that they have chosen to study. For example, Peshkin writes of his study of school and community in a small town in Illinois, 'I hoped . . . to explicate some reality which was not merely confined to other places just like Mansfield' (1982: 63), a hope tellingly reflected in the title of his book, *Growing Up American* (1978), as opposed to 'Growing Up in Illinois' or 'Growing Up in Mansfield'. This desire to have one's work be broadly useful is no doubt often stimulated by concern over the state of education [. . .] today. It is also clearly reinforced by the fact that, unlike most readers of ethnographic reports of exotic cultures, most readers of qualitative reports on American education have had considerable exposure during their own school years to at least one version of the culture described. Thus, unless the researcher chooses a very atypical site or presents an unusually insightful analysis of what is happening, the purely descriptive value of the study may be undercut or discounted.

So far I have argued that qualitative research's shift in both purpose and locale in the last decade or two has contributed to an increased interest in generalizability among qualitative researchers. There is yet one other factor contributing to this trend – the striking rapprochement between qualitative and quantitative methodologies that has occurred in the last decade (Cronbach *et al.*, 1980; Filstead, 1979; Reichardt and Cook, 1979; Spindler, 1982). Exemplifying this trend is the shift in the position of Donald Campbell. Campbell and Stanley at one point contended that the 'one-shot case study', which is one way of describing much qualitative research, has 'such a total absence of control as to be of almost no scientific value' (1963: 176). However, more recently Campbell wrote a paper to 'correct some of [his] own prior excesses in describing the case study approach' (1979: 52) in which he takes the, for many, rather startling position that when qualitative and quantitative results conflict, 'the quantitative results should be regarded as suspect until the reasons for the discrepancy are well understood' (1979: 52).

One result of the rapprochement that has occurred is that qualitative and quantitative researchers are more in contact with each other's traditions than had typically been the case heretofore. As is often the case when a dominant tradition makes contact with a minority one, the culture and standards of the dominant group make a significant impact on the members of the minority group. This trend has most likely been reinforced by the fact that a great deal of the qualitative research on education conducted in the past fifteen years has been embedded within multimethod evaluation projects undertaken by private research firms that have traditionally specialized in quantitative research. Thus the concept of external validity and the associated issue of generalizability have been made salient for qualitative researchers, whose own tradition has not predisposed them to have given the issue a great deal of thought.

RECONCEPTUALIZING GENERALIZABILITY

Although many qualitative researchers have begun to recognize the importance of dealing with the issue of generalizability, it is clear that the classical view of external validity is of little help to qualitative researchers interested in finding ways of enhancing the likelihood that their work will speak to situations beyond the one immediately studied – that is, that it will be to some extent generalizable. The idea of sampling from a population of sites in order to generalize to the larger population is simply and obviously unworkable in all but the rarest situations for qualitative researchers, who often take several years to produce an intensive case study of one or a very small number of sites. Thus most of the work on generalizability by qualitative researchers in this decade has dealt with developing a *conception* of generalizability that is useful and appropriate for qualitative work.

A second approach to the issue of generalizability in qualitative research has been very different. A number of individuals have worked on ways of gaining generality through the synthesis of pre-existing qualitative studies. For example, Noblit and Hare (1988) have recently published a slim volume on meta-ethnography. Substantially earlier, Lucas (1974) and Yin and Heald (1975) had developed what they call the 'case survey method'. Ragin (1987) has presented yet another way of synthesizing qualitative studies, one that employs Boolean algebra. I will discuss these approaches to generalizing from qualitative case studies briefly at the end of this chapter. [This discussion is omitted here.] At the moment, I would like to focus on issues connected with the first approach – that is, with transforming and adapting the classical conception of external validity such that it is suitable for qualitative work.

Important and frequently cited discussions of conceptions of generalizability appropriate in qualitative work can be found in Guba and Lincoln (1981, 1982), Goetz and LeCompte (1984), and Stake (1978). Guba and Lincoln's stance on the issue of generalizability is aptly summarized in two excerpts of their own words. Guba and Lincoln write:

> It is virtually impossible to imagine any human behavior that is not heavily mediated by the context in which it occurs. One can easily conclude that generalizations that are intended to be context free will have little that is useful to say about human behavior. (1981: 62)

They go on to say:

> The aim of (naturalistic) inquiry is to develop an idiographic body of knowledge. This knowledge is best encapsulated in a series of 'working hypotheses' that describe the individual case. Generalizations are impossible since phenomena are neither time- nor context-free (although some transferability of these hypotheses may be possible from situation to situation, depending on the degree of temporal and contextual similarity). (1982: 238)

Given these views, Guba and Lincoln call for replacing the concept of generalizability with that of 'fittingness'. Specifically, they argue that the concept of 'fittingness', with its emphasis on analyzing the degree to which the situation studied matches other situations in which one is interested, provides a more realistic and workable way of thinking about the generalizability of research results than do more classical approaches. A logical consequence of this approach is an emphasis on supplying a substantial amount of information about the entity studied and the setting in which that entity was found. Without such information, it is impossible to make an informed judgment about whether the conclusions drawn from the study of any particular site are useful in understanding other sites.

Goetz and LeCompte (1984) place a similar emphasis on the importance of clear and detailed description as a means of allowing decisions about the extent to which findings from one study are applicable to other situations. Specifically, they argue that qualitative studies gain their potential for applicability to other situations by providing what they call 'comparability' and 'translatability'. The former term

> refers to the degree to which components of a study – including the units of analysis, concepts generated, population characteristics, and settings – are sufficiently well described and defined that other researchers can use the results of the study as a basis for comparison. (1984: 228)

Translatability is similar but refers to a clear description of one's theoretical stance and research techniques.

Stake (1978) starts out by agreeing with many critics of qualitative methods that one cannot confidently generalize from a single case to a target population of which that case is a member, since single members often poorly represent whole populations. However, he then goes on to argue that it is possible to use a process he calls 'naturalistic generalization' to take the findings from one study and apply them to understanding another *similar* situation. He argues that through experience individuals come to be able to use both explicit comparisons between situations and tacit knowledge of those same situations to form useful naturalistic generalizations.

Several major themes can be found in the work of qualitative researchers who have written recently on the concept of generalizability. Whether it is Guba and Lincoln (1981, 1982) writing of fittingness, Goetz and LeCompte (1984) writing of translatability and comparability, or Stake (1978) discussing naturalistic generalizations, the emerging view shared by many qualitative researchers appears to involve several areas of consensus. First of all, there is broad agreement that generalizability in the sense of producing laws that apply universally is not a useful standard or goal for qualitative research. In fact, most qualitative researchers would join Cronbach (1982) in arguing that this is not a useful or obtainable goal for any kind of research in the social sciences. Second, most researchers writing on generalizability in the qualitative tradition agree that their rejection of generalizability as a search for broadly applicable laws is not a rejection of the idea that studies in one situation can be used to speak to or to help form a judgment about other situations. Third, as should be readily apparent from the preceding discussion, current thinking on generalizability argues that thick descriptions (Ryle, cited in Geertz, 1973) are vital. Such descriptions of both the site in which the studies are conducted and of the site to which one wishes to generalize are crucial in allowing one to search for the similarities and differences between the situations. As Kennedy (1979) points out, analysis of these similarities and differences then makes it possible to make a reasoned judgment about the extent to which we can use the findings from one study as a 'working hypothesis', to use Cronbach's (1982) term, about what might occur in the other situation. Of course, the generally unstated assumption underlying this view is that our knowledge of the phenomena under study is sufficient to direct attention to important rather than superficial similarities and differences. To the extent that our understanding is flawed, important similarities or differences may inadvertently be disregarded.

THREE TARGETS OF GENERALIZATION

Given the growing emphasis on generalizability in qualitative research and the emerging consensus about how the concept of generalizability might most usefully be viewed by qualitative researchers, two questions present themselves:

To what do we want to generalize?
How can we design qualitative studies in a way that maximizes their generalizability?

It is to these two questions that I will devote the majority of the rest of this chapter. Although I will use the term *generalize* here and elsewhere, it is important that the reader recognize that I am not talking about generalization in the classical sense. Rather, I use it to refer to the process as conceptualized by those qualitative researchers to whose work I have just referred.

I believe that it is useful for qualitative researchers interested in the study of educational processes and institutions to try to generalize to three domains: to *what is*, to *what may be*, and to *what could be*. I will deal with these possibilities one at a time, providing the rationale for striving to generalize to each of these kinds of situations and then suggesting some ideas on how studies can actually be designed to do this.

Studying what is

From one perspective the study of any ongoing social situation, no matter how idiosyncratic or bizarre, is studying *what is*. But when I use the phrase *studying what is*, I mean to refer to studying the typical, the common, or the ordinary. The goal of describing and understanding cultures or institutions as they typically are is an appropriate aim for much current qualitative research on educational institutions and processes. If policy-makers need to decide how to change a program or whether to continue it, one very obvious and useful kind of information is information on how the program usually functions, what is usually achieved, and the like. Thus the goal of studying *what is* is one important aim for many kinds of summative evaluations. It is also appropriate outside of the area of evaluation for researchers hoping to provide a picture of the current educational scene that can be used for understanding or reflecting on it and possibly improving it. Classic works of this type that focus primarily on *what is* are Wolcott's *The Man in the Principal's Office* (1973) and Jackson's *Life in Classrooms* (1968). If one accepts the goal of designing research to maximize the fit between the research site and *what is* more broadly in society, an obvious question that arises is how this can be accomplished within the context of the qualitative tradition.

Studying the typical

One approach sometimes used is to study the typical (Bogdan and Biklen, 1981; Goetz and LeCompte, 1984; Patton, 1980; Whyte, 1984). Specifically, I would argue that choosing sites on the basis of their fit with a typical situation is far preferable to choosing on the basis of convenience, a practice that is still quite common.

The suggestion that typicality be weighed heavily in site selection is an idea that needs to be taken both more and less seriously than it currently is. When I say that it needs to be taken more seriously than it currently is, I am suggesting that researchers contemplating selecting a site on the basis of convenience or ease of access need to think more carefully about that decision and to weigh very carefully the possibility of choosing on the basis of some other criterion, such as typicality. When I say that the strategy of selecting a typical site needs to be taken less seriously than it may sometimes be, I intend to point out that choosing a typical site is not a '*quick fix*' for the issue of generalizability, because what is typical on one dimension may not be typical on another. For example, Wolcott (1973) chose to focus his ethnographic study of a principal on an individual who was typical of other principals in gender, marital status, age, and so forth. This choice most likely substantially enhanced the range of applicability or generalizability of his study. Yet such an atypical principal operating in an atypical school or an atypical system or even an atypical community might well behave very differently from a typical principal in a typical school in a typical system. The solution to this dilemma cannot be found in choosing typicality on every dimension. First of all, not too many typical principals operate in environments that are typical in every way. So this strategy gains less in the realm of generalizability or fittingness than it might appear to at first glance. More important, even if one could achieve typicality in all major dimensions that seem relevant, it is nonetheless clearly true that there would be enough idiosyncrasy in any particular situation studied so that one could not transfer findings in an unthinking way from one typical situation to another.

Carried to extremes or taken too seriously, the idea of choosing on the basis of typicality becomes impossible, even absurd. However, as a guiding principle designed to increase the potential applicability of research, it is, I believe, useful. This is especially true if the search for typicality is combined with, rather than seen as a replacement for, a reliance on the kind of thick description emphasized by Guba and Lincoln (1981, 1982), Goetz and LeCompte (1984) and Stake (1978). Selection on the basis of typicality provides the potential for a good 'fit' with many other situations. Thick description provides the information necessary to make informed judgments about the degree and extent of that fit in particular cases of interest.

In arguing that qualitative researchers would do well to seek to study the typical, I am not suggesting that we study the typical defined solely by national norms. Research that followed this prescription would greatly increase our knowledge of typical situations, but in a nation as diverse as the United States, it would provide too restricted, pallid, and homogeneous a view of our educational system. My emphasis on typicality implies that the researcher who has decided on the kind of institution or situation he or she wants to study – an urban ghetto school, a rural consolidated school, or a private Montessori school – should try to select an instance of this kind of situation that is, to the extent possible, typical of its kind. Such an approach suggests, for example, that a researcher interested in studying mathematics teaching choose to observe classrooms that use a popular text and generally accepted modes of instruction, rather than falling for convenience's sake into the study of classrooms that may well do neither of these. Furthermore, to the extent preliminary investigation of possible sites suggests that some or all are atypical in certain regards, careful thought about the possible implications of this atypicality for the topic under study may help to aid in site selection.

In sum, the point of my argument here is that choosing a site for research on the basis of typicality is far more likely to enhance the potential generalizability of one's study than choosing on the basis of convenience or ease of access – criteria that often weigh more heavily than they should. However, even if one chooses on the basis of typicality, one is in no way relieved of the necessity for thick description, for it is foolhardy to think that a typical example will be typical in all important regards. Thus thick description is necessary to allow individuals to ask about the degree of fit between the case studied and the case to which they wish to generalize, even when the fit on some of the basic dimensions looks fairly close.

Performing multisite studies

An alternate approach to increasing the generalizability of qualitative research was evident in the sudden proliferation in the 1970s of multisite qualitative studies. Such studies were almost always part of federally funded evaluation efforts focusing on the same issue in a number of settings, using similar data collection and analysis procedures in each place. Well-known examples of this approach include the Study of Dissemination Efforts Supporting School Improvement (Crandall *et al.*, 1983; Huberman and Miles, 1984) and the study of Parental Involvement in Federal Educational Programs (Smith and Robbins, 1984). One of the primary purposes of conducting such multisite studies is to escape what Firestone and Herriott (1984) have called the 'radical particularism' of many case studies and hence to provide a firmer basis for generalization.

The multisite studies conducted in the 1970s were extremely varied, although they were all quite expensive and tended to take several years to complete. At least two kinds of variation have special implications for the extent to which this approach actually seems likely to produce results that are a good basis for generalization to many other situations. The first of these is the number of sites studied. Firestone and Herriott's (1984) survey of twenty-five multisite case study efforts found major variation on this dimension, with one study including as few as three sites and another covering sixty. All other things being equal, a finding emerging repeatedly in the study of numerous sites would appear to be more likely to be a good working hypothesis about some as yet unstudied site than a finding emerging from just one or two sites.

A second dimension on which multisite studies vary, which is also likely to affect the degree of fit between these studies and situations to which one might want to generalize, concerns the heterogeneity of the sites chosen for study. Generally speaking, a finding emerging from the study of several very heterogeneous sites would be more robust and thus more likely to be useful in understanding various other sites than one emerging from the study of several very similar sites (Kennedy, 1979). Heterogeneity can be obtained by searching out sites that will provide maximal variation or by planned comparisons along certain potentially important dimensions. An example of the second strategy can be found in the parental-involvement study previously mentioned. The sites chosen for study were selected to allow comparison between urban and rural settings, between those with high and low reported degrees of involvement, and so forth (Smith and Robbins, 1984). This comparative strategy is potentially quite powerful, especially if there is heterogeneity among cases within each of the categories of interest. For example, if several rather different rural cases all share certain similarities that are not found in a heterogeneous group of urban cases, one has some reasonable basis for generalizing about likely differences between the two settings. Although the most obvious comparative strategy is to select cases that initially differ on some variable of interest as part of the research design, it is also possible to group cases in an *ex post facto* way on the basis of information gathered during the fieldwork. For example, if one were studying numerous very different classrooms and found that student achievement gains were quite high in some and quite low in others, one could compare these two sets of classrooms as a strategy for trying to suggest factors that contribute to high or low gains.

In sum, the possibility of studying numerous heterogeneous sites makes multisite studies one potentially useful approach to increasing the generalizability of qualitative work to *what is*. Yet I am very hesitant to see this approach as the only or even the best solution to the problem. First, such studies can be quite expensive, and the current lull in their funding highlights the extent to which such research is dependent on federal dollars that may or may not be forthcoming. Second, as Firestone and Herriott (1984) point out, budget constraints make it likely that studies including very large numbers of sites are less likely than studies of a relatively small number of sites to be able to devote intensive and prolonged care to studying the details of each site. Thus there is typically a trade-off to be made between the increased potential for generalizability flowing from studying a large number of sites and the increased depth and breadth of description and understanding made possible by a focus on a small number of sites. In suggesting that an increased number of sites leads to increased generalizability, I am assuming that enough attention is paid to each site to ensure that problems of internal validity do not arise. To the extent such problems do arise, generalizability is obviously threatened, since one cannot speak meaningfully of the generalizability of invalid data. The fact that roughly forty percent of the multisite studies surveyed by Firestone and Herriott (1984) involved just one or two short visits to the research site raises serious questions about whether such studies can appropriately be categorized as qualitative research in the usual sense of that term. The term *qualitative research*, and more especially the word *ethnography*, usually implies an intensive, ongoing involvement with individuals functioning in their everyday settings that is akin to, if not always identical with, the degree of immersion in a culture attained by anthropologists, who live in the society they study over a period of one or more years (Dobbert, 1982; Spindler, 1982; Wolcott, 1975). Thus it is conceivable, though not logically necessary, that attempts to gain generalizability through studying large numbers of sites undercut the depth of understanding of individual sites, which is the hallmark of the qualitative approach as it has come to be understood.

Studying what may be

The goal of portraying typical schools – or, for that matter, typical instances of federal educational programs as they now exist – is, I believe, worthwhile. Yet accepting this as our only or even primary goal implies too narrow and limited a vision of what qualitative research can do. I would like to suggest that we want to generalize not only to *what is* but also to *what may be*. Let me explain. Here I am proposing that we think about what current social and educational trends suggest about likely educational issues for the future and design our research to illuminate such issues to the extent possible. Let me use some of my own current research to illustrate this possibility, without implying that it is the best or only example of such an approach.

One very obvious and potentially important trend in education recently has been the increasing utilization of microcomputers in instruction. In fact, microcomputers are being adopted in schools at an almost frantic pace (Becker, 1986) in spite of tight educational budgets and a generally acknowledged tendency on the part of educational institutions to resist change. There is a clear division of opinion about the likely consequences of this trend. At one extreme are those who see computers as having the capability to revolutionize education in absolutely fundamental ways. Proponents of this school of thought make the rather startling claim that 'the potential of computers for improving education is greater than that of any prior invention, including books and writing' (Walker, 1984: 3). Others take quite a different stance, emphasizing the inherent conservativism of the teaching profession with regard to pedagogical change and the failure of other highly touted educational innovations to bring about far-reaching changes. Thus it seemed important to me to design a research project focused on understanding the impact of computer usage on students and classrooms (Schofield and Evans-Rhodes, 1989; Schofield and Verban, 1988). One could approach this issue with an emphasis on what is. For example, it would be possible to choose a school that is presently typical in terms of the uses it makes of computers in instruction. But this strategy encounters an immediate problem if one's goal is to speak to what may be. Changes in both microcomputer technology and in individuals' level of experience with computers have been so rapid in the past decade that a study of what is today could arguably be a study of primarily historical interest by the time it gets conducted, written, and published. In hopes of not just documenting the present, which is rapidly becoming the past, but of speaking to the future, I have made a number of methodological decisions that, in their abstract form, may be of use to others interested in making their work applicable to what may be.

Studying the 'leading edge' of change

First, since it is hard to know what kinds of computer usage will become most typical or popular in the future, I have made a point of studying a broad array of uses rather than just one particular kind. More important, I have not looked only for heterogeneity of usage but for types of usage that are now in their infancy but that many informed observers see as likely to be common in the future. Thus I consciously chose to study a school that not only uses computers as they are currently employed around the country to teach computer programing and word processing in fairly typical ways but that also was the field test site for the kind of artificially intelligent computer-based tutor that researchers in a number of centers around the country are currently developing for classroom use (Feigenbaum and McCorduck, 1983; Lawler and Yazdani, 1987). I see this choice as a step in the direction of increasing the chances that this work will 'fit' or be generalizable to the education issues important at the time the work is published. But this is only a mere first step.

Probing factors likely to differentiate the present from the future

One of the big problems in trying to make one's work applicable to even the fairly near future is, as Cronbach (1975) has so eloquently argued, that people and institutions change. Thus it is logically impossible to see the future even when studying futuristic uses of artificial intelligence, because one is studying that future technology in the context of a present-day institution peopled with individuals who are shaped by the era in which they live.

There is no completely satisfactory solution to this situation, but a partial one emerged as I grappled with the issue. It is to think through how the present and the future are likely to differ. Then the research can be structured in a way that explicitly probes the impact of things that are likely to change over time. Of course, if the analysis of the likely differences between present and future is wrong, this approach will not be particularly useful. But if the analysis is accurate, this strategy has the potential to enhance greatly the usefulness of the study.

Let me illustrate in concrete terms how I have done this. Given the rapidity with which computers are being adopted for use in widely varying arenas of life, especially in schools, it seems a reasonable expectation that one major difference between now and five to ten years in the future is what might be called the 'novelty factor'. Specifically, many of today's high school students are having their first real introduction to the computer, or at least to its use for educational purposes, in their high school classrooms. However, in ten years it is rather unlikely that high school students will be having their first exposure to educational computing in the tenth or eleventh grade. I have used this assumption, which is, I think, relatively uncontroversial, to influence the shape of my study in a way that will allow it to speak more adequately to the future. For example, in interviews students were specifically asked about the impact of novelty on their reactions to the computer and its importance in shaping their feelings about computer usage. Similarly, observers in the study carefully looked for reactions that appeared to be influenced by students' unfamiliarity with the computers. Moreover, I have been careful to find out which students have had prior computer experience and what kind of experience this has been in order to see as clearly as possible whether these students differ from those for whom computer use is a completely novel experience. The fact that students were observed during the full course of the school year allowed assessment of whether any initial differences in students' reactions due to prior experience were transitory or relatively long-lasting. To the extent that novelty is crucial in shaping students' reactions, I will be forced to conclude that my study may not help us understand the future as well as it might otherwise. To the extent that students' reactions appear to be more heavily influenced by things that are unlikely to change in the near future, such as adolescents' striving for independence from adult control, the likely applicability of the findings of the study to the near future is clearly increased.

Considering the life cycle of a phenomenon

The preceding discussion of the possible impact of novelty on students' reactions to educational computing brings up an important point regarding qualitative work and the issue of generalizability. The ethnographic habit of looking at a phenomenon over substantial time periods allows assessment of one aspect of generalizability that quantitative research usually does not – of where a particular phenomenon is in its life cycle and what the implications of this are for what is happening. Qualitative research, when studying a dynamic phenomenon, is like a movie. It starts with one image and then moves on to others that show how things evolve over time. Quantitative research, in contrast, is more typically like a snapshot, often taken and used without great regard for whether that photograph happened to catch one looking one's best or looking unusually disheveled. This point can be illustrated more substantively by briefly discussing a study that I carried out in a desegregated school during its first four years of existence (Schofield, 1989). The study tracked changes in the school by following two different groups of students from the first day they entered the school to graduation from that school three years later. Important changes occurred in race relations over the life of the institution and over the course of students' careers in the school. Such findings suggest that in asking about what happens in desegregated schools and what the impact of such schools is on students, it is important to know where both the students and the institution are in their experience with desegregation. Yet virtually all quantitative studies of desegregation, including, I must admit, some of my own, tend to ignore these issues completely. In fact, as I discovered in reviewing the desegregation literature (Schofield and Sagar, 1983), many do not even supply bare descriptive information on the life-cycle issue. Paying attention to where a phenomenon is in its life cycle does not guarantee that one can confidently predict how it will evolve. However, at a minimum, sensitivity to this issue makes it less likely that conclusions formed on the basis of a study conducted at one point in time will be unthinkingly and perhaps mistakenly generalized to other later points in time to which they may not apply.

Studying what could be

As mentioned previously, I would like to argue that qualitative research on education can be used not only to study *what is* and *what may be* but also to explore possible visions of *what could be*. By studying what could be, I mean locating situations that we know or expect to be ideal or exceptional on some *a priori* basis and then studying them to see what is actually going on there.

Selecting a site that sheds light on what could be

When studying what could be, site selection is not based on criteria such as typicality or heterogeneity. Rather it is based on information about either the *outcomes* achieved in the particular site studied or on the *conditions* obtaining there. Perhaps the best-known example of site selection based on outcomes is choosing to study classrooms or schools in which students show unusual intellectual gains, as has been done in the voluminous literature on effective schools (Bickel, 1983; Dwyer *et al.*, 1982; Phi Delta Kappan, 1980; Rutter *et al.*, 1979; Weber, 1971). For an example of site selection based on the conditions obtaining at the site, a less common approach, I will again make reference to my own work on school desegregation.

When thinking about where to locate the extended study of a desegregated school mentioned previously, I decided not to study a typical desegregated school. First, given the tremendous variation in situations characterized as desegregated, it is not clear that such an entity could be found. Second, there is a body of theory and research that gives us some basis for expecting different kinds of social processes and outcomes in different kinds of interracial schools. In fact, in the same year in which the *Brown v. Board of Education* decision laid the legal basis for desegregating educational institutions, Gordon Allport (1954) published a classic analysis of racial prejudice in which he argued that interracial contact can either increase or decrease hostility and stereotyping, depending on the kind of conditions under which it occurs. Specifically, he argued that in order to ameliorate relations between groups such as blacks and whites three conditions are especially important: equal status for members of both groups within the contact situation, a cooperative rather than a competitive goal structure, and support for positive relations from those in authority. A substantial amount of empirical and theoretical work stemming from Allport's basic insight has been carried out in the past three and a half decades, most of which supports his emphasis on the crucial importance of the specific conditions under which intergroup contact occurs (Amir, 1969; Aronson and Osherow, 1980; Cook, 1978; Pettigrew, 1967, 1969; Schofield, 1979; Schofield and Sagar, 1977; Slavin, 1980; Stephan, 1985).

It is clear that desegregating school systems often take little if any heed of the available theory and research on how to structure desegregated schools in a way likely to promote positive intergroup relations, perhaps at least partly because much of this work is laboratory based and hence may seem of questionable use in everyday situations. Thus selecting a site for study on the basis of typicality might be expected to yield a site potentially rich in sources of insight about the problems of desegregated education but weak in shedding light on what can be accomplished in a serious and sophisticated effort to structure an environment conducive to fostering positive relations between students. Since both scholars in the area of intergroup relations and the public are well aware of the potential for difficulties in desegregated schools, the task of seeing whether and how such difficulties can be overcome seems potentially more informative and useful than that of documenting the existence of such difficulties. Thus I chose to study a site that at least approximated a theoretical ideal. My goal was not to generalize to desegregated schools as a class. Rather it was to see what happens under conditions that might be expected to foster relatively positive outcomes. If serious problems were encountered at such a site, there would be reason to think that problems would be encountered in most places or, alternatively, to revise or reject the theory that led to the site selection. However, if things went well at such a site, the study would then provide an opportunity to gain some insight into how and why they go well and into what the still-intractable problems are.

Of course, the strategy of choosing a site based on some *a priori* theoretical viewpoint or, for that matter, any seriously held expectation about it raises a difficult problem. If one is unduly committed to that viewpoint, one's analysis of both what happens and why may be heavily influenced by it, and one may not ask whether other more fruitful perspectives might emerge from a more dispassionate approach to studying the situation. This is the very danger that has led to the development of such elaborate safeguards in the quantitative tradition as the double-blind experiment. Although such procedures are rarely used in the qualitative tradition, a substantial literature on the issue of internal validity in qualitative research offers assistance with this problem to the researcher who pays it close heed (Becker, 1958; Bogdan and Biklen, 1981; Glaser and Strauss, 1967; Goetz and LeCompte, 1984; Guba, 1981; Guba and Lincoln, 1981; Kirk and Miller, 1986; Miles and Huberman, 1984a, 1984b; Patton, 1980; Strauss, 1987). Furthermore, if one's purpose is not to support or reject a specific *a priori* theory but to discover, using an approach that is as open as possible, what is actually happening in a site that was chosen with the assistance of a particular theory, problems related to internal validity are somewhat mitigated. For example, the fact that I chose to study a school that theory suggested might be conducive to positive relations did not keep me from exploring in considerable depth problems that occurred there (Sagar and Schofield, 1980; Schofield, 1981, 1989).

One characteristic of the school chosen for the study was especially helpful in assessing the degree to which the theory on which the site was chosen was useful. Specifically, for various reasons, conditions in two of the three grades in this school came much closer than conditions in the remaining grade to meeting those that theory suggests are conducive to producing positive relations. Thus it was possible to assess intergroup relations as the children went from one kind of environment to another within the school (Schofield, 1979, 1989; Schofield and Sagar, 1977). This suggests one very useful strategy for studying what may be – selecting an 'ideal' case and a comparative case that contrasts sharply on the relevant dimensions.

Generalizing from an unusual site to more typical ones

Although I indicated above that my goal was to learn about the possibilities and problems associated with a *certain kind* of desegregated education, I would like to argue that studying a site chosen for its special characteristics does not necessarily restrict the application of the study's findings to other very similar sites. The degree to which this is the case depends on the degree to which the findings appear to be linked to the special characteristics of the situation. Some of the findings from the study I have been discussing were clearly linked to unusual aspects of the school and hence have very limited generalizability to other situations, although they may nonetheless be important in demonstrating what is possible, even if not what is generally likely. For example, I found very low levels of overt racial conflict in the school studied (Schofield and Francis, 1982). It would obviously be misguided to conclude on the basis of this study that intergroup conflict is unlikely in all desegregated schools, since the school's emphasis on cooperation, equal status, and the like did actually appear to play a marked role in reducing the likelihood of conflict.

However, other findings that emerged from the study and were also related to atypical aspects of the situation may have a greater degree of applicability or generalizability than the finding discussed above. For example, I found the development of a color-blind perspective and of an almost complete taboo against the mention of race in the school studied (Schofield, 1986, 1989). Since the emergence of the color-blind perspective and the accompanying taboo appeared to be linked to special characteristics of the school, I would not posit them as phenomena likely to occur in most desegregated schools. But I feel free to argue that *when* they do develop, certain consequences may well follow because these consequences are the logical outcomes of the phenomena. For example, with regard to the taboo against racial reference, if one cannot mention race, one cannot deal with resegregation in a strightforward way as a policy issue. Similarly, if one cannot mention race, there is likely to be little or no effort to create or utilize multicultural curricular materials. Thus, although the taboo against racial reference may not occur in a high proportion of desegregated schools, when it does occur the study I carried out gives a potentially useful indication of problems that are likely to develop.

I would now like to turn to a third finding of the study, one so unrelated to the atypical aspects of the situation studied that it is a reasonable working hypothesis that this phenomenon is widespread. After I observed extensively in varied areas of the school and interviewed a large number of students, it became apparent that the white children perceived blacks as something of a threat to their physical selves. Specifically, they complained about what they perceived as black roughness or aggressiveness (Schofield, 1981, 1989). In contrast, the black students perceived whites as a threat to their social selves. They complained about being ignored, avoided, and being treated as inferior by whites, whom they perceived to be stuck-up and prejudiced (Schofield, 1989). Such findings appear to be to be linked to the black and white students' situation in the larger society and to powerful historical and economic forces, not to special aspects of the school. The consequences of these rather asymmetrical concerns may well play themselves out differently in different kinds of schools, but the existence of these rather different but deeply held concerns may well be widespread.

I have gone into some detail with these examples because I think they raise a crucial point for judging the applicability or generalizability of qualitative work. One cannot just look at a study and say that it is similar or dissimilar to another situation of concern. A much finer-grained analysis is necessary. One must ask what aspects of the situation are similar or different and to what aspects of the findings these are connected.

[. . .]

SUMMARY AND CONCLUSIONS

Although qualitative researchers have traditionally paid scant attention to the issue of attaining generalizability in research, sometimes even disdaining such a goal, this situation has changed noticeably in the past ten to fifteen years. Several trends, including the growing use of qualitative studies in evaluation and policy-oriented research, have led to an increased awareness of the importance of structuring qualitative studies in a way that enhances their implications for the understanding of other situations.

Much of the attention given to the issue of generalizability in recent years on the part of qualitative researchers has focused on redefining the concept in a way that is useful and meaningful for those engaged in qualitative work. A consensus appears to be emerging that for qualitative researchers generalizability is best thought of as a matter of the 'fit' between the situation studied and others to which one might be interested in applying the concepts and conclusions of that study. This conceptualization makes thick descriptions crucial, since without them one does not have the information necessary for an informed judgment about the issue of fit.

This paper argues that three useful targets for generalization are *what is*, *what may be*, and *what could be* and provides some examples of how qualitative research can be designed in a way that increases its ability to fit with each of these situations. Studying *what is* refers to studying the typical, the common, and the ordinary. Techniques suggested for studying *what is* include choosing study sites on the basis of typicality and conducting multisite studies. Studying *what may be* refers to designing studies so that their fit with future trends and issues is maximized. Techniques suggested for studying *what may be* include seeking out sites in which one can study situations likely to become more common with the passage of time and paying close attention to how such present instances of future practices are likely to differ from their future realizations. Studying *what could be* refers to locating situations that we know or expect to be ideal or exceptional on some *a priori* basis and studying them to see what is actually going on there. Crucial here is an openness to having one's expectations about the phenomena disconfirmed.

NOTE

Much of the research on which this paper is based was funded by the Office of Naval Research, Contract Number N00 14-85-K-0664. Other research utilized in this paper was funded by Grant Number NIE-G-78-0126 from the National Institute of Education. However, all opinions expressed herein are solely those of the author, and no endorsement by ONR or NIE is implied or intended. My sincere thanks go to Bill Firestone and Matthew Miles for their constructive comments on an earlier draft of this paper.

REFERENCES

Allport, G. W. (1954) *The Nature of Prejudice.* Cambridge: Cambridge University Press.

Amir, Y. (1969) 'Contact hypothesis in ethnic relations', *Psychological Bulletin,* 71: 319–42.

Aronson, E. and Osherow, N. (1980) 'Cooperation, prosocial behavior, and academic performance: experiments in the desegregated classroom', in L. Bickman (Ed.), *Applied Social Psychology Annual,* Vol 1. Beverly Hills, CA: Sage, pp. 163–96.

Becker, H. J. (1986) 'Instructional uses of school computers', *Reports from the 1985 National Survey.* 1: 1–9. Baltimore, MD: Center for Social Organization of Schools, Johns Hopkins University, pp. 1–9.

Becker, H. S. (1958) 'Problems of inference and proof in participant observation', *American Sociological Review,* 23: 652–59.

Berg, B. L. (1989) *Qualitative Research Methods for the Social Sciences.* Boston: Allyn & Bacon.

Bickel, W. E. (1983) 'Effective schools: knowledge, dissemination, inquiry', *Educational Researcher,* 12 (4): 3–5.

Bogdan, R. C. and Biklen, S. K. (1981) *Qualitative Research for Education: An Introduction to Theory and Methods.* Boston: Allyn & Bacon.

Bolgar, H. (1965) 'The case study method', in B. B. Wolman (Ed.), *Handbook of Clinical Psychology.* New York: McGraw-Hill, pp. 28–39.

Brown v. Board of Education (1954) 347 US 483.

Campbell, D. T. (1979) 'Degrees of freedom and the case study', in T. D. Cook and C. S. Reichardt (Eds), *Qualitative and Quantitative Methods in Evaluation Research.* Beverly Hills, CA: Sage, pp. 49–67.

Campbell, D. and Stanley, J. (1963) 'Experimental and quasi-experimental designs for research on teaching', in N. Gage (Ed.), *Handbook of Research on Teaching.* Chicago: Rand McNally, pp. 171–246.

Collins, T. and Noblit, G. (1978) *Stratification and Resegregation: The Case of Crossover High School.* Final report of NIE contract 400-76-009.

Cook, S. W. (1978) 'Interpersonal and attitudinal outcomes in cooperating interracial groups', *Journal of Research and Development in Education,* 12: 97–113.

Crandall, D. P. et al.. (1983) *People, Policies and Practices: Examining the Chain of School Improvement,* Vols 1–10. Andover, MA: Network.

Cronbach, L. J. (1975) 'Beyond the two disciplines of scientific psychology', *American Psychologist,* 30: 116–27.

Cronbach, L. J. (1982) *Designing Evaluations of Educational and Social Programs.* San Francisco: Jossey-Bass.

Cronbach, L. J., Ambron, S. R., Dornbusch, S. M., Hess, R. D., Hornik, R. C., Phillips, D. C., Walker, D. F., and Weiner, S. S. (1980) *Toward Reform of Program Evaluation.* San Francisco: Jossey-Bass.

Denzin, N. K. (1983) 'Interpretive interactionism', in G. Morgan (Ed.), *Beyond Method: Strategies forSocial Research.* Beverly Hills, CA: Sage, pp. 129–146.

Dobbert, M. L. (1982) *Ethnographic Research: Theory and Application for Modern Schools and Societies.* New York: Praeger.

Dwyer, D. C., Lee, G. V., Rowan, B., and Bossert, S. T. (1982) 'The principal's role in instructional management: five participant observation studies of principals in action'. Unpublished manuscript, Far West Laboratory for Educational Research and Development, San Francisco.

Feigenbaum, E. A. and McCorduck, P. (1983) *The Fifth Generation: Artificial Intelligence and Japan's Computer Challenge to the World.* Reading, MA: Addison-Wesley.

Fetterman, D. M. (1982) 'Ethnography in educational research: the dynamics of diffusion', in D. M. Fetterman (Ed.), *Ethnography in Educational Evaluation*. Beverly Hills, CA: Sage, pp. 21–35.

Filstead, W. J. (1979) 'Qualitative methods: a needed perspective in evaluation research', in T. D. Cook and C. S. Reichardt (Eds), *Qualitative and Quantitative Methods in Evaluation Research*. Beverly Hills, CA: Sage, pp. 33–48.

Firestone, W. A. and Herriott, R. E. (1984) 'Multisite qualitative policy research: some design and implementation issues', in D. M. Fetterman (Ed.), *Ethnography in Educational Evaluation*. Beverly Hills, CA: Sage, pp. 63–88.

Geertz, C. (1973) 'Thick description: toward an interpretive theory of culture', in C. Geertz (Ed.), *The Interpretation of Cultures*. New York: Basic Books, pp. 3–30.

Glaser, B. and Strauss, A. (1967) *The Discovery of Grounded Theory*. Chicago: Aldine Publishing.

Goetz, J. P. and LeCompte, M. D. (1984) *Ethnography and Qualitative Design in Education Research*. Orlando, FL: Academic Press.

Guba, E. (1981) 'Criteria for assessing the trustworthiness of naturalistic inquiry', *Educational Communication and Technology Journal*, 29: 79–92.

Guba, E. G. and Lincoln, Y. S. (1981) *Effective Evaluation: Improving the Usefulness of Evaluation Results through Responsive and Naturalistic Approaches*. San Francisco: Jossey-Bass.

Guba, E. G. and Lincoln Y. S. (1982) 'Epistemological and methodological bases of naturalistic inquiry', *Educational Communication and Technology Journal*, 30: 233–52.

Huberman, A. M. and Miles, M. B. (1984) *Innovation up Close: How School Improvement Works*. New York: Plenum Press.

Jackson, P. W. (1968) *Life in Classrooms*. New York: Holt, Rinehart & Winston.

Kennedy, M. M. (1979) 'Generalizing from single case studies', *Evaluation Quarterly*, 3 (4): 661–78.

Kirk, J. and Miller, M. L. (1986) *Reliability and Validity in Qualitative Research*. Beverly Hills, CA: Sage.

Krathwohl, D. R. (1985) *Social and Behavioral Science Research: New Framework for Conceptualizing, Implementing, and Evaluating Research Studies*. San Fransisco: Jossey-Bass.

Lawler, R. W. and Yazdani, M. (Eds) (1987) *Artificial Intelligence and Education: Learning Environments and Tutoring Systems*, Vol 1. Norwood, NJ: Ablex Publishing.

Lucas, W. (1974) *The Case Survey Method: Aggregating Case Experience*. Santa Monica, CA: Rand.

Miles, M. and Huberman, A. (1984a) 'Drawing valid meaning from qualitative data: toward a shared craft', *Educational Researcher*, 13: 20–30.

Miles, M. and Huberman, A. (1984b) *Qualitative Data Analysis: Sourcebook of New Methods*. Newbury Park, CA: Sage.

Noblit, G. W. and Hare, R. D. (1988) *Meta-Ethnography: Synthesizing Qualitative Studies*. Beverly Hills, CA: Sage.

Patton, M. Q. (1980) *Qualitative Evaluation Methods*. Beverly Hills, CA: Sage.

Peshkin, A. (1978) *Growing up American: Schooling and the Survival of Community*. Chicago: University of Chicago Press.

Peshkin, A. (1982) 'The researcher and subjectivity: reflections on an ethnography of school and community', in G. Spindler (Ed.) *Doing the Ethnography of Schooling: Educational Anthropology in Action*. New York: Holt, Rinehart & Winston, pp. 48–67.

Pettigrew, T. (1967) 'Social evaluation theory: convergences and applications', in D. Levine, (Ed.), *Nebraska Symposium on Motivation*, Vol 5. Lincoln, NE: University of Nebraska Press.

Pettigrew, T. (1969) 'Racially separate or together', *Journal of Social Issues*, 25: 43–69.

Phi Delta Kappan (1980) *Why Do Some Urban Schools Succeed? The Phi Delta Kappan Study of Exceptional Urban Elementary Schools*. Bloomington, IN: Phi Delta Kappan and Indiana University.

Ragin, C. C. (1987) *The Comparative Method: Moving beyond Qualitative and Quantitative Strategies*. Berkeley, CA: University of California Press.

Reichardt, C. S. and Cook, T. D. (1979) 'Beyond qualitative *versus* quantitative methods', in T. D. Cook and C. S. Reichardt (Eds), *Qualitative and Quantitative Methods in Evaluation Research*. Beverly Hills, CA: Sage, pp. 1–33.

Rutter, M., Maughan, B., Mortimore, P., Ouston, J. and Smith, A. (1979) *Fifteen Thousand Hours: Secondary Schools and their Effects on Children*. Cambridge, MA: Harvard University Press.

Sagar, H. A. and Schofield, J. W. (1980) 'Racial and behavioral cues in black and white children's perceptions of ambiguously aggressive acts', *Journal of Personality and Social Psychology*, 39: 590–98.

Schofield, J. W. (1979) 'The impact of positively structured contact on intergroup behavior: does it last under adverse conditions?' *Social Psychology Quarterly*, 42: 280–84.

Schofield, J. W. (1981) 'Competitive and complementary identities: images and interaction in an interracial school', in S. Asher and J. Gottman (Eds), *The Development of Children's Friendship*. New York: Cambridge University Press.

Schofield, J. W. (1986) 'Causes and consequences of the colorblind perspective', in S. Gaertner and J. Dovidio (Eds), *Prejudice Discrimination and Racism: Theory and Practice*. New York: Academic Press, pp. 231–53.

Schofield, J. W. (1989) *Black and White in School: Trust, Tension, or Tolerance?* New York: Teachers College Press. (Original work published 1982.)

Schofield, J. W. and Evans-Rhodes, D. (1989) 'Artificial intelligence in the classroom: the impact of a computer-based tutor on teachers and students', paper presented at the 4th International Conference on Artificial Intelligence in Education, Amsterdam, The Netherlands, May.

Schofield, J. W. and Francis, W. D. (1982) 'An observational study of peer interaction in racially-mixed "accelerated" classrooms', *Journal of Educational Psychology*, 74: 722–32.

Schofield, J. W. and Sagar, H. A. (1977) 'Peer interaction patterns in an integrated middle school', *Sociometry*, 40: 130–38.

Schofield, J. W. and Sagar, H. A. (1983) 'Desegregation, school practices and student race relations', in C. Rossell and W. Hawley (Eds), *The Consequences of School Desegregation*. Philadelphia, PA: Temple University Press, pp. 58–102.

Schofield, J. W. and Verban, D. (1988) 'Computer usage in the teaching of mathematics: issues which need answers', in D. Grouws and T. Cooney (Eds), *Effective Mathematics Teaching*. Hillsdale, NJ: Erlbaum, pp. 169–93.

Shaughnessy, J. J. and Zechmeister, E. B. (1985) *Research Methods in Psychology*. New York: Knopf.

Slavin, R. E. (1980) 'Cooperative learning', *Review of Educational Research*, 50: 315–42.

Smith, A. G. and Robbins, A. E. (1984) 'Multimethod policy research: a case study of structure and flexibility', in D. M. Fetterman (Ed.), *Ethnography in Educational Evaluation*. Beverly Hills, CA: Sage, pp. 115–32.

Smith H. W. (1975) *Strategies of Social Research: The Methodological Imagination*. Englewood Cliffs, NJ: Prentice-Hall.

Spindler, G. (1982) 'General introduction', in G. Spindler (Ed.), *Doing the Ethnography of Schooling: Educational Anthropology in Action*. New York: Holt, Rinehart & Winston, pp. 1–13.

Stake, R. E. (1978) 'The case-study method in social inquiry', *Educational Researcher*, 7: 5–8.

Stephan, W. J. (1985) 'Intergroup relations', in G. Lindzey and F. Aronson (Eds), *The Handbook of Social Psychology*, Vol 2. New York: Random House, pp. 599–658.

Strauss, A. L. (1987) *Qualitative Analysis for Social Scientists*. Cambridge: Cambridge University Press.

Walker, D. F. (1984) 'Promise, potential, and pragmatism: computers in high school', *Institute for Research in Educational Finance and Governance Policy Notes*, 5: 3–4.

Weber, G. (1971) *Inner-City Children Can Be Taught to Read: Four Successful Schools*. Washington, DC: Council for Basic Education.

Whyte, W. F. (1984) *Learning from the Field: A Guide from Experience*. Beverly Hills, CA: Sage.

Wolcott, H. F. (1973) *The Man in the Principal's Office: An Ethnography*. New York: Holt, Rinehart & Winston.

Wolcott, H. F. (1975) 'Criteria for an ethnographic approach to research in schools', *Human Organization*, 34: 111–27.

Wolcott, H. F. (1982) 'Mirrors, models, and monitors: educator adaptations of the ethnographic innovation', in G. Spindler (Ed.), *Doing the Ethnography of Schooling: Educational Anthropology in Action*. New York: Holt, Rinehart & Winston, pp. 68–95.

Yin, R. K. (1981) 'The case study crisis: some answers', *Administrative Science Quarterly*, 26: 58–64.

Yin, R. K. (1984) *Case Study Research: Design and Methods*. Beverly Hills, CA: Sage.

Yin, R. K. and Heald, K. A. (1975) 'Using the case survey method to analyze policy studies', *Administrative Science Quarterly*, 20: 371–81.

Yin, R. K. and Yates, D. (1975) *Street-Level Governments: Assessing Decentralization and Urban Services*. Lexington, MA: D. C. Heath.

8

PROBLEMS OF SOCIOLOGICAL FIELDWORK: A REVIEW OF THE METHODOLOGY OF *HIGHTOWN GRAMMAR*

C. Lacey

[. . .] To write about one's own methodology and the problems of doing empirical research is inevitably to make gross assumptions about one's own theoretical orientations and even one's biography. While it is impossible in a short paper to trace out the full implications of these two factors, I think it is important to outline some of the basic strands of my intellectual development. In this way I can provide the material for developing an internal as well as external critique of my methodology and view of sociology. This is the sort of exercise from which both reader and author can benefit. [. . .]

In contrast with the essentially narrow, competitive, crossword-puzzle, problem-solving world of the grammar school in which 'society' is static, or ignored, my interests developed through the political and union activities of my family and in reading Marx, Shaw and Russell. These writers, from very different vantage points, have a purposive, change-orientated view of society. All imply that it is possible to intervene into the dialectic relationship between personality and social structure, or, put in more recent terminology, into the intricacies of the social construction of reality. My concern was to promote those sorts of intervention that would lead towards an egalitarian society. It seemed to me self-evident that greater social and economic equality would lead to greater democracy and greater potential for the full development of individual personality, in turn leading to greater diversity and richness in social life.

This concern has remained a central underlying purpose. It predates my interest in sociology as such and it provides a support for my continuing interest. In fact, I feel sure that my interest in sociology depends on my seeing it as a tool, as a means for progressing towards a realisation of this purpose. If I felt that sociology was not 'useful' in this way, I would probably turn to politics or journalism, or something.

If this perspective – sociology as a 'means' rather than an 'end' – implies that my involvement is peripheral, a dilettante interest, I must challenge the assumption. I see sociology as a vital analytical tool in the reconstruction of our society. As such, I am centrally interested in all aspects of its development, its theory, methodology and technology, its legitimation and status, not just in the eyes of an elite group of academics, but also the wider society. I see sociology developing to provide a basic ingredient in a generally available education in a self-understanding society.[1] In my view, the converse is also true; sociology as an end in itself, as an academic exercise among many others, is to run the risk of reducing its status to that of a hobby for secure academics. [. . .]

My own experience has led to a particular blend or synthesis of methodologies and approaches and, before embarking on the central core of the paper, it is perhaps important to know in outline what these were, up to the point at which I undertook my study of Hightown Grammar.

In 1960, after teaching for three years in Birmingham and London, I joined the Department of Social Anthropology at Manchester to read for an MA. Manchester at that time was diversifying. Max Gluckman had encouraged Tom Lupton to start micro-studies of shop-floor organisation. In particular, they were concerned to apply the careful fieldwork techniques of the social anthropologist to the attainable areas of industrial society. Participant observation is a much maligned word, but in Manchester at that time it involved the fullest possible transfer; that is, the transfer of the whole person into an imaginative and emotional experience in which the fieldworker learned to live in and understand the new world he had chosen. I have not used the term 'role-playing'. I think in retrospect I would use the term 'role-taking' (or role-making in the sense used by Turner) because this implies involvement of the self in an exposed and vulnerable position. There could be no clinical distancing, the fieldworker was expected to enter in and take punishment until he or she had learned to survive.

The analyses of a wide range of fieldwork situations were united by Manchester's own peculiar blend of conflict theory and functionalism. The mix varied. The Marxists pushed criticisms of the structural reification, timelessness and ossification apparent in the earlier studies, and at one time a fruitful line in MAs developed in which classical anthropology was reanalysed using a conflict framework.[2] The idea of the study of Hightown Grammar grew out of this mix of social anthropological fieldwork techniques, a theoretical concern for social processes and social conflict and my own experiences within schools. [. . .]

GENERAL AIMS

It is easy to guess from what I have said already that a major concern of the study would be with the under-achievement of working-class children in grammar schools. Behind this lay an unworked-out set of assumptions that if schools changed sufficiently to allow radically different rates of upward mobility, there would be a chain reaction in which sets of unchallenged assumptions about the structure of our society would be examined and criticised; for example the public schools (privileged education) and eventually the inheritance of wealth (privileged social position). It seemed to me that the internal logic of a meritocratic society would bring about changes that were an essential precursor to the posing of problems relevant to an egalitarian society. Until those steps were taken most people would be unable even to understand this later stage. It would remain in the realms of utopian philosophy until the necessary experiences, gleaned from the 'meritocratic versus inherited social position' battle, had become a common occurrence. I was not unduly worried by some of the results of Dennis Marsden and Brian Jackson's work[3] which revealed the strains experienced by working-class families through the upward mobility of one of their daughters or sons. They were both walking contradictions of the 'defection' argument.

PROBLEMS OF BIAS

Even before the study began a number of colleagues expressed opinions about the viability of the research. There were two strands of this opinion that foresaw as inevitable a broad irreducible streak of bias running through the study.

One group, made up mainly of the more traditional social anthropologists, argued that, given my experience and closeness to schools, I could not obtain the necessary distance and therefore objectivity to make a study.

Another expressed the view that it would be important to 'open up' grammar schools to criticism and implied that a hefty dose of the 'right' bias would be a good thing.

I disagreed with both these views. I could not agree that the 'outsider' had to be totally outside the culture (for some social anthropologists an outsider also meant an outsider from the point of view of race and language in order to achieve 'distance' and make so-called 'objective' judgments). Even at the planning stage of the study I felt disinclined to go along with the notion of 'objectivity'. Instead I saw it as my job to develop views of the system from a number of points of view – those of the parent, the teacher and the child. It was, I believed, through presenting these views and, more importantly, the intersection of these views that the researcher could illustrate the dynamics of the system. This task seemed to me to call for a specific approach to fieldwork requiring sympathy, naïvete, openness, a willingness to help where possible, and an ability to let people talk.

I had rather more sympathy with the second view. After all, every study is constrained by the limitations of the researcher and those limitations extend to the constraints imposed by the researcher's values. These may limit his insights and curb his imagination. This criticism made me determined to go beyond the usual social anthropological methodologies and construct models that could be tested at various points in the analysis. In this way my biases could perhaps lead to omission, but they could hardly lead me to constructing an account based simply on my prejudices. There are many instances of these tests within the book; the connection between 'performance' and 'behaviour' of pupils made by the teachers and the construction of sociometric indicators to test 'differentiation' and 'polarisation', for example. The chapter most affected by social anthropological criticism, and which itself contains an implied criticism of much social anthropological writing, is chapter 7 where case studies are presented within an analytical framework to counteract the tendency to make 'apt illustration' from fieldwork notes. [. . .]

THE FIELD OF STUDY

The merging of one's own value orientations and the work already accomplished in the chosen field of study is a complex interaction to unravel. However, it bears directly on the development of my methodology and needs some explanation.

The major weakness of existing research in the field seemed to me to be its adherence to a simplistic theoretical model, around which elaboration had almost ceased to be useful. Bernstein has described this as an input–output model. I prefer the term a 'black-box' model of research because it describes more accurately the nature of its limitations. The model assumes that in order to demonstrate an effect it was necessary only to show correlations between inputs and outputs. The contents of the black box, the social mechanisms and process, are neglected and not without cost. At whatever level of generality the model is used, societal or institutional, the element of social determinism is extremely strong. There is nothing to counteract it. Nor is there anything inherent in the methodology associated with the model to challenge the notion that the factors considered by the researchers are necessarily the salient ones as far as the social actors are concerned. The framework of variables to be considered is imposed; there is little chance of developing an alternative perspective from these research reports. There is one further drawback to this type of research. It produces descriptions of the school system that document, for example, the under-achievement of working-class children but give very little indication of how the school system or individual teachers can change in order to alter or modify this effect. In fact, because of the 'social determinism' element and the imposition of an analytical framework which rarely contains variables relating to the school or the classroom, the implication for many teachers is that it cannot be changed. The idea that the causes of under-achievement are to be found solely in low material standards or attitudes held by working-class families, I found totally unacceptable. Elaborations of this model can only take place in three directions:

1. Superimposition of different scales of black-box model.[4]
2. Elaboration of input and output variables.
3. A moving black box, a follow-through cohort study.

In the period leading up to the study the major effort of researchers in this field had undoubtedly been in the direction of the elaboration of variables. Asher Tropp had attempted to put almost all the variables anyone had ever heard of in a complex model of causation. Stephen Wiseman had attempted a similar exercise with ecological units and in the USA number crunching proceeded on a grand scale.

It seemed useful, therefore, to work within the framework of established black-box findings and to use if necessary the first alternative of different scales of application of the model, but to work in the opposite direction, that is, from within the black-box out towards the community and wider society. The implication of this direction was that I would need to immerse myself within the system in order to be able to feel, recognise and describe the constraints of the various roles within the school and be able to put together a descriptive model or series of models of the processes that I recognised. The idea was to describe the system from a number of perspectives. Only in this way did I feel that I could include an analysis of how these intersected to produce a social process.[5]

THE RESEARCH STRATEGY

[. . .] The broad strategy which we worked out for Hightown was as follows:

1. To choose the school carefully with advice from HMIs and the local authority and present definite reasons for our choice.
2. To enter the system above the school in the authority system and move down through the authority system to the school.
3. To teach (participate) and observe, but to move slowly out of the teacher role towards a research role with much greater flexibility and access to pupils.

The decision to teach was reached through a number of lines of reasoning:

1. Entry to the school would be facilitated if the headmaster felt he was getting additional, worthwhile teaching assistance.
2. Long-term participation (a three-year period of association was initially proposed) in a school would require the researcher to build up in the first period a fund of goodwill on which to draw to support his later roles. These would be incomprehensible to the staff of the school unless they were developed out of an established relationship. Within the last year of the study it was expected that the contact would be attenuated and a monitoring relationship set up. This attenuation could, it was felt, put some strain on the relationship with the school. If a considerable fund of goodwill had been created, this would not be so marked.

Table 1

Start with	(3 years later)	→ Finish with	Methods
1. 1st year (120 boys)		→ 3rd year	teach and observe
2. 4th year (120 boys)		→ 6th formers or leavers	observe
3. Lower 6th form (50 boys)		→ leavers	teach and observe

3. Most importantly, to gain a teacher perspective as one of the essential elements in putting together a pattern of interacting perspectives.

My operational strategy was designed to examine the 'process' of grammar school education as it developed from the lower school, through the middle school to 'O' level and the sixth form. I therefore selected three points in the school from which I could eventually cover the whole school during a three-year period, albeit at different intensities of participation and observation (see Table 1).

The intention was to teach for the first year and then give up most of my teaching to move towards a freer research role in the second and third years. In the third year in particular I planned to move outside the school into the community and the home.

The plan was far too ambitious. In my desire to include everything I saddled myself with a killing workload and a far too attenuated contact with any one form at any time. It required a tremendous effort to keep going on all fronts and learn in some detail the personal data for 300 boys. By the second term I had given up the detailed study of the sixth form. Looking back, it is easy to see this mistake in the context of a common participant observer syndrome. The feeling develops very vividly at times that the real action, the real social drama is going on somewhere else. While you are in the staffroom there are important discussions in the headmaster's study; while you observe 3A, a really critical series of lessons is being taught in the room next door. The root of this feeling is in the nature of one's task. The participant observer records as accurately as possible selected aspects of the everyday life of people in everyday situations. There is rarely anything dramatic, there is rarely anything of outstanding interest taking place.[6] Classrooms can be incredibly boring places. The interest in the situation emerges as the observer puts together the pieces of an amorphous and intricate puzzle in which even the pieces are not defined. Until this is done the tensions and strains on the researcher are considerable and the 'it is all happening somewhere else' syndrome flourishes. [. . .]

CHANGE OF RESEARCH ROLE

The movement from a teacher role to a freer, research role was accomplished smoothly without too much strain on my relationships with the staff. Several incidents did, however, illustrate the potential dangers of living within the informal worlds of both staff and pupils. Before relating these incidents, it is necessary to describe the actual changes that took place in my research role.

Even during my first year at the school my role differed considerably from a normal teacher role:

1. I was not employed by the local authority and had a special negotiated relationship with the headmaster, which staff and pupils knew about.
2. I observed classes on a regular basis, something other teachers never did.
3. I was more available to staff and pupils, who found me interested in matters not usually discussed by other teachers.

This interest gradually established a flow of information from both staff and pupils about things they thought would interest me, from formal events like public speaking competitions to informal events like fights in the park. My change in role was accomplished by building on these existing differences and moving out of my classroom teaching role (I retained some sixth-form teaching). I held informal discussion groups, which were established during school hours (boys could be excused Religious Education) but continued during lunch-time on an informal basis. I visited the homes of boys to talk over problems with them or their parents. I entered informally into conversations with boys in and around the school and invited boys to my home, which was only a few hundred yards from the school. I entered into informal activities after school and eventually ran a school cricket team (second-year). The final stage of this change of role was never achieved. I had planned to move out of the school and meet boys in clubs, coffee bars and informal out-of-school groups like regular street football games. [. . .]

The change in role brought an increase, gradual at first and then steep, in the amount of information received about pupils. The discussion group ranged over topics from marriage and sex through general questions about the school and its relation to jobs and earning a living, to individual masters and the boys' relationships with them. One of the groups had been 'set up' to include most of the anti-group boys from one fifth-year class and this group of between six and eight boys provided without doubt the most stimulating and entertaining discussions I enjoyed in the school. The discussions had a life of their own.

It was this group that proposed and carried out an experiment within the classroom to 'prove' that Mr Bradley 'had his knife into' Morris, one of the boys in the group. Morris was programmed to keep quiet and work diligently for the first part of the lesson. Then when the classwork had been set and the customary buzz of conversation had established itself, he was to start talking like the rest of the class. According to the boys in the group, Mr Bradley noticed him immediately and told him off. They were delighted with their experiment and its result.

The completely informal, relaxed relationship with this group of boys contrasted with the classroom role of the teacher and the formal relationship generated through the teaching persona. The group was noisy, frank, sometimes lewd, but always (in marked contrast to the classroom) interested and sincere. I was constantly surprised by the degree to which they appreciated their own position in the school, and the way in which they were prepared to examine and discuss it. [. . .]

My participation and involvement in these situations demonstrated more clearly than any other method the way some aspects of the pupil/adolescent world are cut off from the teacher and the school. They also demonstrated the way the teacher role is shaped and constrained by pressures outside the classroom emanating from the community, mediated by the headmaster and to some extent enshrined in the behaviour codes and punishment system.

CLASSROOM OBSERVATION PERSPECTIVE VERSUS TEACHING PERSPECTIVE

I hope it is still clear at this stage that although there were numerous supporting reasons for the decision to teach, the main purpose was to explicitly take on a teacher perspective. This linked into the theoretical orientation of examining the system in action and describing the dynamic interaction of perspectives.

The classroom observation

The question of how much I as an observer altered the teachers' or children's behaviour in the classrooms I observed seemed secondary to the question of how I interpreted what went on. After I had observed all the masters teach it was quite clear that I could fairly easily observe in most of the classes within the school. However, there were some masters who were going to be constantly worried by my presence. One began by asking me 'What are you doing?', asked three or four times 'What shall I tell the boys?', and finished after the lesson by asking pointedly, 'What can you possibly get out of it?' He conveyed such a strong sense of discomfort that I felt I could not possibly impose myself. Afterwards, a group of masters asked me about what went on in his lesson. Hardly waiting for an answer, they told me that he once made a boy stand in the corner for a whole lesson holding a sand bucket in one hand and a water bucket in the other. He tried to teach ecology by linking it with the Queen's progress round Australia. 'What do these boys care about the Queen's visit? He's a nut.' It was quite clear that the man was under pressure from both his fellow teachers and his pupils and I decided I could not increase the pressures he already felt.

The contrast between my observer position, feeling free from the responsibilities of classroom control, and his tense irritability, worried by problems of the classroom and lack of support from his colleagues, highlights the problem of the observer versus the teacher perspective. Remarks from boys that I interpreted as lacking menace or threat obviously stung him into reprisals of sarcasm or anger.

During my first weeks in the school a whole series of incidents made it apparent that the observer role would enable me to achieve a pupil perspective far more easily than a teacher perspective. An example from my field notes illustrates this:

Mr P was shouting at a pupil, already in tears, as I went into the staffroom.

Mr P: (bursting into the staffroom with great energy and in great anger): Hill, been at it again – truanting!
Mr J: What again – not for a whole day!
Mr P: No, he's been in the toilets for my lesson. He'd lost his exercise book and was frightened to face up to it. I asked him whether he thought he'd get away from it – he said 'No'.
Mr J: He was caned about a fortnight ago for truanting.

Later, I left the staffroom and passed the boy in the corridor. Mr P was ranting at him in a loud voice:

Mr P: What sort of trick do you think this is – deceitful, low, sly – shows you've no backbone.

Hill was crying – tears streaming down his face.

Mr J: (later): The only way to cure it is to cane him and cane him every time he does it.

(Later) Mr P laughed about his 'go' at Hill and said it was all a big act.

The teaching perspective

An important finding from teaching at Hightown was that even with a strong desire to break out of an authoritarian mould – as I had – my teaching represented only a modified version, a more permissive version, of this style. And I had not been subjected to pressures from the bottom streams of the third and fourth years.

This experience led me to observe the socialisation of young teachers. I noted their timetables, the gossip about them, the sort of advice they were given and finally, when they were judged to be ready, their induction into the 'hard core', that is the group of teachers who were central to the running of the school.

All these investigations showed that their induction was also structured by the processes of differentiation and polarisation. Young teachers had to deliver their message, define and do battle with the enemy. The enemy had to be the right enemy. Young teachers were sanctioned (as I was) for helping the wrong types. Interestingly enough, they were also sanctioned for being too emotionally involved and too zealous in their punishment of wrong-doers. The contrasting examples of Mr P and Mr L illustrate this last point.

As I described previously, Mr P pointed out that his outburst had been 'all an act'. In doing this he was distancing himself from the person we had all seen ranting in the corridor. That person had been an aspect of the 'mask', the 'teaching persona', and the act had been a necessary unpleasant act that did not, however, reflect on the personal qualities of Mr P. In this Mr P had been successful. Other masters had made it clear that they were on his side by suggesting the cane and also by allowing the remark to go unchallenged. Mr L, describing a similar incident, told how he had caught a boy called Chegwin in some wrong-doing by standing in a doorway and grabbing him as he passed. Mr L spoilt the whole story as far as the rest of the staff were concerned by ending with an emotional outburst: 'I despise him, detest him and loathe him.'

This lack of 'professional distance' led a senior member of staff to interrupt Mr L with a long discourse on how to handle Chegwin. 'He is a decent boy at heart, despite a poor home background, and a limited ability – we will have to ride him with a light rein.' He carried on in this way until Mr L left the room. His departure was marked by the raising of eyebrows, the puffing of cheeks and the shaking of heads.

I still remember vividly incidents like those described by Mr P and Mr L. As an observer of these incidents, I felt little affinity with the teachers – all sympathy for the pupils. Yet, as is clear in the description above, many of these teachers were sincere in their desire to help and encourage their pupils to learn. I had to teach in order to appreciate the strains that on occasion turned reasonable, kindly men into bellowing, spiteful adversaries. They left the staffroom in good order; it was in the classroom that things went wrong.

The section in *Hightown* on the teaching persona was the outcome of that experience. It was only through the creation of a second 'me' that I could survive. Every event within the classroom had to be judged on two criteria: first, its own merit; second, its effect on the classroom order. It is the second criterion that is difficult to understand as an observer.

Why did Mr A suddenly pounce on Jimmy Green? Answer – because Jimmy Green was venturing, perhaps unwittingly, across a threshold that Mr A judged was essential for his control in the classroom. Practically all the teachers at Hightown were domino theorists and most had learned their lesson through hard experience.

Mr L failed to develop this second self. He was progressively sanctioned by other teachers not so much for the intensity of his outbursts or the punishments he inflicted, but for the fact that they were 'real'. They were spiteful and vindictive. Finally, he was humiliated by his exclusion from the staff cricket XI which was to play the school First XI. He had failed to develop a 'teaching persona' acceptable to staff and pupils. My participation as a teacher enabled me to watch with a certain amount of apprehension but with fascination the way in which small group pressures were manipulated by prominent members of staff. The manner of his exclusion illustrated the working of these informal pressures.

The staff team[7] had been put up in the staffroom. Mr L came into the room and all went quiet. He went over to the notice board and looked at this list. He turned angrily to the staff who were there and complained that there were some people in the team who were not really 'staff' (I was not in the room), and with a 'flourish' took out his pen and crossed off his name as twelfth man. As he left the room there were guffaws of laughter and a number of choice comments.[8] Mr L left the school for a job 'nearer home' that did not involve a promotion. I felt it important not to underestimate the pressures on the new staff to conform to the staff mores.

PARTICIPANT OBSERVATION AND OTHER METHODS

The core methodology of the study was without question participant observation and observation. Yet in a sense the most important breakthrough for me was the combining of methods, and the integration of these in the analysis.

The observation and description of classrooms led quickly to a need for more exact information about individuals within the class. I used school documents to produce a ledger of information on each boy, for example, address, father's occupation, previous school, academic record, and so on. I built on this record as more information became available from questionnaires. This information enabled me to check immediately any change taking place in seating arrangements or patterns of association outside the classroom and, most importantly, to interpret the significance of the development within the established structure of the classroom.

During the early period of observation a high proportion of the incidents and interaction I observed were simply not interpretable. I could see one boy punch another, or two boys joking; I could record the interaction between a master and a boy; but very little added up to produce a structure, or even more important, the sorts of processes I was attempting to unravel.

The key series of observations for me was in the music teacher's class as described in *Hightown*. He simplified the pattern of interaction by imposing his mental picture of the class on to the physical layout of the classroom. This idea of the teacher having a crude conceptual picture of the class began to fit into my own developing ideas of the classes I taught. I had vivid impressions of the 'clever boys', the 'good boys', the ones that 'rarely understood', the 'bad boys' and the 'characters', but the others, probably between a half and a third of the class fell into the undifferentiated middle. Even after teaching them for some months, it was difficult to recall their names.

The idea of the master imposing his view of the class on to the pupils in the class followed quickly from this and soon I was looking for a way to check how far this imposition[9] actually affected the way children thought of each other, interacted with each other, maybe even made friends with each other. The idea of using sociometric indicators for this purpose, therefore, evolved from the problem and my relationship with it.

The analysis of the sociometric data was a completely new experience. I can still remember the excitement as one after the other of my ideas about the patterns of relationships held up during the analysis. The conceptualisation of the processes of differentiation and polarisation grew out of this interplay between observation and analysis of sociometric data. Looking back, I now feel that I under-utilised these findings in my subsequent fieldwork (by this time I was also teaching at Manchester University). I collected no direct *interview* evidence on the complexities of the structure. I watched for changes and knew about quarrels, fights and emerging friendships, but I omitted to ask questions about how other boys viewed boys outside their own group. I did this in a formal questionnaire (can't get on with choices and diaries etc.) in a systematic way, but should have done much more in following up particular insights from the analysis in informal but patterned interviews. The next strategy would have been to explain my analysis to some of the boys who were closest to me so that they would also act as observers of the process. I began this with two boys, one who was having difficulty within the sixth form and for whom the analysis provided an explanation of his difficulties, a form of therapy, and one who did in fact start to provide me with a self-generated analysis of his own classroom.

What I did was to 'escalate insights' through moving backwards and forwards between observation and analysis and understanding (see Figure 1). This diagram could obviously be complicated by adding a large number of cycles in this process,[10] as I built upon certain methods and insights to achieve a deeper understanding. An important point to notice is the way certain insights or levels of understanding are associated with certain methods of data collection. In other words, just as methods such as classroom observation or participation as a teacher have important theoretical repercussions, so other methods such as the use of sociometric data and their analysis using sociomatrices can have important effects on the shaping of concepts and the deepening of one's understanding (which is perhaps another way of saying the same thing). I feel very strongly that the world under investigation seen through one method of collecting data becomes enormously distorted by the limitations of that data and the available methods of analysis.

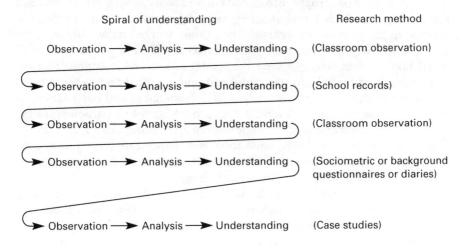

Figure 1

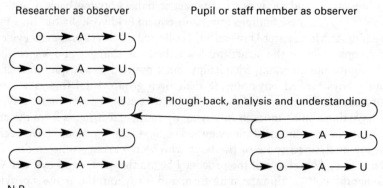

N.B.
Plough-back can occur at the stage when the researcher has developed models.

Figure 2

The extension of this process that I began at Hightown and would certainly advocate in any similar study can be portrayed schematically as shown in Figure 2.

The effect of this strategy is twofold:

1. the pupil or teacher is brought into the analysis as a positive contributor – almost as a research assistant;
2. the system itself is changed in that within it there are new perspectives that might alter it.

This second possibility occurred at Hightown but not in any planned way. It was coincident that while I was studying the school there was a change of headmaster. After a year in which the new head allowed the school to run itself in the established pattern, he introduced fairly radical changes. He de-streamed the third year (which I was studying) and did not stream any of the new intakes. In the span of two years the innovation worked its way through the school which was then completely de-streamed.[11] There is no way for me to assess how far these changes were the result of ideas and intentions that the new headmaster brought to the school and how far what had happened was influenced by the results of my analysis of differentiation and polarisation, of which he was aware. In any event, it does provide us with a paradigm for the study of innovation and an interventionist research strategy (see Figure 3).

In other words, episodes of innovation and change can occur through research and augment that research. These innovations need not occur by chance – they can be planned episodes in research designs.

It will be some time before local government administrators, teachers, pupils, their parents, and researchers have enough confidence in each other to plan this sort of research in a co-operative enterprise. Yet this degree of co-operation is a necessary first step in understanding, if not controlling, the effects of innovation.

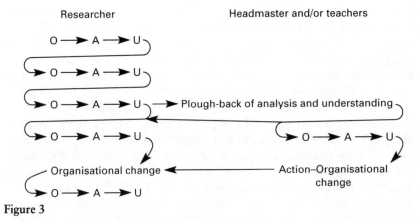

Figure 3

LEVELS OF ANALYSIS

I dealt early on with the problem of bias and my desire to combine so-called subjective participant observation methods with tests of the models produced using so-called objective indicators. There is also a second dimension on which it is possible to obtain a critical appraisal of the explanations produced by the research. The research was planned to integrate a number of levels of analysis from the macro to the micro levels. It is therefore possible to test this research by examining the compatibility of the models produced at these different levels. In the book *Hightown Grammar* I begin by describing the community and the school within the community, and taking an historical view before moving into the school. Within the school I investigate one cohort, then a single class within the cohort, and finally I move on to individual case studies. In the final chapter on staff-pupil relations I link back again to more macro levels when I consider the career and professional aspects of the teacher role. A useful critical exercise is to read the book from this point of view to establish how far the six to eight models used in the description of Hightown Grammar contain mutually contradicting or reinforcing elements. In order to use the book as a sociological tool (as opposed to using it to learn about schools), and it was certainly intended as such, it seems essential to approach the book critically in this way. [. . .]

THE MODELS PRODUCED: SOME SUBSTANTIVE AND METHODOLOGICAL CONSEQUENCES

Models are a form of explanation and are therefore closely related to understanding. The models produced in *Hightown Grammar* have an interventionalist purpose and are therefore designed to be as close as possible to the everyday world of the teacher and the pupil, while still retaining analytical penetration. It was not the intention of the research to be directly interventionalist (the changes initiated by the headmaster ran counter to the planned research design) but to provide teachers and students in general with an insight into their own world that would lead to further debate, the redefinition of problems and the development of new solutions. There was also an attempt to diagnose the points at which intervention is possible.

The model of the classroom as a competitive arena, presented in *Hightown Grammar*, is a good example of this aspect of the study. The analysis shows how the teacher perspective transforms competition between individuals with markedly different resources relevant to the competitive process into a competition of equals. In other words, the dynamics of the classroom situation make demands that cause the teacher (often despite his private feelings) to ignore the fact that the unequal resources of his pupils are relevant to the classroom.

Figure 4 shows the classrooms within the community. The pupil-parent teams are included in shaded areas that represent the size of each team's resources. The teacher frequently conducts the competitive aspects of the classroom process as though the differences made explicit in the diagram do not exist. My interest in the classroom situation has developed out of this early insight. It has involved me in two lines of inquiry and in developing new models of co-operation between sociologists and educationalists.

One line of inquiry has been into the training and professional socialisation of teachers. The question that intrigues me is how far the teacher and the school can modify the classroom role of the teacher in the face of community, professional and situational pressures. The possibilities of change seem to exist at three different levels:

1. A modification of the competitive process, to produce less differentiation and polarisation. This would involve a modification of the teacher's role within the classroom and perhaps some organisational change.
2. A reversal of the usual allocation of resources – that is, a compensatory strategy – in the face of pupil and community pressures.
3. A redefinition of the teacher role and the part played by education within the community.

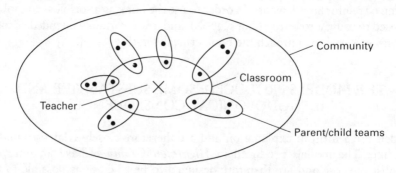

Figure 4

Most innovation and change within our schools aims at levels 1 or 2 above,[12] yet each year a large number of student-teachers leave universities and colleges ideologically committed to level 3 change. This process of change and the way in which the ideological commitment of young teachers merges with the gradually changing practice within our schools have become some of my central sociological concerns. Future research of this problem seems to me to require co-operative work including social scientists, curriculum analysts, pupils and teachers. The practical forms of co-operation have still to be worked out but the theoretical notion behind this co-operation has been suggested earlier in this section.

The second set of ideas that emerged from the Hightown study and have continued to involve me have been the concepts of differentiation and polarisation. These processes resulted from a particular and perhaps peculiar set of pressures on a group of individuals, held together in an organisation over a considerable period of time and for long periods of each work day. They therefore emerged clearly within an observational study and were capable of documentation using sociometric techniques, despite the inaccuracies of the technique and 'noise' created by other processes at work within the classroom. Viewed at a higher level of abstraction these processes are, however, a universal characteristic of human relationships. Actors within social settings pursue social strategies that derive from the actors' experiences and expertise, are relevant to the social situation and are an attempt to achieve the often complex and unworked-out aims of the actor. The peculiar nature of Hightown Grammar rests in the similarity of the pupils' previous experience and expertise, the uniformity and pervasiveness of the academic and behaviour norms imposed by the school and the persistence of the social situation (the classroom) over a period of years.[13] In these conditions the strategies chosen by individual pupils have a regularity and persistence and sometimes a generality that persuades the teacher (or the observer) that what he is observing is the individual and not simply strategies adopted by that individual; that is, strategies that are sometimes chosen, sometimes forced on him in the situation in which he is observed. I think there were times when I made this mistake and there are perhaps points in *Hightown Grammar* when the analysis comes close to obscuring this important distinction. There are times, however, when the distinction is clear. It is made clear by describing incidents where individuals manipulate one set of subcultural understandings in one situation and then partake actively in another – for example, when the teacher leaves the room. It is made clear at a theoretical level by using the term subculture to represent a set of ways of behaving and understanding, and not a group of individuals who are indelibly marked by experiences or personal characteristics. (An important realisation gained during the Hightown study was the extent to which the selection and adoption of a social strategy was part of a competitive process. Another competitive element in the classroom is the battle to define the situation so that strategies over which one has established a claim are seen to be most relevant to the situation.) Changes in the social setting could markedly upset even well-established structures made up of stable patterns of adopted strategies. This was obviously the case within the discussion group I describe in this paper. I also have records of a case study where I experimented with the usual situational constraints affecting the selection and running of a cricket team. My team of 'playground'[14] cricketers brought forth a new set of relationships and behaviours on a Saturday morning that again had little relationship to the usual schoolday patterns.

These insights have had important repercussions on the way I now view adolescent and adult socialisation. I have developed the concept of situationally constrained social strategies in my study of the professional socialisation of teachers, and it has been able to show why, for example, many of the ideas adopted by students during their training year are relatively quickly modified during their early years of teaching.

The connection between the individual and the social setting has been illustrated by these researches. My conception of the problems we face in attempting to change the social world has been sharpened.

The main purpose of this paper was to review my study of Hightown Grammar in broadly methodological terms. In doing so, I illustrated the way in which my own values and preoccupations fed into the research and were developed and refined during and through the process of the research.

Finally I described how these developments directed me into new channels of inquiry.[15]

If a student can obtain a feeling for the movement from ideas to research – a realisation that his deepest concerns about society can become the basis for his research – then he need see no dichotomy between these two. If he can come to see, in time, that the research, grounded in these deep concerns, is his principle means of refining and developing them, then he will hardly settle for their separation.

NOTES

1. See R. J. Frankenberg, 'The sociologically-minded person and the self-understanding society', University of Keele Inaugural Lecture, 1970.

2. See Peter Worsley's MA thesis and Curl Bequest Essay. My own MA thesis would have been an application of Weber's paradigm of authority types to a Nilotic tribe in which institutionalised leadership failed to develop.

3. B. Jackson and D. Marsden, *Education and the Working Class*, Routledge & Kegan Paul, 1962. See also M. Young and P. Willmott, *Family and Kinship in East London*, Routledge & Kegan Paul, 1957, for the effects of upward mobility on the relationships within working-class families.

4. The model can be applied to the education system as a whole (Coleman's 'Equality of opportunity' Report), grammar schools (Early Leaving Report – probably the purest 'black box' design), or individual schools (Julienne Ford's *Social Class and the Comprehensive School*, Routledge & Kegan Paul, 1970).

5. I was anxious to present more than a simple 'underdog' perspective. The discussion between Alvin Gouldner and Howard Becker on this issue is illuminating with

respect to many facets of the problem but overlooks the central issue. If sociologists are involved (for whatever reasons) in 'understanding' social behaviour then it is important to understand the full complexity of the problem. The intersection of perspectives seems essential to this end. See J. D. Douglas, ed., *The Relevance of Sociology*, Appleton-Century-Crofts, 1970, New York.

6. Bill Watson summed up this aspect of fieldwork in a remark made in a seminar. He was describing how he arrived in an African village full of romantic notions of what he would find. 'What did I find? A load of unemployed bums!'

7. The staff team had a regular fixture list and Mr L had played on a number of occasions. He had bought all the correct kit and had taken lessons, in his own time. He was very keen and had let it be known. The staff/school match was a special fixture. The whole school turned out to watch and there was competition for places in the team.

8. The incident was described to me later by teachers who were obviously satisfied by the way things had gone.

9. In *Hightown Grammar* I made a clear distinction between 'differentiation' – imposed by the teacher – and 'polarisation' – a product of pupil interaction. I have modified my position slightly and now see differentiation to be in part produced by intra-group competitive pressures. In other words, the children themselves bring into the classroom some of the criteria which will be used in judging them. They use these criteria to judge each other.

10. The process is portrayed here as inevitably progressive. My filing system shows otherwise. On more than one occasion I worked hard and enthusiastically on a 'new' idea, only to find an almost identical analysis planned or even worked out in my filing system.

11. C. Lacey, 'Destreaming in a "pressured" academic environment', in S. J. Egg-leston, ed., *Contemporary Research in the Sociology of Education*, Methuen, 1975, pp. 148–66.

12. It has been a characteristic of sociologists studying education that they have underestimated the difficulties of bringing about even minor changes. They have not, therefore, made studies of innovation and change in educational institutions. This is an important gap in the literature.

13. Only the family presented the actor with a more consistent set of pressures over a longer period of time.

14. A term sometimes used to describe those boys who played cricket with a soft ball and an asphalt wicket. They specialised in fast bowling and big hitting and were regarded by some teachers (e.g. First XI coach) as poor cricketers in the proper sense. They were not normally chosen as school team members. I chose my second-year school team mainly from 'playground' cricketers. It was outstandingly successful.

15. J. S. Coleman, 'A research chronology', in P. E. Hammond, ed., *Sociologists at Work*, Basic Books, 1964.

9

PRIMARY TEACHERS TALKING: A REFLEXIVE ACCOUNT OF LONGITUDINAL RESEARCH

J. Nias

My research into teachers' lives, life histories and careers has been dominated by accident and opportunity. It started almost by chance growing out of the work in which I was engaged during the 1970s. At that time I was a lecturer at the School of Education at the University of Liverpool, responsible for designing and running a one-year postgraduate Certificate in Education course for graduates who wished to teach children between 7 and 13 years old. Each year there was a substantial cohort of secondary students; the primary group numbered between 12 and 20 and worked in an isolated basement room in a large old building whose upper floors were inhabited by more prestigious courses. The physical conditions under which we all worked were difficult, staffing was limited, the pressure to cover a good deal of professional ground in a short time was intense. As a result, we spent many hours in each other's company and got to know one another well. Once individuals had begun teaching, they would often telephone, call or write, seeking reassurance, support and information from an interested, professionally knowledgeable colleague who did not have the control over their careers which was now vested in their headteachers or inspectors. When, one day, someone who had been teaching for three years returned from many miles away to talk about her experiences in school and, in passing, exclaimed, 'I do wish you could come and see what I am doing now!' I decided to spend a forthcoming sabbatical term visiting past graduates from this course and exploring with them the strengths and weaknesses of their training.

It seemed sensible to limit my enquiries to those who had been teaching for at least two years. By 1974, when I began seriously to listen to 'primary teachers talking', several studies of the probationary year had been published. The early experience of teaching appeared to be similar for all teachers, no matter how long their preparation had been. I was more interested in discovering whether or not students' nine-months PGCE course equipped them to cope with their jobs once they were through the initial traumas of induction than in exploring yet again the apparent inability of any form of training adequately to prepare teachers for the 'reality shock' of classroom life. I also decided to approach those who had left teaching, but not those who, having successfully completed their training, had immediately entered other careers. I reasoned that people who had abandoned the classroom, for whatever reason, might have important things to say about their professional education. Their opinions might be particularly valuable because the views of people who had left teaching had not been solicited by earlier studies of the probationary year.

I contacted by letter or by telephone 37 of my ex-students – 26 were teaching, 11 were not – explaining that I would like to visit them in the following term and talk to them about their experiences in teaching, with particular reference to their PGCE course. I also said that in order to help me understand their circumstances, I would like to spend roughly half a day with them in the classroom. Two (both teaching) said they would prefer me not to visit them, the rest readily agreed. I asked them to make necessary arrangements with their headteachers.

My research was, then, initially conceived as a naive and personal attempt to evaluate the course of which I was tutor, and in particular to discover how ex-students felt that it could be improved. Fortunately, however, while I was waiting for replies to my letters, I conducted two trial visits and interviews with teachers who were working not far from the university. Almost as soon as I began to talk to them I realized that my concerns were of little relevance or importance to them. Instead they wanted to talk to me about what they were doing now and about their pressing memories of earlier encounters with adults in school, not just with their pupils. It did not take me long to realize that there was a mismatch between what they wanted to tell me and what I thought I wanted to know. However, I also realized that they were presenting me with a vivid picture of the lived experience of primary teaching, of a kind and with a richness of detail which I did not think existed in any published form. It would not be impossible, I felt, to listen to what they wanted to tell me and, at the same time, also to acquire some information about the relevance and durability of their professional education.

Accordingly, I reformulated my original aims. My intention became, and remained for the next two years, to capture, as nearly as possible in the words of teachers themselves, a detailed and comprehensive picture of the subjective reality of primary teaching. In the process I hoped also to gain some feedback about the course for which I was responsible, but this was now of secondary importance.

I then approached three more ex-students, with my revised aims in mind and asked them to talk to me about their life in teaching so far. I devised a few very open questions in advance and listed single words on a postcard as an *aide-mémoire* which I could use to ensure that at some point in the interview we covered the ground I was interested in. I used these interviews to help me become progressively more aware of areas that teachers themselves felt it important to talk about (e.g. I initially underestimated the salience of the staff group to teachers with all lengths of service and of the head to teachers in their early years in particular; I did not realize how important it was for all teachers to have someone in or outside school to whom they could talk freely about their professional values). These initial discussions also helped me to modify or eliminate questions which appeared to yield little data. I ended up with about twenty topics on which I wanted further information. These ranged from the very broad (e.g. What is it you like about your job? Have you had all the help you felt you needed in each of your jobs? If so, from whom? If not, do you know why?) to the fairly narrow (e.g. Have you ever consciously modelled your teaching on anyone else's? If so, whose?). These areas, represented by single words on a small, unobtrusive piece of card, remained substantially unchanged during the interviews which I conducted over the next two years. Indeed, I used them to re-interview my first five respondents towards the end of this period. Although I was hesitant about approaching them a second time, since I was conscious of how busy they were, none of them appeared to feel that this second conversation was redundant.

In converting areas of interest into questions which I hoped would elicit relevant information, I was guided by three principles. The first was to make the question sound as natural as possible, since I believed the interviews were likely to yield maximum information if they resembled open-ended conversations. So, I altered my wording to suit the circumstances of the individual or the topic under discussion and did my best to introduce my query smoothly into the flow of talk. The second was to seek for concrete rather than abstract responses; for example, I did not ask, 'What has guided your choice of jobs?' but 'Why did you leave that school? Where did you go next? Was that for any particular reason?' And when I received a reply which contained words or phrases capable of many interpretations (e.g. 'unfriendly staff'; 'inspiring head-teacher'; 'formal teaching') I asked for examples of behaviours or situations which would illustrate these terms. Third, I approached sensitive areas, and especially ones likely to be associated with strong feelings (e.g. shame, love) with indirect rather than direct questions (What changes in your school would enable you to do better what you're trying to do? Why? Can you give me an example of a really good day? Bad day?). I subsequently discovered Lortie's *School Teacher* (1975) and found that he invoked similar principles in collecting data about American teachers' goals and attitudes. His rationale (p. 110) proved useful to me in mounting a post-hoc justification for my choice of questions.

While I was redefining my research focus and discovering by trial and error which aspects of primary teachers' lives were likely to yield the most productive data, I was also arranging visits and interview times for the next term. During that term, I visited thirty-five teachers or ex-teachers, in many parts of England from Devon to North Yorkshire. I spent roughly half a day with each of them in their classes, making unstructured observations which I tried to note down before the interview, as a guide to my own understanding of the individual's professional context. However, I was careful never to take notes in the classroom or even to produce a notebook, since I wished to emphasize that I was there as the teacher's guest, and for my own interest, and not in an evaluation or judgemental capacity. I often found this shared experience a useful starting point, especially if it was some years since I had met the teacher; we would talk for some time about the children or their curriculum before we embarked on personal experiences and individual perspectives.

Interviews sometimes started at lunchtime, if teachers said they could not spare much time after school. Generally, however, they took place at the end of the school day and went on for as long as the individual wanted. We talked in their classrooms, until the caretakers shut us out, and then in their own homes, in pubs, cafes, railway stations, parks and on one occasion, in an art gallery. No one talked for less than an hour and a half, some for as long as five hours. Most interviews lasted for three hours. I encouraged people to give long and, if they wished, discursive replies to my questions and I often used probe or supplementary questions.

The hunger that they all showed to reflect upon their professional lives in the presence of a neutral but friendly outsider was almost insatiable, a fact that in itself taught me much about the loneliness of many teachers' working lives. Nor did I find that they talked less, or less openly, in school than they did in other venues. The pleasures, sometimes the release, of talking seemed to override considerations of place or territory. Indeed, in most cases, the largest part of what I did was to listen, seldom interrupting except to prompt or to offer another line of enquiry.

My interviewees' prolixity caused me formidable recording problems. I had no funds for tape-recording or transcription and, in any case, I was uncertain what effect a tape recorder would have upon the teachers' willingness to be frank (as they were in many cases, to the point of indiscretion). So I took rapid notes in a personal shorthand, recording verbatim whenever I could. This proved difficult to do since I was also attempting to create a relaxed conversational atmosphere and so to maintain as much eye-contact as possible. However, it may be that I found these conditions more potentially inhibiting than my interviewees did, as they continued to talk for as long as I was willing to listen.

I also interviewed eight people over the telephone (two were outside England, six were in the UK but too far away for me to visit), having devised a way of holding the mouthpiece which left me free simultaneously to listen and to take notes. Despite being deprived of contextual and non-verbal cues, I found that these interviews yielded a good deal of valuable data. It is possible that some people found it possible to talk more freely because I was not physically present.

As the interviews progressed I began to realize that I had stumbled, almost unawares, upon a rich seam of data which had the potential to illumine an area about which relatively little was apparently known. However, I was also aware that my previous knowledge of, and my relationship to, my interviewees might be having a distorting effect upon what they said or what I heard. Accordingly, as a rudimentary check upon the subjectivity of my data, I decided to interview a similar number of graduates from PGCE courses in other institutions of higher education. I used an opportunity sample of 30 (8 men and 22 women) who between them had attended seven universities, polytechnics or colleges of education. To my surprise, I found these people were as ready to talk openly to me, as a stranger, as were the teachers who I already knew. Over the next eighteen months I also interviewed a further 21 graduates from my own course who had by this time been teaching for two years or who had changed, after at least two years in the classroom, from teaching into other careers (most often, into parenthood). Altogether, I interviewed 99 people (30 men and 69 women), the balance of sexes being roughly the same among those whom I had taught and those whom I had not.

As a further attempt to release myself from the biases which I knew would creep into data collected in this way, I asked members of both groups if they would be prepared to keep a journal, recording significant events and their reactions to them on one day a week for a term. Twenty-two did this and the perspectives they revealed in their accounts were very similar, no matter where their pre-service education had taken place. However, these diaries were much shorter, terser, and less reflective than their writers were in face-to-face conversations and I found them much less informative than the interviews. I now know much more about professional journals as a research tool than I did then (see, in particular, Holly, 1989) and realize that in hoping I would find a rich alternative source of data in journals voluntarily kept by busy teachers who embarked on this task for my ends not theirs, I was expecting too much. Accordingly, I later used the journals to corroborate patterns or trends which I found in the interviews and not as a prime source of evidence.

The desire to move beyond my own perspective also caused me to try to contact – by letter, telephone or visit – all the headteachers of any school in which any of my interviewees were now teaching or had taught. I succeeded in getting in touch with 70 per cent of these, and had brief (at most thirty minutes, usually much less) conversations with them. I used these exchanges to cross-check factual information and sometimes statements of opinion, and to build up my knowledge of the institutional context from and about which teachers spoke. I also solicited headteachers' views about the efficacy of a shorter-than-normal professional training. Almost all the information I derived from headteachers proved of background rather than of direct value and I made little use of it in interpreting the data or writing up. I do however blush when I consider that I did not seek my interviewees' permission for these conversations and that, unless I was visiting a school, I did not tell them I intended to talk to their heads, or about what. I now have a much greater regard for the ethical rights of participants in research than I had then and would approach this kind of data collection more sensitively than I did and only after prior negotiation.

One more point needs to be made about the interviews conducted in 1975–77: in the course of the next eighteen months, after my initial sabbatical term, they had to be fitted in round a demanding teaching load. Sometimes this would be done travelling at weekends, and visiting schools on Mondays or Fridays, at others I used occasions when the university term began later or finished earlier than the school term. When my interviewees worked reasonably locally, I took advantage of any opportunity provided by, for example, an in-service course at a teachers' centre. In general however, although visits and interviews were not rushed, they were so spaced out that I had repeatedly to think myself anew into the aims of my enquiry and into the questions I was going to ask.

I had virtually completed interviewing when the whole endeavour nearly came to an end. First, the cardboard boxes in which I kept my notes were inadvertently carted away from my office by over-zealous cleaners and I rescued them from the municipal rubbish tip only after a frantic and unsalubrious search. Second, I took a new job in a different part of the country and for a further two years was too busy and preoccupied to start the task of serious analysis. But I went on thinking about the material and the ideas which had begun to form during the period of data collection gradually became clearer. One day I chanced to talk about them during an unplanned conversation with Rob Walker, then at the University of East Anglia. He asked me to share them with some teachers on a higher degree course, one of whom was a teachers' centre warden. The latter in turn asked me to talk to other teachers on in-service courses and soon I started to receive requests for 'copies of papers'. I began to realize that academics and professionals alike were interested in the issues raised by the teachers who had talked so eagerly to me about their lives, albeit several years before.

Spurred on by this interest, over the next six years, in the intervals of a professional life already heavily committed to my own teaching, I nibbled into, chewed and began to digest the huge quantity of data which I had accumulated. Two things made this a formidable task. To start with, I was overwhelmed by the sheer quantity of data. The open-ended nature of much of the questioning and my search for concrete examples also meant that there were few ready-made categories built into the interview responses. Second, therefore, I was faced with sifting relevant information from conversations about many unrelated topics. I wanted to use 'grounded theory' (Glaser and Strauss, 1967), to allow my ideas to emerge from the data, but this seemed a very daunting task. For example, early on I discerned a developmental sequence in teachers' attitudes to their work (it was this which had formed the basis of my early talks to teachers). However, it was clearly a complex idea and I did not feel capable of developing it in written form without a deeper knowledge of other ideas which might also be present in the data. Yet I seemed to lack the time and the means to explore all my evidence in such a comprehensive way.

In the end I embarked on what I hoped would be a relatively straightforward first attempt at category analysis. While interviewing I had repeatedly noted how often my interviewees mentioned their headteachers and how great an impact these people appeared to have on the job satisfaction or dissatisfaction of individual teachers. So I decided to pull out of the data all references to headteachers and see what I could make of it. Patterns began fairly rapidly to emerge and before long I had the outline of a paper which subsequently appeared in an Open University reader as 'Leadership styles and job satisfaction in primary teachers' (Nias, 1980). The final shape of this paper was itself dictated by serendipity. I had just completed the first draft when I happened to meet someone from the Open University with an interest in educational management. He commented on the lack of empirical studies of primary school management and asked if I knew of any unpublished work. I tentatively offered him my draft, it came back to me with a note saying he liked it, but could I make it more 'theoretical'. A week of the holidays spent in the Institute library enabled me to comply with his request and the article (as it had now become) was on its way to publication.

The swift and unexpected success of this first effort gave me encouragement. As soon as I could, I tackled another 'easy' topic: the word 'commitment' (with a number of denotative analogues) appeared in almost every interview. I decided to see what I could discover about its use and to reflect on what this told me about teachers' perspectives and careers. I was soon able to categorize the meanings which people seemed to attribute to it, using conventional methods to test the validity of the categories. I refined and subdivided them, looked for internal consistency, searched for contradictions and negative instances and went on piling up examples until I was thoroughly convinced that a category was saturated. My next tasks were to consider the significance of these 'grounded' themes to an understanding of the subjective reality of teaching and to explain, if I could, why the same word appeared to have several meanings. Once again, I turned, after I had made a preliminary analysis of the data, to what others had written and, as I moved between my own understandings and those of others, patterns began to form. The first draft of the article which subsequently appeared as '"Commitment" and motivation in primary school teachers' (Nias, 1981a) was completed in the departure lounge of Heathrow Airport at the start of my summer holiday.

As the mention of 'motivation' suggests, it was an easy step from here into job satisfaction and dissatisfaction (Nias, 1981b). In any case these topics were relatively straightforward to tackle because all the interviews had contained questions which bore directly upon them.

By this time three further things had happened. I had encountered Peter Woods' illuminating and seminal work on secondary teachers (especially Woods, 1981), we had exchanged papers and ideas and he had encouraged me to go on thinking and writing. This was timely, because I also knew by now that I was into deeper conceptual waters than I had anticipated; as I had worked on the data I had come to realize that the related notions of 'self' and 'identity' were central to any further understandings that I could reach. Yet it was clear that getting a firm grasp on these slippery concepts was likely to prove difficult and time-consuming. I was also therefore ready, thirdly, for the challenge which was presented by an invitation to present a paper at a conference of educational ethnographers in eight months' time.

Once I had embarked on the time-consuming and complex task of understanding the extent and the nature of primary teachers' self-referentialism I was sustained by a combination of intellectual excitement and tenacity. The former arose because I felt that I was generating fresh insights which were genuinely 'grounded' in the data; it was teachers' constant and persistent use of words like 'I', 'me', 'myself' which had first alerted me to the importance of identity and self-image. The latter was needed for two reasons. One was pressure. I was also involved at this time in doing and writing up another, separate research project into alternative understandings of accountability in secondary schools (Elliott *et al.*, 1981). The second was because implicit references to the 'self' and to its salience for primary teachers were scattered through all the data. Analysis was therefore a much slower and more concentrated task than it had been when my attention could be triggered by a few key words or phrases.

I was dimly aware that there were several sub-themes within what I was not certain was a central concept, so I tackled them one by one. However, this was not as straightforward as it appeared. It was clear that to understand any of these sub-themes, I needed to be mentally saturated in the data. Yet I could achieve this only outside term time, since it took between two and four weeks to become immersed in a complex topic, to tease out its implications and to put them into written form. Progress was slow, my friends and family began to complain.

As I wrote this second and more conceptually substantial set of papers I also made deliberate use of a coherent theoretical framework, something which was lacking from my first piecemeal attacks upon the data. I found in symbolic interactionism a productive organizing device and explanatory tool. I would be the first to agree, however, that there are other convincing ways of conceptualizing notions of identity and the self. As I said in the introduction to *Primary Teachers Talking* the choice of theoretical framework is therefore to some extent arbitrary. None the less, I have found this one consistently useful.

In the meantime a decade had passed since my first interviews. At this point the professional interest which the eight published articles had begun to attract, together with my own continuing involvement with the in-service education of teachers, encouraged me to gather some longitudinal data, a development which I had not had in mind when I embarked on the enquiry. I had current or recent addresses for about a sixth of my interviewees, and through them or through previous addresses I contacted over half the original group, asking for their movements to date and whether they would be willing to talk to me again. Fifty-four of them replied, all but three saying they would be ready to meet me (these three were men, still teaching in the same school or neighbourhood in which they had been ten years earlier). I also wrote to fifteen people who had qualified in 1976 or 1977, too late for my original enquiry, but whom I knew were still teaching. Thirteen replied. During 1985, about six months after my original contact with all these people, I conducted a second set of interviews with most of them.

These interviews differed from the first in a number of respects. They took place ten years later in what can loosely be termed 'mid-career' for most of the group. I focused upon a limited number of issues that my experience in in-service education had taught me were likely to be significant: motivation; job satisfaction and dissatisfaction; professional, personal and career development; personal experience of and reflections upon teaching; the place of work in life and future career plans. I also encouraged people to talk freely about any other aspects of their work or career which they felt were important. I did not talk to the headteachers of interviewees, nor, in general, visit their classrooms. Like the first interviews, these were open-ended and loosely structured, but they were shorter; the shortest was about fifty minutes, the longest about three hours. About two-thirds were tape-recorded; for the remaining third I took rapid notes and wrote up a summary as soon as possible thereafter. In both cases, transcripts or summaries were sent to individuals for validation, with the suggestion (of which only three took advantage) that they delete anything they did not want me to use, and with assurances of confidentiality.

The biggest difference of all, however, was that the second group were much more obviously self-selected than the first. I knew by word of mouth what had happened to 29 out of the 45 people who did not reply (4 were in primary schools, 3 were teaching outside primary schools, 13 were raising families, 9 were in other careers including educational psychology), but I did not know why I had not heard from them: did my letter not reach them or were they so disenchanted with me or with their careers that they chose not to reply? Moreover, I had no way of establishing whether the 4 who were still teaching but had not replied, had not done so because they did not receive my letter or because they did not wish to talk about their work, perhaps because they were unhappy in it. By contrast, most of those who answered my letter seemed to be succeeding, in terms of promotion, or were enthusiastically resuming a career after childrearing.

In addition, on this occasion I spoke only to 3 of the 22 people whom I knew had moved to other careers outside teaching (including full-time parenthood). So I do not know whether the 10 married women who indicated an intention to return eventually to teaching had made those plans out of financial necessity or a genuine interest in the work that they had left. Last, during 1975–77 I was in direct or indirect touch for other reasons with many of those whom I interviewed. It is therefore possible that they agreed to my request for information out of courtesy or deference. However, in 1985, only those who were quite happy to be re-interviewed needed to reply to my postal overture.

Thus the second set of evidence on which I drew is heavily biased. With few exceptions it reflects the experience of successful and committed teachers who had been working for between nine and eighteen years (though in the case of married women returners, the years worked varied from five to twelve). What it does not represent is the experiences of those mid-career teachers who may be ready or anxious to change jobs or occupations but are unable to do so. By contrast, the views of such teachers are represented in the first interviews. This difference may be particularly salient because the second interviews were conducted in the spring of 1985, during a period of industrial action for many teachers.

For the second interviews I decided to visit only those who were still working in infant, junior or middle schools. I left the choice of place and time to individuals; 24 chose their place of work, and I met the rest in pubs or in their own homes. The venue did not appear to affect the freedom with which they spoke. However, I also talked to 1 special school teacher (a woman), 3 secondary teachers (2 men and 1 woman), 2 adult education tutors (both women), 5 college lecturers (2 men, 3 women), 1 adviser (a woman) and 3 mothers who had recently given up teaching. Altogether, I conducted 50 interviews (2 of them by telephone). I had been PGCE tutor to all but 2 of those who replied to my original letter and several had, intermittently, kept in touch with me. All of the 50 had at some point taught 4 to 13 year olds (the approximate age range for which they trained) and 36 (13 men, 23 women) were still doing so. There were 17 men, 33 women, 5 headteachers (4 men), 7 deputy heads (of whom 5 were women), 8 women doing part-time or supply work.

Notwithstanding its imperfections, I analysed the resulting data in the ways I have already described, with the difference that I was by now aware of (though I had not fully conceptualized) the importance to individual teachers of their self-image. I started my analysis by looking at the main themes which my questions addressed (e.g. motivation, job satisfaction). However, I found that further patterns emerged (e.g. the conflict between personal and professional lives and how this was resolved; subjective meanings of 'career'). Thus the notion of 'feeling like a teacher' was first worked out tentatively as a conference paper (Nias, 1986), but eventually became of central importance in the book (Chapter 9). Indeed, I found that my ideas were growing even after I had completed the manuscript (e.g. Nias, 1989b was written in 1988 at the request of the journal editor and prompted me to extend my thinking about the concept of 'career').

As analysis proceeded, I also faced the problem of how to integrate all the various ideas. Certain themes (e.g. personal development; reference groups) emerged in both sets of interviews, but some appeared more strongly in early than mid-career or vice versa, and a few (e.g. survival concerns) were peculiar to one, not the other. Moreover, it was very difficult to draw valid or reliable comparisons between the two sets of data. Quantitatively, the numbers of potential interviewees had halved during the intervening decade, though the gender balance within each group remained about the same. There were the issues of self-selection and bias which I have already discussed. Further, a very different political climate surrounded education in 1975–77 and 1985. The first interviews took place soon after teachers had received a substantial pay rise and at a time when morale within the profession was relatively high. The second occurred when salaries were very low and when the industrial action of

1984–86, in which almost all my interviewees were involved in one way or another, was well under way. It has proved impossible to estimate accurately the effect of any or all these factors.

Despite the difficulties posed by the task of analysing the final mass of data collected over ten years – handwritten notes, transcripts or validated summaries of interviews, teachers' written accounts – the task was not without its methodological advantages. The main one was the fact that because there was so much material, patterns appeared fairly readily and could be internally checked and validated. I had no shortage of corroborative evidence and, in consequence, have often been able to generalize with some confidence about my findings, as far as they relate to graduates who trained for one year. In the absence of further evidence it is a matter of speculation whether they also apply to teachers with a longer pre-service education. Other benefits were the wide range of potential illustrative material and the varied nature of the data which helped to keep me from getting bored.

At the time when I undertook the second set of interviews I had no clear idea of what the final outcome might be. I was motivated by my own interest and by that of others and not by the desire to write a book. However, academics and teachers whose opinions I respected repeatedly encouraged me to bring all my work in this area together in one publication. Eventually a chance meeting with a publisher early in 1986 resulted in the offer of a contract. Even then I resisted; I was by this time directing a funded research project which was obviously going to result in substantial publication, and I had no illusions about the work involved in writing one book, let alone two simultaneously. Further, although the fieldwork for the research project had been undertaken during a sabbatical year, by mid-1986 I was back at work full-time. Eventually, however, I was persuaded to sign, though the manuscript was not finally completed until March 1988, three months after its contract date. In the intervening eighteen months it had to compete with my job, two accidents, each of which left me one-handed for several months, arranging publication for the research project, co-authoring the resulting book (Nias, Southworth and Yeomans, 1989), and completing three book chapters to which I had committed myself a long time before. It was a period through which I would not willingly live again. Not least, although I tried hard not to let my teaching suffer, I am sure that it did, so the pressures of multiple authorship were compounded by guilt.

Writing was difficult for many reasons. Since I still write longhand, I was dependent on the help of two excellent and long-suffering typists. Had they not been as efficient and as patient as they were and had they not used word-processors I do not think the book would ever have been completed. I am a slow and painstaking writer most of whose work goes through four drafts. I do not find writing easy, but I like to do it as well as I can. In consequence, producing a manuscript which I feel is fit for publication is hard and tiresome work, inducing broken nights, bad temper and the kind of preoccupation which it is often difficult to distinguish from utter egocentricity. I can truthfully say that whereas data collection is generally enjoyable and analysis is intellectually rewarding, writing is painful drudgery. I persist in it for only two reasons: I feel I have something to say that I want others to read (this itself is normally dependent on other people telling me that they think it is worth saying); and I take a craft pride in the finished product.

Writing for publication, in whatever form, also presented me with the problem of selecting illustrative examples, especially given the constraints of length and the need to balance against each other the reader's likely interest in abstractions on the one hand and living detail on the other. For the most part, I set myself an arbitrary limit of three or four illustrative comments for any given point and pared these down to essentials. I was painfully aware of all the data I did not, and probably shall never directly, use.

The research which resulted in *Primary Teachers Talking: A Study of Teaching as Work* (Nias, 1989a) has never been officially funded. However both my employers directly or indirectly covered the cost of travelling to visit schools, and of postage, and the Cambridge Institute of Education was generous in helping with the cost of tape-recording and transcription. Otherwise I have operated on a self-help basis, staying with friends when I needed to be away from home, squeezing time and resources away from other commitments. I would not however underestimate the importance of institutional backing and I am grateful to have received it. In particular, my colleagues were forbearing and helpful during the tortured months of authorship and I could not have coped without their silent support. The relationships which suffered most obviously during this period were my personal ones.

I have described in detail the sequence of events which has led me more and more deeply over the past fifteen years into a study of primary teachers' lives and careers because this story itself highlights what I feel to be both the weaknesses and the strengths of my research in this area. Among the former I would count: a crude and simplistic methodology; little protection against memory decay over a long period; heavy reliance on one form of data collection; few controls on subjectivity in data collection, recording and analysis; unsophisticated methods for data analysis; lack of attention during the first interviews to the ethical rights of respondents; failure systematically to collect biographical data which might have revealed cohort influences and pointed me towards historical or structural interpretations as well as the sociopsychological one which I finally adopted. In short, judged by most of the accepted canons of qualitative research, my enquiry may be deemed naive, subjective and opportunistic.

Yet it also has its strengths. First, the simplicity of the research design and the relatively uniform format in which the data were presented has freed me to concentrate upon what the teachers themselves had said. My experience as a supervisor and examiner of higher degrees has taught me that operating and justifying complex systems of data collection and analysis can become an end in itself, an excuse not to wrestle with the ideas embedded in the evidence. By contrast, I had to make sense of the testimonies I had collected or abandon the whole enterprise; I could not take refuge in the contemplation of methodological complexities.

Second, the extent and quality of the information I collected challenged me to search for and eventually find connections and relationships between apparently isolated ideas. In seeking not to drown in the data, I found unexpected reefs under my feet.

Third, the fact that I have worked for so long on the material has enabled my ideas to grow slowly, albeit painfully. They have emerged, separated, recombined, been tested against one another and against those of other people, been rejected, refined, reshaped. I have the opportunity to *think* a great deal over fifteen years, about the lives and professional biographies of primary teachers and about their experience of teaching as work. My conclusions, though they are in the last resort those of an outsider, are both truly 'grounded' and have had the benefit of slow ripening in a challenging professional climate.

I wish to stress this point. The more research I do, the more important I realize it is to allow oneself the time to think, at every stage from data collection to interpretation. The corollary is that one has to learn not to feel guilty when one is not directly working on the task. I have found that time spent walking, swimming or gardening, activities initially undertaken out of desperation or physical need, can be immensely productive. Time spent thinking about other things can also be valuable; not all cerebral activity takes place at a conscious level and ideas can form while left to 'compost' slowly.

Thinking however seldom takes place in a vacuum. A fourth benefit of returning again and again to the data over such a long period and in pursuit of different themes is that, to continue the gardening metaphor, one rakes it into such a fine tilth that ideas germinate easily. By the end of fifteen years, I knew my data intimately, a fact which facilitated the search for patterns, interconnections and insights.

In this context I would also like to emphasize the value of chaos as a seed bed for creativity. There were many occasions when I felt overwhelmed by the apparent formlessness or the complexity of the material. If the task had been less messy, I would not have needed to struggle so much and might have been satisfied with premature foreclosure. I have repeatedly found that an acutely uncomfortable period of ambiguity and confusion seems to be a necessary condition for the birth of a new idea. My experience in this respect echoes that of Marshall (1981).

Next, in contrast to the largely solitary nature of cogitation, my employment for the past thirteen years as an in-service teacher educator has given me many opportunities to test my thinking against the perceptions and professional insights of academics and of teachers themselves. In particular I have been able to defend and validate my emerging ideas in discussion with practitioners similar in gender, age, status and experience to those whom I interviewed. I am satisfied that, despite its methodological shortcomings, the picture which I have painted reflects the world which teachers themselves inhabit and yet helps them to see it, and themselves within it, in fresh ways. It seems to have fulfilled one of the main purposes of qualitative research, that is, to provide a 'language for speaking about that which is not normally spoken about' (Hargreaves, 1978, p. 19).

Last, another strength of the research has been the way in which I have been able to cross-fertilize it with other ideas. During the past few years I have drawn on my knowledge of psychotherapeutic groups to write a monograph, commissioned as part of distance learning course materials, by Rob Walker, now at Deakin University, Australia (Nias, 1987). In this publication I used some of the same interview material but interpreted it from a different theoretical perspective. In addition, I have also been a participant observer in a primary school (Primary School Staff Relationships Project, funded by the Economic and Social Research Council 1985–87 (see Nias, Southworth and Yeomans, 1989). This project, and its successor (Whole School Curriculum Development and Staff Relationships in Primary Schools, funded by ESRC 1988–90), used ethnographic methods to explore the workings of primary schools as organizations of adults and the relationships of teachers and non-teaching staff as colleagues. Although these last two pieces of research do not focus directly upon teachers' subjective realities, there are obvious areas of overlap. Simultaneous involvement in various pieces of research and writing has enriched them all, sometimes by confirming central ideas such as the importance to teachers and headteachers of their self-image, at others by challenging or extending particular notions (e.g. what are the conditions which make a staff group both affectively satisfying and task-focused?). I have found it immeasurably beneficial to set the picture that teachers gave in interviews of their own behaviour and careers against a backdrop of fine-grained observation of their life in classrooms and schools, and into the context provided by the literature from a different discipline.

In this account of my research, I have tried both to recount its chequered and often opportunistic growth from a naive and misplaced idea to a published book, and to analyse its methodological strengths and weaknesses. The ways in which a small initial enquiry grew in size and scope and eventually became a piece of longitudinal research really were as dominated by chance as I have suggested. Begun and largely pursued for my own interest, it would not have been carefully conceptualized or written up in a published form had it not been for several serendipitous encounters and the encouragement in which they resulted. Although I find that wrestling with data and with ideas and writing are solitary activities, I owe much of the persistence which has characterized this undertaking to the confidence which others have placed in me.

Methodologically, this work is flawed. Nevertheless, I would argue that its long time-span has given me ample opportunity to reflect upon my data and, in the process, to refine, extend and reconceptualize the ideas which have arisen from them. In addition, methodological simplicity has freed me to think about the interpretation rather than the collection of my evidence. I am sharply aware of the limitations of this longitudinal enquiry. Notwithstanding, I am confident both that I have been able to portray teachers' lives and careers in a way that is convincing to them and also that the book contains ideas which others find practically and theoretically useful. I end, therefore, with a claim and a hypothesis. The claim is this: *Primary Teachers Talking* is not the fruit of 'good' educational research, but the prolonged effort of doing it has given me material to think about and the incentive to think, a process which has resulted in some worthwhile ideas. Had I not undertaken and persisted in the research, however imperfect it may be, I would probably not have had the ideas and would certainly not have shared them with others in writing. The hypothesis therefore is this: the value of this enquiry has been the generation of insights which will be validated not by looking back at the research process but by looking forward, to the uses that other educationalists make of them.

REFERENCES

Elliott, J., Bridges, D., Ebbutt, D., Gibson, R. and Nias, J. (1981) *School Accountability*, Oxford, Blackwell.

Glaser, B. and Strauss, A. (1967) *The Discovery of Grounded Theory*, London, Weidenfeld & Nicolson.

Hargreaves, D. (1978) 'Whatever happened to symbolic interactionism?' in Barton, L. and Meighan, R. (Eds), *Sociological Interpretations of Schooling and Classrooms*, Driffield, Nafferton.

Holly, M. L. (1989) *Writing to Grow: Keeping a Personal-Professional Diary*, New York, Heinemann.

Lortie, D. (1975) *School Teacher: A Sociological Study*, Chicago, University of Chicago Press.

Marshall, J. (1981) 'Making sense as a personal process', in Reason, P. and Rowan, J. (Eds), *Human Inquiry*, Chichester, Wiley.

Nias, J. (1980) 'Leadership styles and job satisfaction in primary schools', in Bush, T., Glatter, R., Goodey, J. and Riches, C. (Eds) *Approaches to School Management*, London, Harper & Row.

Nias, J. (1981a) '"Commitment" and motivation in primary school teachers', *Educational Review* 33, 181–90.

Nias, J. (1981b) 'Teacher satisfaction and dissatisfaction: Herzberg's "two-factor" hypothesis revisited', *British Journal of Sociology of Education* 2, 235–46.

Nias, J. (1986) 'What is it to "feel like a teacher"', paper presented to Annual Conference of British Educational Research Association, Bristol.

Nias, J. (1987) *Seeing Anew: Teachers' Theories of Action*, Geelong, Deakin University Press.

Nias, J. (1989a) *Primary Teachers Talking: A Study of Teaching as Work*, London, Routledge.

Nias, J. (1989b) 'Subjectively speaking: English primary teachers' careers', *International Journal of Education Research: Research on Teachers' Professional Lives* 13, 4, 392–402.

Nias, J., Southworth, G. and Yeomans, R. (1989) *Staff Relationships in the Primary School: A Study of Organizational Cultures*, London, Cassell.

Woods, P. (1981) 'Strategies, commitment and identity: making and breaking the teacher role', in Barton, L. and Walker, S. (Eds), *School, Teachers and Teaching*, Lewes, Falmer Press.

PART 3:

Educational research and practice

10

EDUCATIONAL THEORY

P. H. Hirst

In my contribution to Professor J. W. Tibble's volume *The Study of Education*[1] I sought to characterise educational theory as a domain of practical theory, concerned with formulating and justifying principles of action for a range of practical activities. Because of their concern for practical principles I sharply distinguished domains of practical theory from domains concerned simply with purely theoretical knowledge. The function of the latter is primarily explanation. The function of the former is primarily the determination of practice. The one is concerned with achieving rational understanding, the other with achieving rational action. In this approach I was in major respects at variance with that set out several years previously by Professor D. J. O'Connor in his influential book *An Introduction to the Philosophy of Education*.[2] He had argued that though the term theory could be used for 'a set or system of rules or a collection of precepts which guide or control actions of various kinds',[3] it is better used as in the natural sciences for a hypothesis or logically inter-connected set of hypotheses that have been confirmed by observation. In this sense we have 'standards by which we can assess the value and use of any claimant to the title of "theory". In particular this sense of the word will enable us to judge the value of the various (and often conflicting) theories that are put forward by writers on education.'[4] He concluded: 'we can summarise this discussion by saying that the word "theory" as it is used in educational contexts is generally a courtesy title. It is justified only where we are applying well established experimental findings in psychology or sociology to the practice of education. And even here we should be aware that the conjectural gap between our theories and the facts on which they rest is sufficiently wide to make our logical consciences uneasy. We can hope that the future development of the social sciences will narrow this gap and this hope gives an incentive for developing these sciences.'[5] It seemed to me then, as it seems to me now, in spite of all Professor O'Connor says, critical for the development of educational practice that we hold hard to developing educational theory of a kind that is fully adequate to the nature of the educational enterprise. And to this end we should resist the seductions of a much more limited paradigm of 'theory' taken from another area, however prestigious its claims.

The differences (and agreements) between myself and Professor O'Connor were sharpened in an exchange of papers between us subsequently published in *New Essays in the Philosophy of Education*, edited by G. Langford and D. J. O'Connor.[6] We agree that all theory is concerned with explanation, but to my mind the explanation of human activities in an area like education involves not only the sciences, including the social sciences, but also matters of beliefs and values. Reasons as well as causes enter into the business, mental concepts as well as the empirical concepts of the sciences are involved. If we agree acceptable theories are to be refutable, refutation is for me not confined to the form it takes in the sciences. We agree that educational theory is concerned with 'improving' and 'guiding' practice, but for me that is more than a technical matter for a scientific form of educational theory, on the assumption that the values involved come from outside the theory itself. Of course, if I insist that the debate of educational ends as well as means comes within the theory, because to my mind the development of rational practice demands that debate and because ends and means are not ultimately separable, I must accept that the theory must incorporate all the confusions of contemporary debate about values. I must accept too that at present the logic of practical reasoning is unclear and that the structure of educational theory is therefore uncertain. But I do not despair of our progressively making our educational practice more rationally defensible, indeed I think we are slowly doing that. What is more, I see no reason to think that the logic of practical reasoning will forever elude us. After all, the elucidation of the logic of discourse can only be discerned after the emergence of acceptable paradigms of the discourse. Even in scientific discourse that logic is still a matter of dispute, whilst in the practical domain acceptable sophisticated theories are still in the making.

This second debate with Professor O'Connor has left me unrepentant in seeing educational theory as primarily the domain which seeks to develop rational principles for educational practice. To this end it draws, of course, on all the theoretical knowledge available in the social sciences. Educational psychology and sociology of education are precisely those sub-areas of psychology and sociology that are of use in this way. But it also draws on history, philosophy and much else besides; all that is significant for the formulation and justification of its rational principles. And if educational theory is a composite area of this kind, I remain unrepentant in regarding its unity as the unity of a consistent set of principles of practice at which it aims, not that of one vast theoretical integration of the contributory disciplines.

By the early 1970s, however, it was becoming clear that even if this view of the nature of educational theory is accepted, much more has to be said about the way in which the contributory disciplines are related to practical principles.

Developments at that time within these disciplines only served to accentuate their radically different characters and the limited significance of any one or even all of these domains in the formulation of practical principles. Each discipline, even when concerned with educational practice, clearly has its own concepts, employing these to ask its own distinctive theoretical questions, questions that are essentially, say, philosphical, psychological or historical in nature and not practical. The conclusions reached in each area, however focused on matters of educational practice, are again philosophical, psychological or historical in character and are not themselves principles for practice. The disciplines cannot tackle any given practical questions as such for each tackles questions which are peculiar to itself, those that can be raised only within its own distinctive conceptual apparatus. Psychologists, sociologists or philosophers faced with any matter of practical policy on, say, the grouping of pupils in schools or the use of punishment, can legitimately comment only on different psychological, sociological or philosophical issues that may be at stake. The disciplines each make their own limited abstractions from the complexities of practice. They tackle no common problems of any kind and none of them is adequate to the proper determining of principles for educational practice. Indeed, there seems an inevitable gap between the conceptual framework within which the issues of practice arise and the conceptual frameworks the distinct disciplines employ for their particular purposes. In seeking to characterise the relationship between the disciplines and the principles of educational theory, I have from the start referred to the disciplines as providing reasons, of many different kinds, for the principles. In this the disciplines are seen to be crucial for the justification of what is claimed in the theory. But how can such diverse, partial and limited theoretical studies ever provide a satisfactory justification for any set of practical principles? Even if the account I have given to date is satisfactory as far as it goes, it is certainly in need of further development.

In these early accounts of the nature of theory, uncertainty about what more might be said led to ambiguities that I now consider can be removed, at least to some significant extent. In particular, my view that the disciplines can provide justification for practical principles which in their turn justify particular educational activities in individual circumstances was interpreted by some in very simplistic ways that must surely be rejected. Taken as giving a methodology for developing rational educational practice, it is clear that this scheme, of proceeding from disciplines to principles to particular activities, simply will not work. As has already been indicated, the disciplines we have deal with certain aspects abstracted from complex practical situations, dealing with these in dissociation from each other. There is no reason whatever to suppose that these abstractions when put together begin to give any adequate understanding of the situation for practical purposes, nor even that they ever could. What other new disciplines might come to contribute to our understanding we cannot at present know, but further, we are not able to see how such an array of disciplines can provide a comprehensive base for the determination of practical principles. It is not just that at present the disciplines we have are too un-developed and full of disputes for such a method of developing principles to be workable, true though that is. It is rather that the very character of the disci-plines seems such that they must prove inadequate as a basis for practical principles.

[. . .] Any adequate account of educational theory must, I now consider, reject more firmly than I once saw certain central tenets of rationalism in favour of a more complex theory of rational action.

On the rationalist account, which I now wish to reject explicitly, rational action is seen as necessarily premeditated. Action waits on prior reflection. The justification of any action is therefore a matter of the justification of the prior decision in the light of the beliefs and principles on which it was based. Gilbert Ryle long ago argued against this account in terms of his distinction between 'know how' and 'know that'.[7] Not all forms of intelligent 'know how' presuppose that the person possesses the 'know that' of the relevant principles. In telling examples he pointed out that good cooking came before relevant recipes and that valid deductive arguments were used and known to be valid before their principles were formulated. Rational action can, and in certain respects must, precede rational principles, the latter being the result of reflection on rational actions. That is not to say that principles, once formulated, are not useful in promoting rational action, or that the range of rational action cannot be extended by modifying the principles of such action in specific ways. What is being denied is that an adequate account of rational action in general can be given simply in terms of principles determined prior to action and justified independently of such action.

A distinction similar to Ryle's has been made by Michael Oakeshott in his analysis of all human activities requiring skill of any sort.[8] By means of this distinction he not only builds up further criticism of rationalism, but begins to develop an alternative account of rational action. All activities, he claims, involve two kinds of knowledge. There is, on the one hand, what he calls technical knowledge, a knowledge of rules, techniques and principles that can be formulated comprehensively in propositions, which can be learned, remem-bered and put into practice. On the other hand there is practical knowledge which exists only in use, which is not reflective and cannot be formulated in rules. Its normal expression is in a practice of some sort, in a customary or traditional way of doing things. These two kinds of knowledge Oakeshott considers distinguishable but inseparable, both being involved in every con-crete activity. Together they make any skill or act what it is. He explicitly denies, however, that technical knowledge tells us what to do and practical knowledge how to do it. Even in knowing what to do there is involved not only an element of technical knowledge but one of practical knowledge too. The propositions of technical knowledge could not exist without a practical knowl-edge of how to decide certain questions. Doing anything, therefore, depends on and exhibits knowing how to do it and only part of that knowledge can subsequently be reduced to propositional technical knowledge. What is more, these propositions are not the cause of the activity, nor are they directly regulative of it. Rules and principles cannot be applied to situations by the exercise of knowledge of another kind, practical knowledge. For practical knowledge is not simply some blind unstructured executive competence that applies rules and principles. Practical knowledge consists of organised abilities to discern, judge and perform that are so rooted in understanding, beliefs, values and attitudes that any abstracted propositional statements of those elements or of rules and principles of practice must be inadequate and partial expressions of what is involved. Practical knowledge is acquired by living within the organised social world to which we belong, structured as it is by institutions and traditions of great variety. In education, as in any other area of activity, we come to understand the activity, its problems and their answers from engagement in the activity itself. We have to penetrate the idiom of the activity by practising it. Then, gradually, by a variety of means, we can improve and extend our knowledge of how to pursue it, analysis of the activity and reflection on its rules and principles having their part to play in that process.

On this view, the justification of any individual educational activity cannot be seen simply in terms of an appeal to a set of practical principles. Not merely, as previously seen, because the very existence of principles presupposes the acceptance of at least some activities as independently justified. But now because practical principles are seen to be necessarily inadequate even for an understanding of any activity let alone for justifying it. Justification must be seen, in Oakeshott's words,[9] as 'faithfulness to the knowledge we have of how to conduct the specific activity we are engaged in', and that is different from 'faithfulness to the principles or rules of the activity'. We may easily be faithful to the latter whilst losing touch with the activity itself. 'Rational conduct is acting in such a way that the coherence of the idiom of the activity . . . is preserved and possibly enhanced.' Rules and principles are only 'abridgments' of the coherence of the activity. And if justification of any activity by approach to principles is inadequate, justification of practical principles by an appeal to academic disciplines is equally called in question. The validity of practical principles must, on this view, stem from their being abstracted from practice, rather than some independent theoretical foundation.

Oakeshott's distinction between technical and practical knowledge draws attention to the nature of practical principles and their relationship to practices and individual activities in a way that makes my earlier outline of the nature of educational theory much too simple. What is not clear, however, is the extent and the way in which he considers the understanding, beliefs, values, attitudes and principles embedded in activities to be incapable of formulation in propositions. Is it that this whole constellation of elements is just too complex ever to be analysed except partially? Is it that it is too subtle and mysterious ever to be amenable to propositional formulations that are anything but distortions? Is it that practical knowledge demands the structuring of capacities in patterns that are in principle capable of conceptualisation but whose incorporation cannot itself be propositionally described? On all these views, rational practices and activities can only be learnt in the exercise of the capacities. But if non-distorting conceptualisation is, at least in principle, possible, even if only partial in its concerns, individual activities can with increasing conceptualisation be subjected to ever more critical analysis and perhaps even to limited forms of justification. And if that conceptualisation can, at least in principle, be comprehensive then justification of a much more rigorous kind is at least possible.

What Michael Polanyi has had to say about the tacit element in all human undertakings is perhaps illuminating here.[10] In any activity of understanding or doing he distinguishes what we are attending to focally, what is before the mind, and that which is tacitly or implicitly known. We attend from the tacit to the focal, the activity demanding an integration of these elements. All activities involve the use of many clues, beliefs and judgments which we do not attend to or apply, which indeed we cannot attend to in performing the activity. They are necessarily held tacitly on this occasion. It is not, however, that these tacit elements cannot in principle be made explicit and on other occasions be entertained focally, though in then considering them explicitly, other elements of a tacit nature will be involved. But when we attend to a tacit element explicitly, we fail to capture its meaning in the integration process in which it functions tacitly. Using these terms, Oakeshott's practical knowledge can be seen as involving tacit elements of understanding, values and principles which are all, at least in principle, capable of being made explicit and can therefore be made subject to critical evaluation. But the integration of these elements within practical knowledge involves their incorporation into an organisation that is, in Polanyi's view, essentially and necessarily unspecifiable. Nevertheless, though Polanyi holds that in the last analysis all knowledge and practical activity rest on irreducible tacit elements, this does not make knowledge or action a merely subjective matter. He maintains firmly that one always acts from the tacit elements to a focal, public truth claim, performance or action in all domains, and that each can have its own critique. What such a critique has always to recognise is that here is no ultimate certainty in any domain but a commitment to tacit elements at a lower level. In activities like education, the complexity of the elements is greater than in the case of, say, technology, for education operates at a higher level incorporating lower levels of knowledge and skill as tacit elements. The existence of the tacit in higher levels of understanding and activity is not seen as excluding rational criticism in these domains any more than its existence in science excludes such criticism there. What is needed is rather a recognition of the complexities of critique at higher levels.

What these considerations from Ryle, Oakeshott and Polanyi indicate forcefully is that we must reject totally the idea that rational action is a matter of bringing about a state of affairs whose character is fully predetermined and justifiable. We must accept rather a view of reason as of its nature able to provide only a partial explicit characterisation of action even when that action is premeditated. Formal justification of even premeditated action is therefore at its best partial. But we must accept further that our understanding of action is in large measure necessarily derived from an analysis of what is judged to be successful action before we understand, let alone formulate explicitly, the rules or principles that it embodies. [. . .]

In keeping with this view, if we are to develop rational educational practice, it now seems to me we must start from a consideration of current practice, the rules and principles it actually embodies and the knowledge, beliefs and principles that the practitioners employ in both characterising that practice and deciding what ought to be done. The practical discourse in which what is going on can be expressed will have much in common with the discourse of everyday practical activities. It will include particular technical terms, beliefs and principles concerned with specifically educational practices and institutions, but these will be embedded within a much wider general body of discourse. Getting at current practice and policy will necessarily involve articulating accurately the concepts and categories that practitioners use implicitly and explicitly, for it is only from descriptions and principles formulated in these terms that an overt rational critique of practice is possible. Any analysis of educational practice achieved in this way constitutes what I shall call the 'operational educational theory' of those concerned. Such an analysis can of course be undertaken to cover a limited or wide range of educational activities. It can relate these in varying degrees to other, non-educational activities, beliefs and principles. I can be concerned with the practice of, say, an individual, a school or an LEA. Of course, any such explicit analysis is only a partial expression of what occurs. But it sets out elements of practice, belief and principle that are to a greater or lesser degree susceptible to overt rational criticism.

In examining the particular actions or activities of an individual practitioner, critical examination can be made in terms of the understanding of the situation employed, the principles used in deciding what to do, the anticipated consequences of different possibilities, the actual consequences and so on. This may be questioning of the individual's action and judgment in the light of all that he can be seen to bring to the situation, both explicit and implicit, or it may be a challenge to the person's operational educational theory in terms of its coherence or the justification of its elements. The first form of questioning is very much an assessment of performance, of the exercise of know how, and an attempt to make explicit the operational rationale of what was done in the particular case in terms of the practitioner's own general operational theory. How far this critique will be possible will vary in particular cases because of their possible uniqueness in crucial respects. It will also vary according to the personal characteristics of the individual concerned. It must, too, be remembered that the burden of much that has been considered earlier implies that the inability of the practitioner or an outsider to provide a satisfactory explicit rationale for an action or activity is of itself no measure of its success. Nevertheless, it is equally true that judgment and action can be trained to be more adequate in relation to a person's existing knowledge, beliefs, principles and capacities through consideration of the operational rationale of particular incidents.

Consideration of particular actions or activities and their rationale may, however, raise critical consideration of the understanding and principles with which the practitioner in general approaches these situations. The question then is no longer whether particular judgments or actions were the best that could be taken by this practitioner in the circumstances in which the situation arose, but whether the understanding, principles and capacities that he could bring were themselves justifiable. It is with the critique of 'operational educational theory' in this sense that educational theory in its wider sense is concerned. Educational theory is thus directed at more rational educational practice by the continuous attempt to develop operational educational theory composed of elements that are as far as possible rationally defensible. But if this pursuit is not to be misunderstood, the complex character of operational educational theory and its partial characterisation of practice must be kept firmly in mind. In general the concepts employed in operational theory will be those used by practitioners as a result of their formal and informal education, training and socialisation. Many of these concepts will be those of everyday life, developed to capture complex situations and activities as existential wholes, whilst taking for granted a common recognition of their detailed characters and their context. The concepts of specifically educational situations and activities will be of exactly the same character. Much of the understanding within this level of theory will have been developed in the context of immediate practical experience and will be co-terminous with everyday understanding. In particular, many of its operational principles, both explicit and implicit, will be of their nature generalisations from practical experience and have as their justification the results of individual activities and practices. In many characterisations of educational theory, my own included, principles justified in this way have until recently been regarded as at best pragmatic maxims having a first crude and superficial justification in practice that in any rationally developed theory would be replaced by principles with more fundamental, theoretical, justification. That now seems to me a mistake. Rationally defensible practical principles, I suggest, must of their nature stand up to such practical tests and without that are necessarily inadequate. This demand stems from the fact that only principles generated in relation to practical experience and that are operationally tested can begin to do justice to the necessarily complex tacit elements within practice. Indeed, I would now argue that the essence of any practical theory is its concern to develop principles formulated in operationally effective practical discourse that are subjected to practical test.

But if the practical testing of principles of this character is central to all practical theories, including educational theory, we must recognise that neither the formulation nor the testing involved is a self-contained enterprise. The activities and practices of everyday life are developed and modified in a wide context of knowledge, beliefs and values about men and their physical and social context. The very concepts in which our implicit and explicit understanding of practice occurs are tied in with concepts of knowledge and understanding of many kinds. Men have developed knowledge and understanding not only in relation to immediate practice, but in the pursuit of scientific, historical, religious and other forms of explanation. These employ their own conceptual schemes in pursuit of their own forms of rationally defensible claims. The concepts and principles of everyday practice and its discourse become modified progressively in the light of scientific advances, changes in our psychological and sociological understanding, and so on. If practical principles are to be rationally defensible they must therefore be seen to be formulated and tested in ways that incorporate wider beliefs and values that are rationally defensible rather than erroneous. In relation to practical affairs, therefore, it is the job of such disciplines as psychology, sociology and philosophy to provide a context of ever more rationally defensible beliefs and values for the development and practical testing of practical principles.

But if practical discourse is itself limited in its capacity to articulate the principles of practice, the discourses of these other disciplines, which have been developed for other purposes, will of themselves be unable to provide any directly helpful forms of conceptualisation for the promotion of rational practice. Their proper significance is, by virtue of their nature, going to be indirect. Any attempt to derive defensible practical principles from the findings of, say, research psychology, must founder on the gross inadequacy of such findings in relation to the complexities, both implicit and explicit, that characterise practical activities. Any attempt to implement such ill-conceived principles can only serve to distort practice into indefensible activities.

Looked at in these terms, the role of such separate disciplines as, say, sociology of education and philosophy of education within the domain of educational theory as a whole must be the appropriate form of criticism of the sociological and philosophical elements that are significant for the formulation and practical testing of practical principles. It is their job to aid these processes in every way possible. It is not their job to be individually or collectively the basis for the direct formulation of practical principles. In so far as they may suggest forms of practice, these will require reformulation in the light of past practical experience of appropriate kinds if they are to have any serious hope of rational defence through practical testing.

The logic of educational theory I therefore now see as demanding the justification of what is done in any particular case by reference to knowledge, understanding and practical principles, which principles have been subject to the test of practical experience. The knowledge, understanding, practical principles and forms of practical test which are thus appealed to incorporate and make use of elements that are open to rational criticism in various contributory disciplines. The justification of these elements in the disciplines is in principle necessary but not sufficient for the justification of the practical principles. It is therefore as mistaken to think of the practical principles of educational theory being justified by appeal to the disciplines as it is to think that a theory in physics is justified by appeal to the validity of the mathematical system it employs.

[. . .]Since my article in 1966 for the volume edited by Professor Tibble, the characterisation of the nature of educational principles and their justification has emerged as far more problematical than I then recognised. The significance of the tacit elements in all action can now be seen to be fundamental to any adequate account of practice and its principles. Likewise, the fact that we are ourselves products of the social situations we have created and that our understanding of these situations is central to their being what they are means that the practitioner's view of what is occurring must be recognised as central. These features can to some extent be discerned progressively in writing on educational theory, in certain exploratory approaches within educational research and in new emphases within the teaching of educational studies. There has come to be a focus on the actual practices of education and the discourse practitioners use. It is not so much that what I wrote in 1966 was mistaken as that what I omitted led to a distorting emphasis. Educational theory I still see as concerned with determining rationally defensible principles for educational practice. The adequate formulation and defence of these principles I now see as resting not simply on appeal to the disciplines, but on a complex pragmatic process that uses its own appropriate practical discourse. How best we might give an account of the logic of such discourse and its principles remains I think uncertain, though I have indicated how I think we should approach the matter.

Perhaps the most promising discussions of this now focal question are to be found quite outside the particular context of educational theory, in the contemporary study of critical theory, particularly the work of Habermas and his critics. Habermas has sought to outline the fundamental framework within which rational practical discourse can take place by articulating the basic presuppositions of speech acts. This sets out certain normative conditions for rational decisions and consensus. His approach in formulating these principles that underlie all practical activities can also be used in the context of more particular areas. As one of his most able expositors and critics, Thomas McCarthy, has expressed it:

> As Habermas sees it, the basic idea behind this approach is that speaking and acting subjects know how to achieve, accomplish, perform, produce a variety of things without explicitly adverting to, or being able to give an explicit account of, the structures, rules, criteria, schemata on which their performances are based. The aim of rational reconstruction is precisely to render explicit the structures and rules underlying much 'practically mastered, pre-theoretical know-how', the tacit knowledge that represents the subject's competence in a given domain . . . if the tacit, pre-theoretical knowledge that is to be reconstructed represents a universal know-how . . . our task is the reconstruction of a 'species competence'. Adopting this approach, Habermas advances a proposal for a universal or formal pragmatics.[11]

In another passage he writes:

> Communication that is oriented towards reaching understanding inevitably involves reciprocal raising and recognition of validity claims. Claims to truth and rightness, if radically challenged, can be redeemed only

through argumentative discourse leading to rationally motivated consensus. Universal-pragmatic analysis of the conditions of discourse and rational consensus show these to rest on the supposition of an 'ideal speech situation' characterised by an effective equality of chances to assume dialogue roles.[12]

There is much dispute about many features of Habermas's programme. Whether or not his particular exposition of the ethics of speech acts is correct, and this is far from obvious, it is by no means clear that such an ethic is in any ultimate sense the necessary foundation of rational practice. And just what the implementation of such an ethic means logically and methodologically in the rational critique of more specific practices like those of education, it is not easy to envisage. However, it certainly suggests self-critical, reflective and reconstructive analysis and judgment by different groups of practitioners, operating at different and progressively more deep and wide-ranging levels of presupposition, using the disciplines to maximum degree. That kind of activity, whatever particular form it may come to take, can hardly fail to contribute illuminatingly to rational educational practice. And if practice does indeed precede theory in this area as in others, perhaps this will in due course bring us further understanding of educational theory. Certainly, at present it seems to me to afford us the most hope.

NOTES

1. P. H. Hirst, 'Educational Theory', in J. W. Tibble (Ed.), *The Study of Education*, London, Routledge & Kegan Paul, 1966.

2. D. J. O'Connor, *An Introduction to the Philosophy of Education*, London, Routledge & Kegan Paul, 1957.

3. Ibid., p. 75.

4. Ibid., p. 76.

5. Ibid., p. 110.

6. G. Langford and D. J. O'Connor (Eds), *New Essays in the Philosophy of Education*, London, Routledge & Kegan Paul, 1973, Papers 3 and 4.

7. G. Ryle, *The Concept of Mind*, London, Hutchinson, 1949.

8. M. Oakeshott, *Rationalism in Politics*, London, Methuen, 1962. See the papers 'Rationalism in Politics' and 'Rational Conduct'.

9. Ibid., pp. 101–2.

10. See particularly, M. Polanyi and H. Prosch, *Meaning*, University of Chicago Press, 1975.

11. T. McCarthy, 'Rationality and Relativism', in J. B. Thompson and D. Held (Eds), *Habermas – Critical Debates*, London, Macmillan, 1982, p. 60.

12. Quoted in Thompson and Held (Eds), op. cit., pp. 255–6.

11

WHAT IS AN EDUCATIONAL PRACTICE?

W. Carr

It has become rather fashionable these days to extol the virtues of educational practice. Teacher-education should be more firmly based on it, educational theorising made more relevant to it, and teacher educators should have more experience of it. Given this state of affairs, it is surprising to find that educational philosophers who willingly argue about the meaning of 'educational theory' seem rather reluctant to discuss how the concept of 'educational practice' ought to be understood.[1] Indeed, it seems to be assumed that the meaning of 'educational practice' is so straightforward and clear that we can safely rely on our common-sense understanding when we use the term in educational discussions and debates. The possibility that our common-sense may, in this instance, be in need of philosophical examination does not seem to have been seriously considered or explored.

But suppose it were the case that our common-sense understanding of educational practice was radically ambiguous and incoherent. Suppose, further, that the defects in our concept of educational practice not only pre-date modern forms of educational theorising, but actually paved the way for their evolution and growth. If this were the case, if, that is, our concept of educational theory *and* our concept of educational practice both emanated from the same dubious historical source, then we could expect certain difficulties to arise. We could, for example, expect to find that all our efforts to make educational theory 'practically relevant' were constantly breaking down. Despite our best intentions, the 'gap' between theory and practice would stubbornly remain. We could also expect to find that any philosophical enquiry into the meaning of 'educational practice' which simply concentrated on how this concept is now used, would fail to detect the inherited weaknesses which our modern concept contained. Indeed, a philosophy of education committed to this kind of 'conceptual analysis' would offer nothing but an empty silence concerning the numerous philosophical puzzles to which our ambiguous and incoherent understanding of educational practice inevitably gave rise.

The argument of this paper is that these suppositions are largely true, and hence that our contemporary concept of educational practice is the end-product of an historical process through which an older, more comprehensive and more coherent concept has been gradually transformed and changed. Given this thesis, it is not my intention to treat the title of this paper as an invitation to analyse the ways in which the concept of educational practice is presently understood. On the contrary, I intend to regard it as an open invitation to allow the history of the concept to expose possibilities of meaning which are very different from those now encountered in contemporary use.

In order to respond to the question in this way, I have set myself three specific tasks. The first is to show why attempts to analyse the concept of 'practice' which focus on its relationship to 'theory' fail to furnish us with a satisfactory understanding of what an educational practice is. The second is to argue that this failure is in part due to the absence of any historical exegesis of the concept of 'practice' – a state of affairs which itself exemplifies the common belief that concepts can be philosophically analysed apart from their history. The third is to show that once we are prepared to give historical depth to philosophical analysis, it becomes possible to spell out a core concept of practice which not only illuminates some of the incoherences in our present conception of educational practice, but also offers a more satisfactory understanding of why it is that education is understood as a practice at all.

II

In education, as elsewhere, the notion of 'practice' is used in different and, sometimes, incompatible ways. It is used, for example, to refer both to an activity undertaken in order to acquire certain capacities and skills ('teaching practice') and to an activity which demonstrates that these competences and skills have already been acquired ('good practice'). Normally, this ambiguity does not give rise to confusion: the context in which the notion occurs is sufficient to indicate the particular way it is being used.

What do give rise to some confusions, however, are those occasions when the concept of 'practice' is defined and understood in terms of its relationship to theory. The most common way of understanding this relationship is, of course, as one of opposition. On this view, 'practice' is everything that 'theory' is not. 'Theory' is concerned with universal, context-free generalisations; 'practice' with particular context-dependent instances. 'Theory' deals with abstract ideas; 'practice' with concrete realities. Theorising is largely immune from the pressures of time; practice is responsive to the contingent demands of everyday life. Solutions to theoretical problems are found in knowing something; practical problems can only be solved by doing something. As one exponent of this 'oppositional' view puts it, 'a theoretical problem does not specify any occasion or situation in which it must be solved . . . but a practical problem can only be solved by taking action in a certain situation at a certain time'.[2]

When applied to the field of education, however, this view of practice is always unsatisfactory. For example, certain educational problems (What should I teach? What should I include in the 'core' curriculum?) are clearly 'practical' in the sense that they are problems about what to do. At the same time, however, they are 'general' rather than 'particular', 'abstract' rather than 'concrete', and relatively 'context-free'. Conversely, there are many educational problems that are 'specific', 'immediate' and 'context-dependent' (what are the major impediments to the introduction in this school of GCSE?) even though they are 'theoretical' in the sense that they are requests for knowledge rather than action. The situation is further complicated by the fact that there are numerous educational situations in which the practical point at issue is what to do about some theoretical claim (should I group pupils on the assumption that claims about innate differences in intelligence are true?). In such cases, the practical situation may call for immediate action based on a timeless question that has been debated 'in theory' since the time of Plato.

Thus, the general weakness of this 'oppositional' view is that it generates criteria for 'practice' which, when applied to the notion of an *educational* practice, exclude too much. By seeing 'theory' and 'practice' as mutually exclusive and diametrically opposed concepts, it tends to neglect these aspects of educational practice which are not constrained by criteria of immediacy, particularity, context-dependency and the like. And, by emphasising the difference between knowledge and action, it tends to ignore the essential role in educational practice that theoretical generalisations and abstract ideas can play. In short, by making the twin assumptions that all practice is non-theoretical and all theory is non-practical, this approach always underestimates the extent to which those who engage in educational practices have to reflect upon, and hence theorise about, what, in general, they are trying to do.

The predictable reaction to these deficiencies has been the emergence of various accounts of educational practice which focus on its dependence on, rather than its opposition to, theory. Drawing on familiar philosophical arguments about the indispensability of conceptual schemes or the role of 'paradigms' in everyday life,[3] these analyses emphasise that, since all practice presupposes a more or less coherent set of assumptions and beliefs, it is, to this extent, always guided by a framework of theory. Thus, on this view, all practice, like all observation, is 'theory-laden'. 'Practice' is not opposed to theory, but is itself governed by an implicit theoretical framework which structures and guides the activities of those engaged in practical pursuits.

It follows from this kind of analysis that since all practice is theory-laden, this will be just as true for the most simple practice (e.g. asking a pupil a question) as for those more complex cases in which the dependence on theory is more explicit and overt (e.g. using micro-computers to implement Skinnerian principles of learning). It thus needs to be emphasised that, on this account, the notion of 'theory-guided practice' can be used in two quite different ways. In the first place, it can be used to make the point that all practice necessarily presupposes a conceptual framework. But secondly, it may also be used to describe those occasions when practitioners appropriate externally produced theory to guide them in their practical pursuits.

Just as the problem with the oppositional view of educational practice is that it excludes too much, so the general problem with the 'theory-guided' view is that it excludes too little. Indeed, on this view, educational practice can be guided both by a 'theory' that is nothing other than tacit, implicit and unarticulated common-sense as well as the 'theory' that is produced through systematic disciplined enquiry. But the most important difficulty with this view is that it does not adequately recognise that educational practice is never guided by theory alone. This is so because 'theory', whether implicit and tacit or explicit and overt, is always a set of general beliefs, while 'practice' always involves taking action in a particular situation. Although practice may be guided by some implicit theoretical principles about what, in general, ought to be done, the decision to invoke or apply such principles in a particular situation cannot itself be guided or determined by theoretical beliefs. For this would entail an infinite regress of first-order theoretical precepts (about what, in general, ought to be done) guided by second-order meta-theoretical precepts (about if and when to apply first-order theoretical precepts) and so on. Because practitioners are not subject to this infinite regress, their judgements about the applicability of general principles to particular situations cannot themselves be determined by theoretical principles or rules.

If educational practice cannot be reduced to a form of theorising, can educational theorising be reduced to a form of practice? One of the most influential attempts to pursue this line of thought is Gilbert Ryle's well-known attempt to assert the autonomy of practice.[4] Ryle develops his argument by showing that since one cannot 'know-that' something is the case unless one already 'knows how' to do a vast number of things, "'know-how' is a concept logically prior to 'know that'".[5] This not only entails that 'practice is not the step-child of theory'[6] but quite the reverse; 'efficient practice precedes the theory of it'.[7] Indeed, Ryle concludes that theorising is itself a form of practice, requiring skill, competence and know-how of various kinds. ('Theorising is one practice among others and is itself intelligently or stupidly conducted').[8]

The fact that Ryle is so effective in refuting the idea that practice is guided by some prior act of theorising should not conceal how, by equating practice to 'knowing how' to perform various operations or skills, he employs it in a way that is more narrow and restricted than might first appear.[9] Nor should it cause us to forget that an educational practice always involves much more than 'knowing how' to do something in this Rylean sense. For a definitive feature of an *educational* practice is that it is an ethical activity undertaken in pursuit of educationally worthwhile ends. Moreover, as Professor Peters has so frequently pointed out, these ends are not some independently determined 'good' to which educational practice is the instrumental means. Rather they define the rules of conduct, or, in Peters' phrase, the 'principles of procedure' which constitute a practice as an educational practice and justify its description in these terms.[10]

To engage in an educational practice it is thus never sufficient (though it is always necessary) to 'know-how' to do a variety of things. We can, for example, consistently assert that a certain teaching method is competently and skilfully performed (e.g. the techniques of behaviour-modification) yet deny that it is an educational practice. To make this assertion is not to claim that this form of teaching is ineffective but that it is incompatible with those ethical principles by which any educational practice must be informed. This is not to say that, in order to engage in an educational practice, these ethical principles need to be translated into a set of codified rules which can then be used to guide practice in an educationally worthwhile direction. It is simply to point out that the educational character of any practice can only be made intelligible by reference to an ethical disposition to proceed according to some more or less tacit understanding of what it is to act educationally. Where this disposition is present, a practitioner may, irrespective of his 'know how' or skill, practise in an educational way. But where it is absent, a practitioner who 'knows how' to practise in a Rylean sense, will be quite incapable of practising in an educational sense at all.

The simple lesson of the argument so far is that the three accounts of practice I have identified are all inadequate for determining how the concept of educational practice ought to be understood. One conclusion that could be inferred is that it reinforces the suspicion that a question like 'what is an educational practice'? is wholly misconceived. 'Practice' has such a plethora of meanings that the search for criteria which can provide our concept of educational practice with some kind of definitive meaning presupposes that it has a unity and simplicity which it patently does not.

But another, less obvious, conclusion may be that it is not the question that is misconceived but our presumptions about how it is to be answered. For it may be plausible to suggest that the reason why these accounts of practice do not enable us to make our concept of an educational practice more intelligible is not that they are false. It may well be that the three features of a practice to which they draw attention (its opposition to theory, its dependence on theory, its independence of theory) are all necessary features of an educational practice as well. But by accentuating only one of these features, to the exclusion of the others, each of these different accounts may only be offering an incomplete, one-sided, version of what an educational practice may be. Once they are looked at in this way, these accounts of practice no longer appear as three incompatible alternatives from which we have to choose. They can instead be seen to be three incomplete analyses of a practice each of which is limited by two false assumptions.

The first of these is that the meaning and significance of practice can only be determined by clarifying how it relates to theory, so that to understand what a practice is, it is always necessary to understand this relationship. The second shared assumption, is that 'practice' is a stable and static concept, so that in any philosophical analysis of its meaning, its history will only be of incidental or antiquarian interest. But once these two assumptions are challenged, it becomes possible to interpret the criteria of 'practice' provided by each of these analyses in a very different way. It becomes plausible to interpret them, not as mutually exclusive criteria, but as three essential features of a historically prior concept of practice for which problems about its relationship to theory do not arise.

To interpret matters in this way is thus to suggest that the various criteria surrounding our present concept of practice are nothing other than the fragmented relics of a previous concept of practice which, though it can no longer find adequate expression, nevertheless continues to convey something of its original meaning and assert something of its original form. It is also to suggest that we ought to be able to produce a historical reconstruction of this concept which will enable us to clarify some of the ambiguity surrounding its contemporary meaning and use. But is it appropriate to try to answer a question like 'what is an educational practice?' in this way? Much of the contemporary philosophy of education asserts that it is not. Indeed, the intellectual predilections now cultivated by the academic study of education, encourage us to believe that philosophical analysis is one thing and the history of ideas is something else. But are we right to construe the relationship between the philosophy and the history of education in this way? To this question I now, albeit briefly, wish to turn.

III

An ancient statue of a Roman god will have a history. It is a history of a stable and unchanging object which has continued to exhibit the same essential features over time. As such, it reminds us of the time and place in which it was produced and so helps us to understand the particular culture and form of social life which it expresses and represents. The concepts we use to describe this statue will also have histories. But the history of concepts like 'religious', or 'god', is not the history of an unchanging object displaying the same essential features throughout time. Concepts are not kept in museums to remind us of the particular form of life in which they have their origins or roots. They continue to be used and, in continuing to be used, they change. How concepts like 'religious' and 'god' are used at any given time and place will vary as social life varies. Conversely, as changes in social life occur so changes in the meaning of concepts will occur as well.[11]

The simple reason why this is so is that conceptual structures and social structures are neither separable nor distinct.[12] Concepts are socially embedded and a form of social life is partially constituted by concepts. So, for example, the differences between the ancient Greek concepts of 'democracy', 'citizen' and 'justice' and the contemporary English usages of these terms, signifies not simply a linguistic difference, but a difference between two forms of social life. Thus, one important way of understanding the concept of 'practice' available to any given historical period would be to uncover the rules governing its use in language and social life. Similarly, one important way of identifying changes that are occurring in our own culture may be by noting changes in the way that the concept of 'practice' is now being used.

The fact that conceptual change and social change are two elements in one essentially dialectical process should not encourage us to assume that this process can somehow occur without direct human intervention. Nor, in particular, should it cause us to overlook the important part that philosophical enquiry can play in influencing this process. For if a philosophical analysis can succeed in revealing that the way in which a concept is being used is in need of major modification or revision, then it may thereby assist in the process of changing its everyday interpretation and use. Philosophical analysis of what concepts mean and changing social life are thus not necessarily independent tasks. Indeed, it may well be that the role now played by the concept of 'practice' in social life is partially due to the way in which it has been analysed by philosophers in some previous era.[13]

To see the history of the concept of 'practice' in these terms is thus to recognise the limitations of any philosophical enquiry which restricts itself to analysing that version of the concept which our own cultural milieu happens to provide. It is also to concede that the only sure antidote to this kind of conceptual parochialism is to bring our own contemporary understanding of the concept of practice face to face with a historical account of how it has been understood in the past. Unless we are prepared to allow the history of the concept of practice to break down our present-day preconceptions in this way, then we may be deprived of important clues for detecting possible confusions and distortions in the way the concept is now used.

Interpreted as a request for historical intelligibility (rather than an analysis of contemporary usage), the question 'what is an educational practice?' presages a form of enquiry committed to the combined tasks of historical reconstruction and philosophical critique. What we could expect such an enquiry to reveal is that the concept of an educational practice is largely explicable in terms of four characteristic historical features.

The first is that our present concept of an educational practice has its origins within the conceptual structures of a form of life which has long since disappeared and, hence, that it can only be made fully intelligible by understanding it as a survival from a social context very different from our own.

The second is that, in this transition from one social context to another, what it means to talk of education as a practice will have changed. Thus, we should be prepared to find that, in the transition from the context in which it was originally at home to our own contemporary culture, an educational practice became something other than it once was. But what, thirdly, we should also expect to find, is that such changes in the concept will not be so complete as to eradicate its original meaning or totally detach it from its historical roots. So it should be unsurprising to discover that, as new conceptions of an educational practice emerge, fragments of an older concept will continue to assert themselves and break through. The history of concepts is one of continuity as well as change.

What, finally, we would expect a full-length history of the concept of an educational practice to reveal are those occasions where changes to its meaning may have been assisted by abstract philosophical beliefs about the nature of education itself. It is only by first appreciating the extent to which our present concept of an educational practice relies on the educational ideas and arguments of our philosophical ancestors that we can critically assess the extent to which this present-day concept can be philosophically vindicated and sustained.

The question 'what is an educational practice?' can now be recast in the following more precise and more answerable form: can we discover a historically specific concept of 'practice' which enables us to reconcile the seemingly irreconcilable range of criteria governing its present use? Can we recover from history a core concept of practice which is more compelling for education than our own? The answer I intend to provide is that we can, and that it turns out to be the classical concept of 'practice' which has always exercised a decisive influence on education and which has only been finally discarded in our own modern times. This concept of practice owes much to the philosophy of Aristotle. It was he who initiated the search for the forms of knowledge and rationality appropriate to practical action. And it is only through a historical understanding of his account of 'practice' that we shall be able to appreciate why it is that education is now construed as a practice at all.

IV

Although the Greek word *praxis* has a meaning roughly corresponding to our term 'practice', the conceptual structures within which it had its proper place are very different from our own. For, in its classical context, 'practice' referred to a distinctive way of life – the *bios praktikos* – a life devoted to right living through the pursuit of the human good. It was distinguishable from a life devoted to *theoria* (*bios theoretikos*) – the contemplative way of life of the philosopher or the scientist – in terms both of its end and the means of pursuing this end.[14]

Thus, the Greek distinction between theory and practice has very little to do with the way in which the distinction is now drawn. It is not a distinction between knowledge and action, thinking and doing, 'knowing that' and 'knowing how'. Rather, it is a way of articulating two different forms of socially embedded human activities each with its own intellectual commitments and its own moral demands. It is thus unsurprising to find that in their discussions about *theoria* and *praxis*, the Greeks rarely found it necessary to discuss the relationship between the two. For them, the modern philosophical problem of whether theory and practice are, or are not, independent of each other, would probably have made little sense.[15]

A problem about practice to which the Greeks did attach philosophical importance, was that of clarifying the forms of knowledge and rationality appropriate to practical thought and action. One way of reading the *Nichomachean Ethics* is as a brilliant attempt to resolve this problem by elucidating the epistemological presuppositions of *praxis*. In doing this, Aristotle not only opened up that tradition of 'practical philosophy' which henceforth was to provide the *bios praktikos* with its major source of theoretical expression and support. He also articulated a range of conceptual distinction which now enables us to distinguish beliefs about 'practice' which belong to this tradition from beliefs which do not.

The most important of these distinctions is not between theory and practice but between two forms of human action – *praxis* and *poiesis* – a distinction which can only be rendered in English by our much less precise notions of 'doing something' and 'making something'. *Poiesis* – 'making action' – is action the end of which is to bring some specific product or artifact into existence. Because the end of *poiesis* is an object which is known prior to action, it is guided by a form of knowledge which Aristotle called *techne* – and what we would now call technical knowledge or expertise. *Poiesis* is thus a species of rule-following action. It is what Weber was to call 'purposive-rational' action and what we would call instrumental action. For Aristotle and the Greeks, the activities of shipbuilders, craftsmen and artisans were paradigm cases of *poiesis* guided by *techne*.

Although 'practice' (*praxis*) is also action directed towards the achievement of some end, it differs from *poiesis* in several crucial respects. In the first place, the end of a practice is not to produce an object or artifact but to realise some morally worthwhile 'good'. But, secondly, practice is not a neutral instrument by means of which this 'good' can be produced. The 'good' for the sake of which a practice is pursued cannot be 'made', it can only be 'done'. 'Practice' is a form of 'doing action' precisely because its end can only be realised 'through' action and can only exist in the action itself.

Thus, thirdly, practice can never be understood as a form of technical expertise designed to achieve some externally related end. Nor can these ends be specified in advance of engaging in a practice. Indeed, *praxis* is different from *poiesis* precisely because discernment of the 'good' which constitutes its end is inseparable from a discernment of its mode of expression. 'Practice' is thus what we would call morally informed or morally committed action. Within the Aristotelean tradition all ethical, political and social activities were regarded as forms of practice. And so too, of course, was education.

Another way in which practice differs from *poiesis* is that its ends are neither immutable nor fixed. Instead, they are constantly revised as the 'goods' intrinsic to practice are progressively pursued. Thus, while it is always possible, and frequently desirable, to produce a theoretical specification of what the ends of *poiesis* should be, the ends of practice cannot be determined in this way. Rather, what they are at any given time, can only be made intelligible in terms of the inherited and largely unarticulated body of practical knowledge which constitutes the tradition within which the good intrinsic to a practice is enshrined. To practise is thus never a matter of individuals accepting and implementing some rational account of what the 'aims' of their practice should be. It is always a matter of being initiated into the knowledge, understandings and beliefs[16] bequeathed by that tradition through which the practice has been conveyed to us in its present shape.[17]

A 'practice', then, is always the achievement of a tradition, and it is only by submitting to its authority that practitioners can begin to acquire the practical knowledge and standards of excellence by means of which their own practical competence can be judged.[18] But the authoritative nature of a tradition does not make it immune to criticism. The practical knowledge made available through tradition is not simply reproduced; it is also constantly re-interpreted and revised through dialogue and discussion about how to pursue the practical goods which constitute the tradition.[19] It is precisely because it embodies this process of critical reconstruction that a tradition evolves and changes rather than remains static or fixed. When the ethical aims of a practice are officially deemed to be either uncontentious or impervious to rational discussion, the notions of practical knowledge and tradition will tend to be used in a wholly negative way.[20]

Rational discussion about how the ethical ends of a practice were to be interpreted and pursued was what Aristotle took 'practical philosophy' to be all about.[21] It is the 'science' which seeks to raise the practical knowledge embedded in tradition to the level of reflective awareness and, through critical argument, to correct and transcend the limitations of what within this tradition has hitherto been thought, said and done. Thus the persistence, within this kind of practical philosophy, of incommensurable historical 'philosophies' about what the aims of a practice should be is neither a sign of its irrationality nor a source of intellectual embarrassment. On the contrary, it is the continuing presence of contesting philosophical viewpoints that provides the oppositional tension essential for critical thinking to perform its transforming role. Once deprived of this critical tension, 'practical philosophy' will quickly degenerate into a chronologically arranged catalogue of philosophical creeds and its relationship to practice will become increasingly difficult to discern.

Although, for Aristotle, practical philosophy is a 'science', it is not a 'theoretical science' entirely devoted to pursuing knowledge of the 'good'. Nor is it a 'productive science' yielding ethically neutral knowledge of effective skills and techniques. Rather it is a 'practical science' yielding knowledge of how to promote the good through morally right action. However, although practical philosophy offers generalisations about the ends of a practice and how they ought to be pursued, this kind of knowledge is never sufficient to determine what a practitioner ought to do. For, in the first place, such knowledge is always imprecise: it merely states the general directions that practical action ought to take. And, secondly, while practical philosophy can only provide general guidance, practice is itself always particular and has to take account of the changing conditions under which it has to operate. For these reasons practical philosophy cannot be used simply as a source of theoretical statements from which practical implications can be logically inferred. For these reasons, also, practical philosophy cannot achieve the status of an 'exact' science, and has to rest content with providing guidance of a 'more or less' or 'in most cases' character.

Since the ends of a practice always remain indeterminate and cannot be fixed in advance, it always requires a form of reasoning in which choice and judgement play a crucial role. This form of reasoning is, for Aristotle, distinguishable from technical forms of reasoning by virtue of its overall purpose, and the structure of the reasoning it employs.

The overall purpose of technical reasoning is to consider the relative effectiveness of action as a means to some known end – as, for example, when a teacher has to decide between 'phonic' and 'whole-word' approaches to the teaching of reading solely on the basis of their effectiveness in producing some specific outcome. By contrast, the overall purpose of practical reasoning is to decide what to do when faced with competing and, perhaps, conflicting moral ideals. Practical reasoning is thus most clearly exemplified in the thoughts and actions of those faced with a moral conflict or a moral dilemma. It is required, for example, when an individual has to decide whether to put loyalty to a friend before patriotic duty, or when a teacher has to decide whether it is educationally more desirable to segregate pupils on the basis of their ability or to adopt a 'mixed-ability' approach. More generally, practical reasoning is required when practitioners have to decide on a course of action where it may only be possible to respect one value at the expense of another. In such cases, a practitioner cannot resort to a form of reasoning which relies on technical calculations to determine what course of action is correct. Practical reasoning is not a method for determining *how* to do something, but for deciding what *ought* to be done. This form of reasoning is, for Aristotle, 'generically different' from technical reasoning and involves proceeding in a measured or 'deliberative fashion'.[22]

Although, in deliberative reasoning, both the means and ends of action are open to question, what is deliberated upon is not ends but means. However, it would be quite wrong to infer from this that means and ends can be characterised independently of each other. For, in choosing between alternative means, practitioners must also reflect on the alternative ethical ends which supply them with criteria for their choice. If the alternative means are simply different ways of achieving the same ethical end, then the question is simply an instrumental question about their relative effectiveness. Where, however, alternative means are means to different ethical ends, then the practitioner has to deliberate about these ends as possible alternative means to some further all-embracing end. Thus, deliberation is not a way of resolving technical problems for which there is, in principle, some correct answer. Rather, it is a way of resolving those moral dilemmas which occur when different ethically desirable ends entail different, and perhaps incompatible courses, of action.

The formal structure of deliberative reasoning is that of the practical syllogism where the major premise is a practical principle stating what in general ought to be done (e.g. people with personal difficulties ought to be treated with consideration) and the minor premise asserts a particular instance falling under this major premise (this person has just lost his wife). Thus, the method of deliberative reasoning is, like the hypothetico-deductive method of scientific reasoning, effected through a syllogistic argument in which a particular case is subsumed under a general principle. But the practical syllogism differs from the ordinary syllogism in at least two crucial respects.

First, the conclusion of a practical syllogism is not a statement prescribing 'what ought to be done' which is analogous to the statements describing 'what is the case' with which ordinary syllogisms conclude. The conclusion of a practical syllogism is an *action* which, precisely because it issues from a deliberate process of moving from premises to conclusions, is the outcome of a process of reasoning rather than shrewd guess-work or pure chance. Secondly, this action, though the product of deductively valid reasoning, is not 'right' action in the sense that it has been proved to be correct. It is 'right' action because it is *reasoned* action that can be defended discursively in argument and justified as morally appropriate to the particular circumstances in which it was taken.[23] Moreover, in deliberative reasoning, it is always conceded that there may be more than one ethical principle that can supply the content to a major premise and that there is no formula for methodically determining which one should be invoked in a particular practical situation. It is for this reason that Aristotle insists that collective deliberation by the many is always preferable to the isolated deliberation of the individual.

It is for this reason, also, that good deliberation is entirely dependent on the possession of what Aristotle calls *phronesis*, which we would translate as 'practical wisdom'. *Phronesis* is the virtue of knowing which general ethical principle to apply in a particular situation. For Aristotle, *phronesis* is the supreme intellectual virtue and an indispensable feature of practice. The *phronimos* – the man of practical wisdom – is the man who sees the particularities of his practical situation in the light of their ethical significance and acts consistently on this basis. Without practical wisdom, deliberation degenerates into an intellectual exercise, and 'good practice' becomes indistinguishable from instrumental cleverness. The man who lacks *phronesis* may be technically accountable, but he can never be morally answerable.

Hence, 'practical wisdom' is manifest in a knowledge of what is required in a particular moral situation, and a willingness to act so that this knowledge can take a concrete form. It is thus a comprehensive moral capacity which combines practical knowledge of the good with sound judgement about what, in a particular situation, would constitute an appropriate expression of this good. For this reason 'judgement' is an essential element in practical wisdom. But it is not the judgement of the umpire impartially applying a set of codified rules.

Rather, it is that form of wise and prudent judgement which takes account of what would be morally appropriate and fitting in a particular situation.[24]

'Judgement' is thus a crucial term in the equation linking deliberation and practical wisdom with action. Deliberating well is a mark of *phronesis*, and *phronesis* is the union of good judgement and action. What is distinctive of the *phronimos* is that his deliberations lead, by way of judgement, to practice. And what is distinctive of practice is that it bears a constitutive relationship to practical knowledge, deliberation and the pursuit of the human good. It is this concept of practice from which our own concept has evolved and, if my argument is at all plausible, it is this concept of practice which will better enable us to answer the question posed in the title of this paper. It is to this question that I now wish to return.

V

One of my main aims has been to show how a self-conscious awareness of the historical roots of the concept of practice helps us to understand why current attempts to analyse the concept run into the sort of difficulties that they do. Another has been to show how these difficulties are largely the product of the widespread assumption that practice can only be adequately analysed by means of an a-historical enquiry into the kind of relationship to theory that it may, or may not, have. Because of this, the conceptual distinctions crucial for any philosophical elucidation of what constitutes an educational practice are always drawn at the wrong point. For what the history of the concept clearly reveals is that the important conceptual distinctions are not those between theory and practice, knowledge and action, or 'knowing-how' and 'knowing-that'. Rather, they are distinctions between different kinds of action (*poiesis* and *praxis*, ethically enlightened action and technically effective action), and the forms of knowledge appropriate to them (*techne* and *phronesis*, technical knowledge and practical knowledge). What, in effect, I have tried to show is that the failure to recognise the importance of these distinctions has left our concept of practice confused. As a result, our understanding of why education is construed as a practice has become increasingly difficult to articulate and describe.

Once the importance of these distinctions is acknowledged, it becomes clear why characterisations of educational practice which focus on its relationship to theory always break down. It becomes clear, for example, that, since educational practice is always guided by some theory about the ethical goods internal to that practice, it cannot be made intelligible in terms of an opposition to theory. But at the same time, it becomes equally clear why this does not mean that educational practice can be sufficiently characterised as a theory-guided pursuit. For what is distinctive of an educational practice is that it is guided, not just by some general practical theory, but also by the exigencies of the practical situation in which this theory is to be applied. Thus, the guidance given by theory always has to be moderated by the guidance given by *phronesis* – wise and prudent judgement about if, and to what extent, this 'theory' ought to be invoked and enacted in a concrete case.

The fact that educational practice cannot be properly characterised as 'theory-dependent' or 'theory-guided' should not be taken to add credibility to the view that it is simply a species of theory-free 'know-how' of a Rylean kind. What is distinctive of *praxis* is that it is a form of reflexive action which can itself transform the 'theory' which guides it. *Poiesis* is a form of non-reflexive 'know-how' precisely because it does not itself change its guiding *techne*. For *praxis*, however, theory is as subject to change as is practice itself. Neither theory nor practice is pre-eminent; each is continuously being modified and revised by the other.

Educational practice cannot be made intelligible as a form of *poiesis* guided by fixed ends and governed by determinate rules. It can only be made intelligible as a form of *praxis* guided by ethical criteria immanent in educational practice itself: criteria which serve to distinguish genuine educational practices from those that are not, and good educational practice from that which is indifferent or bad. While some people now want to reduce educational practice to a kind of 'making action' through which some raw material can be moulded into a pre-specifiable shape, educational practitioners continue to experience it as a species of 'doing action' governed by complex and sometimes competing ethical ends which may themselves be modified in the light of practical circumstances and particular conditions. It is in these terms that many educational practitioners understand their work. And it is in terms provided by the concepts and language of *praxis* that many of them would want to define and defend the essential features of their educational and professional role.

It is, also, something like this concept of practice that permeates Professor Peters' successive attempts to vindicate a view of education as a non-instrumental process concerned to promote intrinsically worthwhile ends.[25] Indeed, it seems to me that many of the standard criticisms of Peters' original analysis arise primarily because what he was actually analysing was not 'the' concept of education, but the conception of education as a form of *praxis* which was undergoing historical transformation and change. Thus, it is interesting to note that the counter-examples adduced to refute Peters' original analysis [26] refer either to a concept of education used in a form of life in which the notion of *praxis* was not available (i.e. Spartan education), or to those modern uses of education which indicate how the concept of education as a form of *praxis* is now being displaced (i.e. vocational education, specialist education). It is not surprising, therefore, that the burden of Peters' attempts to accommodate these counter-examples has to be borne by a historical analysis designed to show how major social changes – such as the impact of industrialism and the emergence of mass schooling – have led to changes in the ways in which the concept of education is now used.[27]

'What is an educational practice?' The answer I have tried to provide is one which is firmly grounded in those developments in post-analytic philosophy which seek to re-establish the classical concept of 'practice' in the modern world.[28] Clearly, any further elaboration of this answer would benefit from a close inspection of the attempts in curriculum theory, evaluation and research to create a renewed awareness of educational practice as the achievement of a tradition rather than as a form of craft-knowledge or technical expertise.[29] It is equally clear that to suggest, as I have, that R. S. Peters' philosophy should be placed in the context of this tradition[30] is not only to propose that the recent history of the philosophy of education needs to be rewritten. It is also to anticipate a discussion about the future of the philosophy of education, which starts from a view about 'what a practice is' rather than a view about 'what philosophy is'. It is thus to foreshadow the re-emergence of educational philosophy as a species of 'practical philosophy' explicitly committed to that concept of practice which has always provided education with its primary definition. Within our dominant contemporary culture, this concept of practice has been rendered marginal and now faces something approaching total effacement. As new concepts of educational practice are emerging, so the older concepts of practical wisdom, deliberation and judgement are being eroded. By re-affirming its traditional commitments and roles, the philosophy of education may be better able to promote the integrity of educational practice and oppose all those cultural tendencies which now undermine and degrade it.

NOTES

1. As far as I can tell, neither the *Journal of Philosophy of Education*, nor its predecessor, contains any papers explicitly concerned with the concept of educational practice. What is available in the general philosophical literature, and what has influenced the argument of this paper more than anything else, are the various discussions of 'practice' in the work of Hans-George Gadamer, see in particular, Gadamer (1967, 1980b, 1981).
2. Gauthier (1963), p. 2.
3. This is a strategy I tried to employ in my own (1980) attempt to explain the gap between theory and practice in education. It also forms part of Professor Hirst's (1983) analysis of educational theory.
4. Ryle (1949)
5. Ibid.
6. Ibid.
7. Ibid.
8. Ibid.
9. Several critical studies make this point. See, for example, Martin (1961), pp. 59–62.
10. See, in particular, Peters (1959, 1965).
11. This is of course a Wittgensteinian insight which was developed with considerable skill by Winch (1968).
12. The relationship between conceptual change and social change is discussed in some detail by Skinner (1980).
13. This view of the role of philosophy in social change has its roots in Hegel. For a fuller account see Taylor (1984).

14. The history of the concept of practice is covered in some detail by Lobkowicz (1967).

15. Historical explanations of how and why this became a problem are offered by Lobkowicz (1977) and Gadamer (1967, 1981).

16. What Gadamer (1980a) refers to as 'pre-judgement', 'for-conceptions' and 'prejudices'.

17. The epistemological role of the notion of tradition has been stressed by writers as diverse as Oakeshott (1966), Gadamer (1980a), MacIntyre (1981) and Bernstein (1983).

18. Gadamer (1980a) puts the point vividly: 'That which has been sanctioned by tradition has an authority that is nameless . . .' (p. 249). The authoritative nature of tradition is also central to the arguments of Oakeshott (1966) and MacIntyre (1981).

19. Again, the point is eloquently put by Gadamer (1980a): 'Tradition is not simply a precondition into which we come, but we produce it ourselves, in so much as we understand, participate in the evolution of tradition and hence further determine it ourselves' (p. 261).

20. The claim that our own modern culture has discarded tradition for just these reasons is, of course, central to the argument of MacIntyre's *After Virtue* (1981).

21. See Gadamer (1980b) both for an account of Aristotle's notion of 'practical philosophy' and an argument for its modern revival.

22. Aristotle's fullest account of deliberation and practical reasoning is to be found in the chapter on 'Practical wisdom and excellence in deliberation' in the *Nichomachean Ethics* (Book VI: Ch. 9).

23. As Aristotle puts it, 'He who deliberates well, deliberates correctly' (NE 1142b).

24. For a detailed exposition of Aristotle's notion of judgement see Beiner (1983) Chapters 4 and 5.

25. Peters (1966, 1967).

26. Woods & Dray (1973).

27. See in particular 'Education and the educated man' in Peters (1977).

28. Ball (1977), Rorty (1979), Gadamer (1980a, 1981), MacIntyre (1981) and Bernstein (1983).

29. Schwab (1969), Van Manen (1977), Reid (1978), Elliott (1980, 1985), Langford (1985) and Carr & Kemmis (1986).

30. Something like this interpretation of Peters' philosophy is developed with considerable conviction by Elliott (1986). See also Carr (1986).

REFERENCES

Aristotle (1955) *The Nichomachean Ethics* (trans. J.A.K. Thomson) (London, Penguin).

Ball, T. (Ed.) (1977) *Political Theory and Praxis – New Perspectives* (Minneapolis, University of Minnesota Press).

Beiner, R. (1983) *Political Judgement* (London, Methuen).

Bernstein, R. J. (1971) *Praxis and Action* (Philadelphia, University of Pennsylvania Press).

Bernstein, R. J. (1983) *Beyond Objectivism and Subjectivism: Science Hermeneutics and Praxis* (Oxford, Blackwell)

Carr, W. (1980) The gap between theory and practice, *Journal of Further and Higher Education*, 4, pp. 60–69.

Carr, W. & Kemmis, S. (1986) *Becoming Critical: Educational, Knowledge and Action Research* (Lewes, Falmer Press).

Carr, W. (1986) R. S. Peters' philosophy of education, *British Journal of Educational Studies*, 34, pp. 268–274.

Elliott, J. (1980 Implications of classroom research for professional development, in: E. Hoyle & J. Megarry (Eds) *World Yearbook on Education, 1980: Professional Development of Teachers* (London, Kogan Page).

Elliott, J. (1985) Educational theory, practical philosophy and case study (Norwich, Centre for Applied Research in Education) (mimeo).

Elliott, R. K. (1986) Richard Peters: a philosopher in the 'older style', in: D. E. Cooper (Ed.) *Education Values and Mind: Essays for R. S. Peters* (London, Routledge & Kegan Paul).

Gadamer, H. G. (1967) Theory, technology, practice: the task of the science of man, *Social Research*, 44, pp. 529–561.

Gadamer, H. G. (1980a) *Truth and Method* (trans. G. Bardey & J. Cummings) (New York, Seabury Press).

Gadamer, H. G. (1980b) Practical philosophy as a model of the human sciences, *Research in Phenomenology*, 9, pp. 74–85.

Gadamer, H. G. (1981) What is practice? The conditions of social reason, in: H. G. Gadamer, *Reason in the Age of Science* (trans. F. G. Lawrence) (Cambridge, Mass., MIT Press).

Gauthier, D. P. (1963) *Practical Reasoning* (Oxford University Press).

Hirst, P. H. (1983) Educational theory, in: P. H. Hirst (Ed.) *Educational Theory and its Foundation Disciplines* (London, Routledge & Kegan Paul).

Langford, G. (1985) *Education, Persons and Society: A Philosophical Enquiry* (Basingstoke, Macmillan).

Lobkowicz, N. (1967) *Theory and Practice: History of a Concept from Aristotle to Marx* ((Notre Dame, University of Notre Dame Press).

Lobkowicz, N. (1977) On the history of theory and praxis, in: T. Ball (Ed.) *Political Theory and Praxis: New Perspectives* (Minneapolis, University of Minnesota Press).

MacIntyre, A. C. (1981) After Virtue: A Study in Moral Theory (London, Duckworth).

Martin J. R. (1961) On the reduction of 'knowing that' to 'knowing how', in: B. Othanel Smith & R. H. Ennis (Eds) *Language and Concepts in Education* (Chicago, Rand McNally).

Oakeshott, M. (1966) *Rationalism in Politics and Other Essays* (London, Methuen).

Peters, R. S. (1959) Must an educator have an aim?, in: R. S. Peters, *Authority, Responsibility and Education* (London, George Allen & Unwin)

Peters, R. S. (1965) Education as initiation, in: R. D. Archambault (Ed.) *Philosophical Analysis and Education* (London, Routledge & Kegan Paul).

Peters, R. S. (1966) *Ethics and Education* (London, Allen & Unwin).

Peters, R. S. (1977) *Education and the Education of Teachers* (London, Routledge & Kegan Paul)

Reid, W. A. (1978) *Thinking about the Curriculum* (London, Routledge & Kegan Paul).

Rorty, R. (1979) *Philosophy and the Mirror of Nature* (Princeton, Princeton University Press).

Ryle, G. (1949) *The Concept of Mind* (London, Hutchinson).

Schwab, J. J. (1969) The practical: a language for curriculum, *School Review*, pp. 1–24.

Skinner, Q. (1980) Language and social change, in: L. Michaels & C. Ricks (Eds) *The State of the Language* (Berkeley, University of California Press).

Taylor, C. (1984) Hegel, history and politics, in: M. Sandel (Ed.) *Liberalism and its Critics* (Oxford, Blackwell).

Van Manen, M. (1977) Linking ways of knowing with ways of being practical, *Curriculum Inquiry*, 6, pp. 205–228.

Winch, P. (1968) *The Idea of a Social Science* (London, Routledge & Kegan Paul)

Woods, J. & Dray, W. H. (1973) Aims of education – a conceptual enquiry, in: R. S. Peters (Ed.) *The Philosophy of Education* (Oxford, Oxford University Press).

12

ACTION RESEARCH

S. Kemmis

Action research is a form of research carried out by practitioners into their own practices. In this article, the definition and character of action research is outlined with reference to its history. The resurgence of interest in educational action research is discussed. Action research is then distinguished from other forms of contemporary educational research through an examination of the 'objects' of action research: educational practices. These are not understood by action researchers as 'phenomena', 'treatments', or expressions of practitioners' perspectives, but rather as praxis. Examples of practices studied by action researchers are given. Research techniques employed by action researchers are noted; it is argued that action research is distinguished not by technique but in terms of method. Criteria for evaluation of action research are then outlined. The role of outside facilitators in educational action research is discussed, and different kinds of intervention by outsiders are shown to influence the form of action research studies. The article concludes with a discussion of the relationship between action research, policy research, and the control of education, suggesting that action research is a participatory democratic form of educational research for educational improvement.

THE DEFINITION AND CHARACTER OF ACTION RESEARCH

Action research is a form of self-reflective enquiry undertaken by participants in social (including educational) situations in order to improve the rationality and justice of (a) their own social or educational practices, (b) their understanding of these practices, and (c) the situations in which the practices are carried out. It is most rationally empowering when undertaken by participants collaboratively, though it is often undertaken by individuals, and sometimes in cooperation with 'outsiders'. In education, action research has been employed in school-based curriculum development, professional development, school improvement programmes, and systems planning and policy development. Although these activities are frequently carried out using approaches, methods, and techniques unrelated to those of action research, participants in these development processes are increasingly choosing action research as a way of participating in decision making about development.

In terms of method, a self-reflective spiral of cycles of planning, acting, observing, and reflecting is central to the action research approach. Kurt Lewin, who coined the phrase 'action research' in about 1944, described the process in terms of planning, fact finding, and execution.

> Planning usually starts with something like a general idea. For one reason or another it seems desirable to reach a certain objective. Exactly how to circumscribe this objective and how to reach it is frequently not too clear. The first step, then, is to examine the idea carefully in the light of the means available. Frequently more fact-finding about the situation is required. If this first period of planning is successful, two items emerge: an 'over-all plan' of how to reach the objective and a decision in regard to the first step of action. Usually this planning has also somewhat modified the original idea.
>
> The next period is devoted to executing the first step of the overall plan. In highly developed fields of social management, such as modern factory management or the execution of a war, this second step is followed by certain fact-findings. For example, in the bombing of Germany a certain factory may have been chosen as the first target after careful consideration of various priorities and of the best means and ways of dealing with this target. The attack is pressed home and immediately a reconnaissance plane follows with the one objective of determining as accurately and objectively as possible the new situation.
>
> This reconnaissance or fact-finding has four functions: It should evaluate the action by showing whether what has been achieved is above or below expectation. It should serve as a basis for correctly planning the next step. It should serve as a basis for modifying the 'overall plan'. Finally, it gives the planners a chance to learn, that is, to gather new general insight, for instance regarding the strength and weakness of certain weapons or techniques of action.
>
> The next step again is composed of a circle of planning, executing, and reconnaissance or fact-finding for the purpose of evaluating the results of the second step, for preparing the rational basis for planning the third step, and for perhaps modifying again the over-all plan. (Lewin 1952 p. 564).

Lewin documented the effects of group decision in facilitating and sustaining changes in social conduct, and emphasized the value of involving participants in every phase of the action research process (planning, acting, observing, and reflecting). He also saw action research as based on principles which could lead 'gradually to independence, equality, and cooperation' and effectively alter policies of 'permanent exploitation' which he saw as 'likely to endanger every aspect of democracy' (Lewin 1946 p. 46). Lewin saw action research as being essential for the progress of 'basic social research'. In order to 'develop deeper insights into the laws which govern social life', mathematical and conceptual problems of theoretical analysis would be required, as would 'descriptive fact-finding in regard to small and large social bodies'; 'above all', he argued, basic social research 'would have to include laboratory and field experiments in social change' (Lewin 1946 p. 35).

Lewin thus presaged three important characteristics of modern action research: its participatory character, its democratic impulse, and its simultaneous contribution to social science and social change. In each of these three areas, however, action researchers of the 1980s would take exception to Lewin's formulation of the significance of action research. First, they would regard group decision making as important as a matter of principle rather than as a matter of technique; that is, not merely as an effective means of facilitating and maintaining social change but also as essential for authentic commitment to social action. Second, though this is partly a matter of changing historical conditions, contemporary exponents of action research would object to the notion that participants should or could be 'led' to more democratic forms of life through action research. Action research should not be seen as a recipe or technique for bringing about democracy, but rather as an embodiment of democratic principles in research, allowing participants to influence, if not determine, the conditions of their own lives and work, and collaboratively to develop critiques of social conditions which sustain dependence, inequality, or exploitation in any research enterprise in particular, or in social life in general. Third, contemporary action researchers would object to the language in which Lewin describes the theoretical aims and methods of social science ('developing deeper insights into the laws that govern social life' through mathematical and conceptual analysis and laboratory and field experiments); this language would now be described as belonging to positivistic science (determinist, technicist) and incompatible with the aims and methods of an adequate and coherent view of social science, especially educational science.

Carr and Kemmis (1983 p. 158) argue that there are five formal requirements for any adequate and coherent educational science:

1. it must reject positivist notions of rationality, objectivity, and truth;
2. it must employ the interpretive categories of teachers (or the other participants directly concerned with the practices under inquiry);
3. it must provide ways of distinguishing ideas and interpretations which are systematically distorted by ideology from those which are not, and provide a view of how distorted self-understandings can be overcome;
4. it must be concerned to identify and expose those aspects of the existing social order which frustrate rational change, and must be able to offer theoretical accounts which enable teachers (and other participants) to become aware of how they may be overcome; and

5. it must be based on an explicit recognition that it is practical, in the sense that the question of its truth will be determined by the way it relates to practice.

Unlike a number of other forms of contemporary educational research, contemporary action research meets these requirements.

THE RESURGENCE OF INTEREST IN ACTION RESEARCH

Lewin's early action research work was concerned with changes in attitudes and conduct in a number of areas of social concern (for example, in relation to food habits and factory production in the later years of the Second World War, and in relation to prejudice and intergroup relations immediately after the War). His ideas were quickly carried into education, when his co-workers and students (and often Lewin himself) began working with educationists on issues of curriculum construction and the professional development of teachers. Teachers College, Columbia University became a centre for action research in education. Stephen Corey, at one time Dean of Teachers College, became an influential advocate (Corey 1953). Kenneth Benne, Hilda Taba, and Abraham Shumsky were other early exponents of educational action research.

After enjoying a decade of growth, educational action research went into decline in the late 1950s. Although some action research work in education has continued in the United States, Nevitt Sanford (1970) argued that the decline was attributable to a growing separation of research and action (or, as it might be put today, of theory from practice). As academic researchers in the social sciences began to enjoy unprecedented support from public funding bodies, they began to distinguish the work (and the status) of the theorist–researcher from that of the 'engineer' responsible for putting theoretical principles into practice. The rising tide of post-Sputnik curriculum development, based on a research–development–diffusion (R,D, and D) model of the relationship between research and practice, legitimated and sustained this separation. Large-scale curriculum development and evaluation activities, based on the cooperation of practitioners in development and evaluation tasks devised by theoreticians, diverted legitimacy and energy from the essentially small-scale, locally organized, self-reflective approach of action research. By the mid-1960s, the technical R,D, and D model had established itself as the pre-eminent model for change and practically inclined educationists were increasingly absorbed into R,D, and D activities.

Perhaps the greatest impetus to the resurgence of contemporary interest in educational action research came from the work of the 1973–1976 Ford Teaching Project in the United Kingdom, under the direction of John Elliott and Clem Adelman. This project, initially based at the Centre for Applied Research in Education, University of East Anglia, involved teachers in collaborative action research into their own practices, in particular in the area of inquiry/discovery approaches to learning and teaching (Elliott 1976–77). Its notion of the 'self-monitoring teacher' was based on Lawrence Stenhouse's (1975) views of the teacher as a researcher and as an 'extended professional'. It seems that Stenhouse had been influenced by certain action research work carried out at the Tavistock Institute of Human Relations. Lewin and his co-workers at the Research Center for Group Dynamics (established at the Massachusetts Institute of Technology and subsequently moved, after Lewin's death in 1947, to the University of Michigan) had collaborated with Tavistock social psychologists in founding the *Journal of Social Issues*.

Since his involvement in the Ford Teaching Project, John Elliott has continued to develop action research theory and practice, and has established the Classroom Action Research Network (publishing its own *Bulletin*) from the Cambridge Institute of Education.

Interest in action research is also growing in Australia and in continental Europe, and, once again, in the United States.

There are a number of reasons for this resurgence of interest. First, there is the demand from within an increasingly professionalized teacher force for a research role, based on the notion of the extended professional investigating her or his own practice. Second, there is the perceived irrelevance to the concerns of these practitioners of much contemporary educational research. Third, there has been the revival of interest in 'the practical' in curriculum, following the work of Schwab and others on 'practical deliberation' (Schwab 1969). This work has revived interest in, and provided legitimacy for, practical reasoning (as against technical or instrumental reasoning) as the basis for decisions about educational practice. Fourth, action research has been assisted by the rise of the 'new wave' methods in educational research and evaluation (interpretive approaches, including illuminative evaluation, democratic evaluation, responsive evaluation, case study methods, field research, ethnography, and the like), with their emphasis on participants' perspectives and categories in shaping educational practices and situations. These methods place the practitioner at centre stage in the educational research process: actors' understandings are crucial in understanding educational action. From the role of critical informant to an external researcher, it is but a short step for the practitioner to become a self-critical researcher into her or his own practice. Fifth, the accountability movement has galvanized and politicized practitioners. In response to the accountability movement, practitioners have adopted the self-monitoring role as a proper means of justifying practice and generating sensitive critiques of the working conditions in which their practice is conducted (conditions often created by the policy makers who hold them accountable for their actions). Sixth, there is the growing solidarity of the teaching profession in response to the public criticism which has accompanied the postexpansion educational politics of the 1970s and 1980s; this, too, has fostered the organization of support networks of concerned professionals interested in the continuing development of education even though the expansionist tide has turned. And finally, there is the increased awareness of action research itself, which is perceived as providing an understandable and workable approach to the improvement of practice through critical self-reflection.

THE OBJECTS OF ACTION RESEARCH

The 'objects' of educational action research are educational practices. These are not construed by action researchers as 'phenomena' (by analogy with the objects of physical science, as if their existence was somehow independent of practitioners), nor as 'treatments' (by analogy with technical or agricultural research, as if they were mere techniques, valued only as alternative and more or less efficient means to a single set of known and universally desired ends), nor as expressions of practitioners' intentions and perspectives (by analogy with the objects of interpretive research, as if their significance could be understood solely by reference to the points of view of practitioners as these meanings emerged in response to historical circumstances).

Practice, as it is understood by action researchers, is informed, committed action: *praxis*. Praxis has its roots in the commitment of the practitioner to wise and prudent action in a practical (concrete historical) situation. It is action which is informed by a 'practical theory', and which may, in its turn, inform and transform the theory which informed it. Practice is not to be understood as mere behaviour, but as strategic action undertaken with commitment in response to a present, immediate, and problematic action context. Practical action is always risky; it requires wise judgment by the practitioner.

As one theorist of practical action remarks, 'practical problems are problems about what to do . . . their solution is only found in doing something'. In this sense the significance of practices can only be established in context: only under the 'compulsion' to act in a real historical situation can a commitment have force for the practitioner, on the one hand, and definite historical consequences for actors and the situation, on the other. Action is thus both a 'test' of commitment and the means by which practitioners can determine the adequacy of their understandings and of the situations in which practice occurs.

Since only the practitioner has access to the commitments and practical theories which inform praxis, only the practitioner can study praxis. Action research, as the study of praxis, must thus be research into one's own practice. The action researcher will embark on a course of action strategically (deliberately experimenting with practice while aiming simultaneously for improvement in the practice, understanding of the practice and the situation in which the practice occurs); monitor the action, the circumstances under which it occurs, and its consequences; and then retrospectively reconstruct an interpretation of the action in context as a basis for future action. Knowledge achieved in this way informs and refines both specific planning in relation to the practice being considered and the practitioner's general practical theory. The interpretations of other participants in the situation will be relevant in the process of reconstruction; they may be treated as the perspectives of relevant 'others', in which case they inform the practitioner about the social consequences of the practice, or be regarded as the perspectives of coparticipants in the action, in which case they can inform collaborative reconstruction and contribute to the discourse of a community of practitioners researching their joint (collaborative) practices. The crucial point, however, is that only the practitioner can have access to the perspectives and commitments that inform a particular action as praxis, thus praxis can only be researched by the actor him/herself. The dialectic of action and understanding is a uniquely personal process of rational reconstruction and construction.

If it is only practitioners who can research their own practice, a problem seems to arise about whether the practitioner can understand his or her own praxis in an undistorted way – whether understandings reached will be biased, idiosyncratic (some would say 'subjective'), or systematically distorted by ideology. This problem is illusory. First, this way of construing the problem suggests that there is some medium in which praxis can be described and analysed in ways which are entirely unrelated to the values and interests of those doing the observing (for example, value-free, neutral, or 'objective' observation categories). This is an illusion created by the image of a value-free, 'objective' social science which cannot by definition be a science of human praxis which must always embody values and interests. Moreover, the study of praxis (informed action) is always through praxis (action with and for understanding) – it, too, is an embodiment of values and interests (in the improvement of praxis). Second, this way of construing the problem fails to acknowledge that the purpose of the critical self-reflection undertaken by the practitioner is to discover previously unrecognized distortions of interpretation and action (for example, the taken-for-granted assumptions of habit, custom, precedent, and coercive social structures and the limitations on action these assumptions produce). It is important to recognize that the medium in which these distortions are expressed (language) is itself social praxis and always subject to influence by values and interests. In short, the dialectic of reconstituting meanings from actions by interpretation is always a process of relative emancipation from the dictates of habit, custom, precedent, and bureaucratic systematization; it is never a complete emancipation from injustice and irrationality. Undistorted communication is purely ideal–typical: it is never achieved, though the practitioner seeking to understand her or his praxis is bound to pursue the ideal in order to discover concrete and particular distortions influencing his or her practice. This dialectical process of reconstruction is a key part of the critical self-reflection of the action researcher.

A range of practices have been studied by educational action researchers. Some examples may suffice to give a picture of how action research has helped practitioners to understand their own practices more deeply. In studies of inquiry/discovery teaching, practitioners have come to understand how, even despite their aspirations, they have used questioning strategies which maintain student dependency on teacher authority rather than create the conditions for autonomy. In studies of the organization of remedial reading, practitioners have come to understand the contradictions of withdrawal practices that preserve rather than overcome the labelling of students as in need of 'remediation', which mystify the reading process rather than make it transparent to students, and which deskill students in terms of progress in other subjects by interrupting subject teaching to focus on reading skills out of context. In studies of teacher–student negotiation of curriculum, practitioners have come to understand that an overemphasis on student interest as the basis for curriculum formation may fragment the social relations of teaching and learning, and deny students access to the discourse of established fields of knowledge. Studies of assessment practices have helped practitioners to understand that notions of ability and achievement can confirm students in failure rather than create the conditions for further learning. Investigations of learning in the classroom, undertaken by students, have helped them to understand how their roles as learners may either imprison them in dependency on teachers or create the conditions for self-directed and collaborative learning. And studies of teaching and learning in higher education, undertaken collaboratively by students and teachers, have helped them to revise their working relationships so as to achieve their joint aspirations more completely.

METHODS, TECHNIQUES, AND THE EVALUATION OF ACTION RESEARCH

Action research is not distinguished by the use of a particular set of research techniques. While it is common for educational action researchers to keep focused diaries about specific aspects of their practice, to make audiotape records of verbal interactions in classrooms or meetings, to carry out group interviews with students after particular lessons, and so forth, these techniques for recording are not particularly distinctive. Similarly, the techniques for analysis of data (such as content analysis of artefacts like audiotapes of interactions or portfolios of student work, analysis of the relative frequencies of different classroom events, or critical–historical analyses of classroom records to produce interpretations of the interdependence of circumstance, action, and consequence in the classroom) are not unique to action research. It is true, however, that in general the techniques for generating and accumulating evidence about practices, and the techniques for analysing and interpreting this evidence more closely resemble the techniques employed by interpretive researchers (ethnographers, case study researchers, historians, etc.) than empirical–analytic researchers (correlational analysis, comparative experiments, etc.). This is so primarily because the 'objects' of research are actions (practices) and the viewpoints and historical circumstances that give these actions meaning and significance; the 'objects' of action research are not mere behaviours.

What distinguishes action research is its method, rather than particular techniques. The method is based on the notion of a spiral of self-reflection (a spiral of cycles of planning, acting, observing, and reflecting). It is essentially participatory in the sense that it involves participants in reflection on practices. It expresses a commitment to the improvement of practices, practitioners' understandings, and the settings of practice. And it is collaborative, wherever possible involving coparticipants in the organization of their own enlightenment in relation to social and political action in their own situations.

The rigour of action research does not derive from the use of particular techniques of observation or analysis (for example, measuring instruments or statistical analyses) or the use of particular metatechniques (for example, techniques for establishing the reliability or validity of measures, or for ascertaining the power of tests). Rigour derives from the logical, empirical, and political coherence of interpretations in the reconstructive moments of the self-reflective spiral (observing and reflecting) and the logical, empirical, and political coherence of justifications of proposed action in its constructive or prospective moments (planning and acting).

As in Habermas's (1974) critical social science, three separate functions in the mediation of theory and practice must be distinguished in action research. These supply criteria for the evaluation of action research studies. Separate criteria are relevant for evaluation in relation to each function, and each requires certain preconditions. First, at the level of scientific discourse, action researchers are engaged in the formation and extension of critical theorems about their practices and their situation, that is, in the formulation and articulation of their own practical theories. This can take place only under the precondition of freedom of discourse. Here the criterion is true statements; the truth of statements is evaluated through discourse which raises, recognizes, and redeems 'validity claims': claims that what is stated is comprehensible, true (accurate), truthfully or sincerely stated, and right or appropriate (in its normative context). Second, at the level of enlightenment of those engaged in the self-reflective process, action researchers are involved in applying and testing their practical theories in their own action in their own situations. This can take place only under the precondition that those involved commit themselves to proper precautions and assure scope for open communication aimed at mutual understanding. Here the criterion is authentic insights, grounded in participants' own circumstances and experience. Finally, at the level of the organization of action, action researchers are engaged in the selection of strategies, the resolution of tactical questions, and the conduct of 'political struggle' (that is, social and strategic action in a social and political context). This can only occur if decisions of consequence depend on the practical discourse of participants. Here the criterion is prudent decisions. Evaluating the quality of action research requires analysis at each of these 'levels' of discourse, the organization of enlightenment, and the organization of action.

These criteria provide the most stringent basis for the evaluation of action research. Typically, however, action research in progress tends not to be evaluated formally in this way. Variants of the questions 'Is it true?', 'Does it make sense in terms of our experience?', and 'Is it prudent?' are more likely to be asked by action researchers in the course of their work. This is an important observation since action research as it is actually practised by teachers and others is a part of their own social process. As such, it tends to be informal and convivial rather than formalistic and overtly 'theoretical'.

'FACILITATING' ACTION RESEARCH

Since action research is research into one's own practice, it follows that only practitioners and groups of practitioners can carry out action research. It is common, however, for 'outsiders' to be involved in action research, providing material, organizational, emotional, and intellectual support to practitioners. The relationships established between outside 'facilitators' and action researchers can have profound effects on the character of the action research undertaken, however. To varying degrees, they influence the agenda of issues being addressed in the research and the 'ownership' (authenticity) of the questions asked, the data-gathering and analytic techniques employed, and the interpretations and findings of particular studies. The intervention of outsiders may introduce significant distortions in each of the three definitive characteristics of action research: the degree to which it is practical, collaborative, or self-reflective. Indeed, it can be argued that some of what passes for action research today is not action research at all but merely a species of field experimentation or 'applied' research carried out by academic or service researchers who coopt practitioners into gathering data *about* educational practices for them. This point needs to be emphasized since the rising popularity of action research in the 1980s (as in the late 1950s) has prompted many educational researchers aspiring to 'relevance' to go out into the field to work with practitioners in the investigation of contemporary educational practices. Forgetting the origins of action research, they have appropriated the term and carried out studies paradigmatically opposed to the nature and spirit of action research.

At worst, these facilitators have coopted practitioners to work on externally formulated questions and issues which are not based in the practical concerns of practitioners. To the extent that it can be described as action research at all, this form may be described as technical action research. It employs techniques (for example, techniques based on a technology of group dynamics) to create and sustain commitment to investigation of issues raised by the outsider, and it frequently concerns itself with the relative efficiency and effectiveness of practices (instrumental reasoning). It is sometimes carried out in order to test the applicability of findings from studies undertaken elsewhere. Such studies may contribute to the improvement of practices, of practitioners' understandings, and the situations of practice (both from an external point of view and from practitioners' own perspectives), but they run the risk of being inauthentic for the practitioners involved, and they may create conditions for the legitimation of practices by reference to outsiders' reputations or ascribed status as 'experts' or 'authorities' rather than being based in the practical discourse of practitioners themselves.

More often, outsiders form cooperative relationships with practitioners, helping them to articulate their own concerns, plan strategic action, monitor the action, and reflect on processes and consequences. This is sometimes described as a 'process consultancy' role. In such cases, outsiders may work with individual practitioners or with groups of practitioners interested in common practices. Where the aim is the improvement of individuals' own practices, however, the relationships between participants may still be mediated by the outsider. In these situations, the research may be described as practical action research (action research which sharpens individual practical reasoning). It can and typically does contribute to the improvement of practices, practitioners' understandings, and the situations in which practice occurs, but it need not develop collaborative responsibility for practices within participant groups.

Emancipatory action research, by contrast, shifts responsibility for practice and the action research process to the participant group. In this case, the group takes joint responsibility for action and reflection. The work of the group expresses a joint commitment to the development of common practical theories, authentic insights, and prudent decision making (based on mutual understanding and consensus). This kind of action research may be described as 'emancipatory' because the group itself takes responsibility for its own emancipation from the dictates of irrational or unjust habits, customs, precedents, coercion, or bureaucratic systematization. Here outsiders are unnecessary; where they do participate in the work of the group, they do so on the basis that they share responsibility equally with other members (not as legitimating authorities nor merely as process facilitators).

Historically, it is possible to discern a shift from technical to practical to emancipatory action research from the late 1940s to the early 1980s, judging from reports of educational action research over the period. Arguably, the ideal of emancipatory action research has existed from the beginning; as the 'ownership' of the idea of action research has shifted from the academy to the profession itself, so the concrete relationship between outsiders and practitioners in particular action research projects has changed (from cooption to cooperation to collaboration). In some places in the world, the profession has sufficiently well-developed organizational structures to foster the development of emancipatory action research which can exist without conspicuous support from outsiders; in these areas, the profession is able to resist the legitimating role of the academy with respect to practice and to take a nondoctrinaire, critical, and self-reflective stance on the bureaucratic control of curriculum and pedagogy (and, in particular, the nexus of policy making and policy research).

ACTION RESEARCH, POLICY RESEARCH, AND THE CONTROL OF EDUCATION

The choice of research methods depends on the presumed character of the object of the research (e.g. a 'natural' phenomenon, a product of 'subjective' views of participants, a product of historical and ideological process). Moreover, these presumptions will tend to be confirmed by the conduct of educational inquiries not because of any principled 'correctness' of the presumptions, but because the presumptions will appear to be vindicated merely by the practice of research. In this way, research practice alone (and ultimately research traditions) conventionalizes and legitimates the paradigmatic presumptions of researchers.

Educational research is generally justified by reference to its contribution to educational reform. In this sense, almost all educational research is policy research; that is, it has the aim of influencing educational practices through influencing local or systemwide policies about curriculum and pedagogy. Three points need to be made about this nexus of research and reform: (a) it assumes that researchers understand the nature of education as an object of research (including its nature as a social enterprise); (b) it assumes that researchers understand the social nature and consequences of educational reform; and (c) it assumes that researchers understand the research enterprise itself as inherently social and political, that is, as an ideological activity.

Different approaches to educational research have different perspectives on how reform relates to research. Put at its simplest, different approaches to educational research have different theories of educational change which underpin them. These theories of educational change embody different assumptions about the control of education.

Empirical–analytic research views educational events and practices as 'phenomena' susceptible to 'objective' treatment. It views schooling as a delivery system whose effectiveness and efficiency can be improved by improvements in the technology of the system. Its form of reasoning is technical, instrumental (means–ends) reasoning. Its interest is in the technical control of education systems, and this technical rationality readily expresses itself in an interest in hierarchical bureaucratic control of the social relations between systems personnel and between teachers and students.

Interpretive research sees education as a historical process and as a lived experience for those involved in educational processes and institutions. Its form of reasoning is practical; it aims to transform the consciousness of practitioners and, by so doing, to give them grounds upon which to reform their own practices. Its interest is in transforming education by educating practitioners; it assumes a relationship between educational researchers and educational practitioners based on mutual trust which leaves practitioners free to decide how to change their practices in the light of their own informed practical deliberation.

Critical social scientific research, including emancipatory action research, views education as a historical and ideological process. Its form of reasoning is practical (like that of interpretive research) but also critical: it is shaped by the emancipatory intent to transform educational organizations and practices to achieve rationality and social justice. It is predisposed towards ideology–critique: the recognition and negation of educational ideologies which serve the interests of specific groups at the expense of others and which mask oppression and domination with the appearance of liberation.

Empirical–analytic and interpretive research preserve a 'gap' between theory and practice. They institutionalize the separation of theory and practice in the separate roles of the researcher–theorist and the practitioner. Critical social scientific research requires the development of self-reflective communities of practitioner–theorists committed to critically examining their own practices and improving them in the interests of rationality and social justice. While the first two forms of educational research employ theories of change which are concretely realized in political relationships which seek to bring practitioners' practices into line with theorists' theories (explicitly in the case of empirical–analytic research and implicitly in the case of interpretive research), critical educational research does not. In this latter case, the development of practical theories is carried out by practitioners as part of the process of change; indeed, all change in the latter case is transformation by practitioners of existing conditions, perspectives, and practices in the interests of rationality and social justice.

Educational action research is a form of educational research which places control over processes of educational reform in the hands of those involved in the action. In principle, this control can be shared collaboratively by communities of teachers, students, administrators, parents, and others. In practice, most action research projects have involved only one or two, and occasionally three, of these groups.

It would be an exaggeration to argue that emancipatory action research in education is the only defensible form of educational research or the only form of educational research capable of bringing about stable transformations of educational practice towards more rational and more just educational arrangements in contemporary society. An argument can be mounted, however, that educational action research is grossly underutilized as an approach to educational reform in a democratic society and that it is, or should be, a key part of the role of the professional educator. Participatory democracy involves substantial control by people over their own lives, and within that over their work. Emancipatory action research is one means by which this ideal can be approached.

BIBLIOGRAPHY

Carr, W. & Kemmis. S. (1983) *Becoming Critical: Knowing through Action Research.* Deakin University Press, Geelong, Victoria.

Corey, S. M. (1953) *Action Research to Improve School Practices.* Teachers College, Columbia University, New York.

Elliott, J. (1976–77) Developing hypotheses about classrooms from teachers' practical constructs: an account of the work of the Ford Teaching Project. *Interchange* 7(2): 2–22.

Habermas, J. (1974) *Theory and Practice.* Heinemann, London.

Lewin, K. (1946) Action research and minority problems. *J. Soc. Issues* 2(4): 34–46.

Lewin, K. (1952) Group decision and social change. In: G. E. Swanson, T. M. Newcomb & E. L. Hartley (Eds) *Readings in Social Psychology*. Holt, New York, pp. 459–73.

Sanford, N. (1970) Whatever happened to action research? *J. Soc. Issues* 26(4): 3–23.

Schwab, J. J. (1969) The practical: a language for curriculum. *Sch. Rev.* 78: 1–23.

Stenhouse, L. (1975) *An Introduction to Curriculum Research and Development*. Heinemann, London.

13

THE POLITICS OF METHOD: FROM LEFTIST ETHNOGRAPHY TO EDUCATIVE RESEARCH

A. Gitlin, M. Siegel and K Boru

Leftist educators, concerned with the way schools help reproduce societal inequalities such as those associated with class, race, and gender, have of late become uneasy about their influence on schooling and their relation to the educational community as well as other political groups. Apple (1986), for example, argues that leftist scholarship has a relatively underdeveloped tradition of applied or middle-range work which runs the risk of cutting leftist educators off from a large segment of the educational community (p. 200). He also notes that the work of these scholars is often written in a style that makes it inaccessible to practitioners. Aronowitz and Giroux (1985), on the other hand, suggest that the left has become so embedded in the 'language of critique' that they have in many ways edited themselves out of policy debates. They suggest a shift in perspective which focuses on the 'language of possibility'. And Shapiro (1987) notes that the left must re-think its agenda if it is to contribute more forcefully to current political discourse.

It is not the purpose of this paper to examine these proposals; rather, we point to what appears to be an important oversight – the lack of attention paid to research method. The question of method is of fundamental importance because it helps define relations between academics and the educational community at large. A consideration of these relations is likely to tell us much about the current and future directions of the left. What we hope to show in this paper is that an uncritical acceptance of ethnography contributes to the impotence of the American educational left.

In the last two decades, ethnography has become the dominant methodology of the American educational left. Its current popularity can be traced to several historical factors. First, economic determinist analyses of schooling, which did little or nothing to expose how schools reproduced inequalities or provided alternative possibilities, were criticized and scholars began to look for methodologies that would open up the 'black box' of schooling. Ethnography, with its emphasis on long periods of observation and participation in particular contexts, seemed to offer a method that satisfied this need. Second, methodological debates about the limitations of positivism opened the way for all researchers, including those on the educational left, to see naturalistic research as a legitimate alternative.

The use of this new method in both leftist scholarship and education in general has led to vigorous debate. For the most part the debate has centered on the concept of 'objectivity'. This emphasis is very clear in LeCompte and Goetz's (1982) classic piece on reliability and validity in ethnographic research. They translate the traditional categories of reliability and validity into ethnographic terms, showing how ethnographers establish the trustworthiness of their findings. Clearly, a consideration of ethnography's 'objectivity' is an attempt to gain legitimacy in relation to the more positivist paradigm. Still, this focus has obscured the relation between method and what the researcher is trying to achieve through the method – its political moment. We strive to put the political moment back in the methodological debate by considering the potential of ethnography to foster emancipatory change – the express purpose of the left. By doing so, we hope to build on an emerging body of work that is attempting to reconceptualize research and strengthen the role the left plays in the practice of schooling (Carr & Kemmis, 1986; Simon & Dippo, 1986). This work is historically rooted in the concept of action research, first articulated by Kurt Lewin in the 1940s, further developed by Lawrence Stenhouse in the 1970s, and currently being addressed by such scholars as Wilfred Carr and Stephen Kemmis.

We begin with an historical overview that traces some of the major debates that have evolved within the ethnographic tradition. By doing so, we start to see what strands the American educational left draws on as well as what debates within the field of anthropology they seem to have ignored. This section is followed by a brief account of what is meant by emancipatory change. An analysis follows of how the use of ethnography relates to this purpose. Specifically, we show how the separation of understanding and application, and of researchers and those researched, contributes to the failure of the left to move in the direction of emancipatory change. This critique provides the basis for an alternative approach, outlined in the final section, which we call 'educative research'.

Before beginning, however, a caveat is necessary. By linking method and purpose, we do not mean to suggest that any approach to research could, by itself, achieve emancipatory change at a societal level. It is unlikely that wide-ranging changes in our inequitable class society can occur without a fundamental shift in our economic structure. Nor are we implying that schools are the best or only site for such efforts. Our intent, instead, is to understand to what extent research can be reconceptualized so that those connected to schools can begin to change schooling in emancipatory ways.

A HISTORY OF THE SELECTIVE TRADITION

Leftist ethnographers (and educational ethnographers more generally) have borrowed methodological procedures from the field of anthropology. What is unsettling about this trend, is its selective nature. Ethnographic methods have been appropriated and debates over rigor have been waged without due attention to the historical, ideological, and textual matrix that constitutes ethnographic practice. It is common, for example, for researchers to speak of 'the ethnographic method' as if there were no alternatives within anthropology, no history, no continuing epistemological questions. In taking ethnographic practices for granted, leftist ethnographers have put themselves in the position of treating method as if it were rhetorically and ideologically innocent, that is, as technique. This has left them unable to identify the ways in which these practices interfere with the achievement of their political goals. A brief look at the history of the ethnographic tradition leftists have selected shows that they have cut themselves off from a rich debate on questions which are central to their project. Questions about whether to intervene in a culture and what kinds of social relations to enter into with members of the culture are essential for all ethnographers and ought not to be classified as issues of validity and reliability. Our point, instead, is that methodological issues are substantive as well. A reading of the recent literature on ethnography suggests that anthropologists are no longer comfortable with their own ethnographic tradition; it seems prudent, therefore, to outline their concerns and see what might be learned from the emerging conversation.

Categorical distinctions between self and other have served as the foundation for ethnographic work, but these foundations have begun to crumble under the weight of doing ethnography in an increasingly complex world (Marcus & Fischer, 1986). Present-day cultures are no longer neatly bounded, and the 'natives' now 'talk back', writing their own ethnographies and scrutinizing those written about them (Drummond, 1981; see Marcus & Fischer, 1986). In an attempt to discover better ways to examine 'otherness', anthropologists have turned their attention to the history of textual practice. What they have found is that it is a history of textual practice because what ethnographers do is write (Geertz, 1973; see Clifford & Marcus, 1986). Ethnographers do not so much *describe* culture as *inscribe* it in discourse; indeed, the 'end of description' (Tyler, 1985) has been announced. The claim, instead, is that ethnographies can never be mere descriptions because the act of writing binds together politics and poetics (Clifford, 1983; Clifford & Marcus, 1986). In a sense, then, the tradition that leftist ethnographers have selected is as much a way of writing as it is a way of collecting data. By looking at the way ethnographies historically have been written, leftist ethnographers may discover that ethnography has never been a neutral undertaking; it was only written as if it were. This insight may provide an opening for considering how new sorts of social relations can contribute to emancipatory aims.

Bronislaw Malinowski usually is credited with establishing ethnography as the *sine qua non* of cultural anthropology (Erickson, 1986), but travelers and missionaries produced good ethnographies as well (Tyler, 1985). For a discipline trying to establish itself as a 'science', such apparently biased and theoretically naive works posed a threat. Malinowski's move was to establish the ethnographer's authority and neutrality by adopting narrative realism as the textual strategy and structural-functionalism as the theoretical lens (Boon, 1981).

Ethnographies were supposed to show the interrelationships among a culture's institutions and beliefs as well as the way such connections contributed to the persistence of the social system. Anthropologists spent long periods in the field gathering the data necessary to this project. Often, gaining access to the group studied required that ethnographers ally themselves with colonial administrators, and although this move succeeded in separating ethnographers from missionaries, it was not ideologically innocent. Caught up in the European expansion, ethnographers and colonial administrators together effectively maintained the status quo (Tyler, 1985; see Pratt, 1986).

Narrative realism was the textual strategy ethnographers used to establish their authority as fieldworkers (Clifford, 1983). As Boon (1981) notes, narrative realism is characterized by transparency of description so that the author-as-fieldworker is present, whereas the author-as-author is absent. Like travel writers, ethnographers began their texts with 'arrival scenes' (Pratt, 1986), detailing the fieldworker's first interaction with the 'natives'; the message to readers was 'You are there, because I was there' (Clifford, 1983, p. 118). Once this authority was signaled, however, the ethnographer-as-author vanished, leaving the impression that the patterns presented were objective descriptions, untainted by either the ethnographer's presence or the rhetorical decisions made.

The shift to interpretive anthropology in the 1960s meant that ethnographers became interested in cultural meanings – in the 'native's point of view' (Erickson, 1986; Marcus & Fischer, 1986). Structural-functionalist accounts of culture were replaced by 'thick descriptions' (Geertz, 1973) of what events meant to the participants. This movement forced ethnographers to ask the epistemological question of how one knows another's point of view, and soon they were engaged in a lively debate over fieldwork practices. One of the outcomes of this debate was the appearance of a new genre of books in which fieldworkers recounted their experiences as participant-observers. Paul Rabinow's *Reflections on Fieldwork in Morocco* (1977) is now a classic. These portraits of ethnographers at work quickly showed that fieldwork was laced with issues of politics and social relations and was nothing like the orderly and neutral undertaking represented in written reports. But these works remained marginal, separate from the substantive texts defined as ethnographies. Hence, it is fair to say that even though Clifford Geertz (1973) identified writing as the most pervasive fieldwork practice, interpretive ethnographers continued to rely on textual strategies associated with narrative realism.

The current debates among anthropologists suggest some discomfort with this tradition, which leftist ethnographers have selected. The making of ethnographic texts has become the starting point for a broader discussion of knowledge and representation in a shifting, complex world, and experiments in ethnographic writing are underway (Clifford, 1983; Clifford & Marcus, 1986; Marcus & Fischer, 1986). Narrative realism is being challenged by reflexive and intersubjective modes of knowledge production, as the question of who speaks for whom becomes paramount. These debates are important to the work of leftist ethnographers for two reasons. First, they show how textual practices transformed fieldwork from a political and social activity to a rational one. Second, they point to the role the ethnographer plays in the production of knowledge. Anthropologists have made it clear that we *are* there when we enter the field and when we write. For leftist ethnographers, the challenge is not only to acknowledge this presence but to act in ways that bring method and purpose into alignment.

PURPOSE: EMANCIPATORY CHANGE

The concept of emancipatory change is implicit in most leftist literature. Unfortunately, the meaning of this term rarely is discussed in detail, making it difficult to say precisely what the left means by emancipatory change. It is possible, however, to make a few general statements.

Schools are unique and important institutions because they are both productive and reflective. By 'productive', we mean that schools help produce a set of attitudes or dispositions, forms of legitimate or high status knowledge, as well as skills which help to structure societal relations. Working class students, for example, often are inculcated with attitudes such as obedience and the need for extrinsic rewards, while important parts of their history are ignored (Apple, 1979; Bowles & Gintis, 1976). These attitudes, along with a lack of knowledge about the struggles of the working class, are likely to help legitimate oppressive relations wherein workers have little or no control over their work; this perpetuates an alienating division of labor between those who conceptualize the work and those who execute it (Braverman, 1975). At the same time, schools reflect the type of structured relations found in society, such as those associated with class, race, and gender. They are not immune from the sexism and racism found in our society.

Emancipatory change is concerned with the productive aspect of schools as well as the particular sets of relations found within. Specifically, emancipatory change reflects a movement away from oppressive relations of all kinds – relations that limit people's control over their work, deny certain groups access to debates, and obstruct opportunities for a quality life – and a movement toward more egalitarian and democratic relations. Where schools, for example, use pedagogical approaches that steer students from working class backgrounds into working class jobs (Anyon, 1981), emancipatory change involves the development of alternative pedagogies that would begin to alter this oppressive trend. And where teachers' work becomes increasingly proletarianized, and women teachers in particular are denied opportunities for advancement, emancipatory change would attempt to empower teachers so as to achieve more control over their work and expand the opportunity structure for women.

Emancipatory change is also concerned with the commodities produced in schools because commodities reflect anonymous relations. Apple (1986) suggests that the use of a particular curriculum represents a relation between teachers and students, just as turning on a light bulb represents a relation between miners and management (pp. 82–83). For this reason, the development of alternative curricula, which can transform authoritarian relations that leave students powerless and silent, is of central importance to notions of emancipatory change.

In sum, emancipatory change is within the reach of those who live and work in schools. It is not simply change for its own sake but, rather, change that reflects democratic and egalitarian interests. Importantly, these interests have not and cannot be precisely defined out of context for their meaning is always worked out in particular contexts at particular times. As Giroux (1981) notes, the goals of emancipation are not 'like shopping lists that one draws up before going to the supermarket: they are goals that are struggled for and defined in specific contexts, under specific historical conditions' (p. 220).

The central issue for this paper, therefore, is to discuss ways the educational left has used ethnography to serve emancipatory interests. And, if ethnography proves inadequate to the challenge of transforming relations of domination, how can the method be reconceptualized better to serve this end?

THE SEPARATION OF UNDERSTANDING AND APPLICATION

Interpretive ethnography is more interested in problems of cultural meaning than in social action (Marcus & Fischer, 1986). This becomes clear when one looks at the typical practice of educational ethnographers. In basic terms, educational ethnography involves a trained researcher with a background in anthropology going into a school to observe everyday life. The ethnographer sits in the classroom taking notes and periodically asks questions of students, teachers, or administrators which try to capture how they think about particular classroom events. At times the ethnographer extends the study so that it includes interviews with parents and community members. While there is no universal agreement about how the researcher should observe, it is generally recommended that the constructs and patterns found should 'emerge from the data' and should not be imposed on the observations (Spradley & McCurdy, 1972). Further, although the ethnographer can operate anywhere along the line between observer and participant, the ethnographer's position should put the subjects at ease, help develop trust, and, most importantly, affect the setting as little as possible (Agar, 1980).

Everhart (1983) in his book *Reading, Writing and Resistance*, exemplifies this type of ethnographic stance toward research. Constructs were not imposed on the data but emerged from the research process. As he notes, 'This study began with no preconceived hypothesis to test and with but a general frame of reference to guide it' (p. 276). Gaining trust and acceptance was also thought to be an important part of the research process.

> The fieldworker attempts to be accepted by them [those being researched], to become part of their everyday lives, to experience the things they do, and to better understand the values that affect what they do (Everhart, 1983, p. 278).

And care was taken to avoid disrupting the natural flow of events.

> Many times extensive notetaking was either impossible (such as field trips) or would, I felt, affect the natural flow of the situation (such as during lunch). In these situations, I would jot down key words or quotes as soon as practical, and fill in the information at the end of the study (Everhart, 1983, p. 283).

For Everhart and others who approach research in this way, understanding and application are separate moments. There are two reasons for this separation. First, these ethnographers try to 'capture' essential, repeated practices, not to change them. There are, in fact, many cautions in the literature about going outside the role of the researcher (Agar, 1980; Spindler, 1974). Second, the research labor is divided between the researcher, who 'understands' the situation, and those studied, who have the opportunity to apply the 'understanding'. Clearly, Everhart is one of many current educational ethnographers who accepts this separation. As he notes,

> The fieldworker attempts to become partly socialized by those being studied so as to *understand better* their lives, all the while remaining the outsider who attempts to call into question everything seen and heard (Everhart, 1983, p. 278; emphasis in original).

The problematic nature of this separation obtains for all ethnographies, but when the purpose is emancipatory change, it is devastating. This can be illustrated by looking at a prominent educational ethnography, Ray Rist's (1970) study of a group of ghetto children. Over a three-year period Rist observed a tracking structure set up by the teacher that allowed little mobility; the mobility that did occur was downward. This informal tracking system was based primarily on dress and appearance and was developed after only eight days of interaction with the students. What Rist observed was the crushing of 30 ghetto children because of basic prejudices about what makes a good student. The question therefore can be raised: Does this study serve emancipatory interests; has it altered school relations, the commodities produced, or the attitudes and skills of the students, and, if so, in what ways? Clearly, the study did not influence the observed students. This is not surprising given that the research tradition Rist comes out of assumes that researcher intervention limits the trustworthiness and understanding of the research data. In a sense, Rist's hands were tied. To give feedback to the teacher or to talk to the students would have been seen as compromising the integrity of the research method. It could be argued, however, that the understanding gained from this study helps other teachers avoid some of the effects of the self-fulfilling prophecy that Rist observed and therefore can alter the oppressive implications for ghetto students. In this case, the claim for emancipatory change is a long-run proposition based on a notion of consciousness-raising; teachers will change their practices by simply reading the account.

Unfortunately, Rist's study, like most other ethnographies, has had little influence on teachers' consciousness, their behavior, or schooling in general. Courtney Cazden (1983) noted this trend in her presidential address to the Council on Anthropology and Education and wondered aloud why anthropological explanations of school failure have done so little to change this pattern. Though she identified two projects that had a positive impact on school practices, neither was emancipatory in any sense. One of the reasons schools have not been influenced by ethnographies is that ethnographers do not try to arrive at a shared understanding of the situation. The work of Habermas is instructive. Bernstein (1983) summarizes Habermas' arguments.

> It is an illusion to think that we can assume the position of disinterested observers by bracketing all our preunderstandings . . . we can only [understand others] by adopting the performative attitude of one who participates in the process of *mutual understanding* [our emphasis] (p. 182).

Habermas' position suggests that mutual understanding, because of its commitment to arriving at a shared interpretation, is linked to the democratic and egalitarian ends which are so much a part of emancipatory interests. His arguments also throw into doubt the epistemological dualism inherent in the type of ethnography described above. It is impossible for the researcher to understand the 'subject' unless she/he enters into a dialogue with the 'subject' aimed at mutual understanding. And this type of dialogue is unlikely if it is assumed that the role of the researcher is to understand and the role of the 'subject' is to apply this understanding or, worst of all, to be 'understood'. Further, even if one argues that the researcher can gain understanding without dialogue, there is the question of how one communicates the 'understanding' of the researcher to those studied. This is especially difficult to do if the problem of the researcher is not a problem for those studied.

This difficulty is evident in Willis' (1977) influential ethnography, *Learning to Labour: How Working Class Kids Get Working Class Jobs*. For Willis, the problem is why working class kids get working class jobs. But he ignores the way that educational problems arise 'out of practical educational activities . . . and occur when the practices employed in educational activities are in some sense inadequate to their purpose'. (Carr & Kemmis, 1986, p. 110). As a consequence, Willis' thesis that teachers facilitate the exchange of credentials for control is unlikely to affect them unless they see their activities as inadequate for the purpose of flattening hierarchical class relations. Specifically, if teachers do not see the inadequacy of their activities, or if they have a different purpose in mind, they are left in the position of knowing more about what to change but not necessarily how to move in that direction. Researchers must consider 'the shared educational values and beliefs of those engaged in educational pursuits' (Carr & Kemmis, 1986). To do otherwise is to ignore the ways in which reality is already permeated by the interpretations, beliefs, and intentions of educational practitioners (Carr & Kemmis, 1986). This does not mean that we accept the beliefs or purposes of those studied at face value; the point, instead, is that consciousness-raising or change of any sort is not likely to occur unless researchers formulate problems through a dialogue that considers and critiques both the 'subject's' and the 'researcher's' view of reality.

Finally, the separation of understanding and application has ramifications for the development of a politics of change, which is essential for any genuinely emancipatory end. Mary Metz's (1978) oft-cited ethnographic study is a case in point. Metz's purpose is 'to identify the character and connections of crucial social variables which shape the life of all public schools . . . particularly for my primary interest in authority and control' (p. 22). Her focus on authority and control suggests a political purpose of some sort. In collecting her data on schooling, however, Metz takes a number of precautions to minimize the political moment in the formation of understanding itself. She allows her politics to emerge only in her thoughts of how to ameliorate the conditions she describes.

> The schools may ameliorate these problems by recruiting staffs whose beliefs and whose racial, social and personal characteristics will refute the children's despair as much as possible. They can design their curriculums to counteract the children's attitudes. They can change the recruitment of student bodies so these children will not be segregated (Metz, 1978, p. 254).

In effect, Metz insists upon the separation of understanding and application and therefore cannot consider how one changes curriculum, recruits radical staff members, or radicalizes the staff at the school. Her suggestions for practice do not include a consideration of possible impediments to the realization of her political purpose – to say nothing of the viable possibilities. The results of maintaining a dichotomy between knowing and acting are thus disappointing for they offer little sense of how change might be accomplished.

In contrast to these studies, several leftist scholars are beginning to challenge the separation of application and understanding. Simon (1983), for example, is working with a group of scholars and practitioners to study the relationship between school and work. This research group not only recognizes the contradictory nature of school practices but importantly attempts to intervene by building upon contradictions within working class experience and schooling. Weiler (1988), a feminist scholar, also is attempting to link application and understanding in her study of women and school change.

> Feminist research is politically committed. In rejecting the possibility of value-free research, feminists instead assert a commitment to changing the position of women and therefore society (p. 59).

What distinguishes Weiler's position from others who also recognize the politics of method (McLaren, 1986), is that a dialogue between researcher and participants is seen as an essential part of helping both parties rethink their ideology and practice. As Weiler (1988) notes,

> This kind of qualitative research into individual lives rests on certain implicit intentions or goals. One of these is to provide an opportunity for the women who are objects of study to discuss their work and to discuss the researcher's observation and analysis. The goal in this case is to provide an opportunity for reflection and a chance to dialogue about the nature of feminist teaching (p. 70).

While we see Weiler's work and feminist methodology in general as helping reconceptualize traditional assumptions about method, there are still gaps between the intent of the method and its practice. In particular, Weiler's important work on feminist teachers leaves out what is unique and important about her study – the dialogue between the researcher and participants. The reader, therefore, is left in the dark about what new insights resulted from the dialogue, how the dialogue encouraged a particular set of practices, and the constraints imposed on these practices.

In sum, while the ethnographies cited surely have value inasmuch as the issues presented can trickle down and jog the thinking and actions of others, for the most part they are extremely limited in achieving emancipatory ends because the researchers' 'understanding' of reality is imposed. Focusing on problems which are often not shared by the participants and maintaining the passive stance of interpretive ethnography separates knowledge from action and researchers from those 'researched'. This prevents educators from gaining insights into the changes that might be possible, as well as the impediments to emancipatory change likely to be encountered.

SEPARATION OF RESEARCHER AND RESEARCHED

If ethnographers separate understanding from application, their only stance toward the object of study can be one of detachment. The difficulty of maintaining this detachment is acknowledged widely among ethnographers, but novice fieldworkers nonetheless are cautioned against 'going native', that is, being so drawn into the 'native's' perspective as to lose all objectivity. Our position on this matter is somewhat different. The danger, for us, is not 'going native', but detachment. The question is not whether the data are biased; the question is whose interests are served by the bias. As we leave behind the goal of objective knowledge, we are forced to consider the role social relations have in mediating the construction of knowledge.

The idea that it is possible to know an object without considering the way a subject participates in the production of that knowledge is especially ironic when noted in the work of leftist ethnographers. The very researchers who seek to show how structural inequalities are anything but natural have carried out research 'as if there were no subject-object relation, as if the subject were simply absent, as if the research reported were a reflection of the externally objective facts of the case' (Wexler, 1987, p. 82). Indeed, Wexler (1987) suggests that leftist ethnographies are not unlike the activity of watching television; both proceed on the assumption that knowledge is unmediated and spectatorship is possible.

Gitlin's (1983) study of the relationship between teachers' work and school structure illuminates the problematic nature of this dichotomy. Gitlin spent 35 days as a participant-observer in a middle school and conducted extensive interviews with the teachers. In addition, he gathered data about the school's history on the assumption that such information would help to explain patterns noted in field notes and taped interviews. He found that teachers' work was constrained but not completely determined by school structure. The primary constraint affecting the teachers' work was the form the curriculum took. This form, which consisted of predetermined, sequentially ordered objectives measured by pre- and post-tests, affected teachers' relationships with their students as well as their decisions about what to teach. Teachers centered on managing the required pre- and post-tests rather than on guiding and motivating individual students. Yet, teachers resisted this form. Gitlin (1983) writes,

> One example of resistance was observed during a spelling period where a teacher was so busy trying to keep up with the never-ending line of students waiting to have work marked or evaluated that she was clearly frustrated. When the frustration reached a certain level, the teacher simply stood up and told the students to put their work away and gather as a group. When they had done so, she asked, 'What would you like to know about me?' (p. 202).

However, Gitlin (1983) argues that such instances were the exception rather than the rule and concludes that most teachers were likely to accommodate school reality.

> The perspective encouraged by the work structure narrowed teachers' roles so that it was difficult for them to ask questions about how reality is or should be constructed. This narrow focus made it more likely that they would accommodate school reality as opposed to trying to transform it (p. 210).

This statement is particularly striking; it is a case of a leftist ethnographer arguing that teachers need to challenge the status quo while he himself maintains the status quo through his realist approach to ethnography. Gitlin's report is a clear case of fieldwork as television watching. He watches the workings of the school and reports his findings as if they were natural rather than constructed through the interaction of his theoretical perspective and the teachers' work lives. Little is said about what events mean to the participants themselves; instead, the researcher uses his privileged position and theoretical presuppositions to say what things mean. In this case, Gitlin is unable to move toward emancipatory aims because his traditional approach to ethnography does not permit him to step into the picture and initiate a dialogue that might erode his own privileged status. It seems clear to us that he will be unable to join teachers in the transformation of their work lives unless his methodological actions are directed toward the creation of a dialogical community that resists subject-object dualism.

Similar methodological practices can be identified in Apple and King's (1979) study of how kindergartners learn to be students. They argue that 'Meanings of objects and events become clear to children as they participate in the social setting' (p. 52). Therefore, they continue, 'to understand the social reality of schooling, it is necessary to study it in actual classroom settings' (p. 53). Despite a nod to the social construction of meanings, Apple and King eliminate any personal reference or political positioning except in a brief mention of methodological procedures.

Apple and King's (1979) study is replete with statements about what events mean – about the way in which young children sort out work from play in school – and the reader is expected to view these interpretations as givens. Though the substantive point aims directly at showing how there is nothing innocent about attending kindergarten, the authors imply that the ethnographer is neutral and that ethnographic practice *is* somehow innocent. To say that the ethnographer is never neutral is too simple, though, for it suggests that the problem of realism could be solved by including a paragraph stating the researcher's orientation and methodological decision points. A paragraph such as that would do little to challenge the social relations between teachers and researchers which prevent any real changes in schooling (see Popkewitz, 1984). If, on the other hand, the authors had entered the classroom with their political agenda explicit and with the goal of entering into a collaborative relationship with the teacher, one which would permit them to co-determine problems and issues, they might have opened up a dialogue on the process of 'becoming a student'. This kind of dialogue might eventually allow them to work with the teacher and students to develop a curriculum that empowers participants and allows them to interact in a democratic fashion – in other words, a curriculum reflecting emancipatory interests. In that case, their report might have emphasized the struggle to create that kind of project and not simply to 'report the findings'.

This tendency to separate the researcher from the participants can be found in more recent ethnographies as well. Though more aware of the constructed, reflexive nature of their research, leftist ethnographers continue to adopt the role of a spectator. For example, Valli (1986) describes her attempt to maintain rapport while at the same time not disrupting the workings of the vocational education program she studied. Valli concludes that cooperative educational programs, which include both classes and work experiences, offer a curricular space for students to examine taken-for-granted aspects of their work experiences. Yet her method actually prevented her from developing the sort of relationship with teachers and students that might have contributed to this transformative project.

To summarize, Gitlin (1983), Apple and King (1979), and Valli (1986) fall prey to the danger of a naive realism by editing themselves out of their texts. They assume that non-reflexive, spectator-like research is possible and even essential to the task of writing thick descriptions. In a sense, these researchers use the language and authority of conventional positivist research. What they lose in this process is the opportunity to contest the oppressive relations found in schools or those relations of domination that are reproduced by the school system. As Wexler (1987) notes, 'What realism insists upon is the stability of the object. Whatever now reinforces the stabilizing desire, as a regime of knowledge, and even more perniciously when it does so in the name of both science and radical change, operates as a blockage to the emergence of the alternative social order, and of new social relations' (p. 115).

EDUCATIVE RESEARCH: AN ALTERNATIVE CONCEPTUAL FRAMEWORK

In calling for educative research, we propose two things: first, that the research fosters the establishment of a dialogical community, which we see as intimately tied to democratic and egalitarian interests, and, second, that it contribute to rather than stand outside of these interests. Carr and Kemmis (1986) articulate this position in their call for a critical educational science. They state,

> A critical educational science . . . takes a view of educational research as critical analysis directed at the *transformation* of educational practices, the educational understandings and educational values of those involved in the process, and the social and institutional structures which provide frameworks for their actions. In this sense, a critical educational science is not research *on* or *about* education, it is research *in* and *for* education (p. 156; emphasis in original).

In the same way, educative research also is research *in* and *for* education. We use the term 'educative' not only to highlight its connections with schooling but to suggest that this type of research pushes all those involved to see the world differently and to act on these new insights. Fay (1977), in his description of the educationist approach, puts it this way,

> Changing people's basic understanding of themselves and their world is a first step in their radically altering the self-destructive patterns of interaction that characterize their social relations (p. 204).

Central to the idea of educative research is a conception of application and understanding as bound up in a single moment. For this reason, praxis is fundamental to educative research. Praxis has been an elusive concept made to serve a variety of purposes and interests. One common sense view of praxis is the application of science, narrowly conceived, to technical tasks. Experts use science to legitimate what is real knowledge and practitioners apply their advice. Linking theory and practice in this way not only privileges 'scientific' results over practical reasoning but fails to confront the divisions between practitioners and those thought to be experts; in this situation practitioner understanding is ignored and changes are imposed on her/his work. Praxis of this sort serves conservative interests by legitimating relations of domination.

To confront this problematic sense of praxis, others have suggested that individuals or groups should be involved in both the development of theory and its application. Within this framework, intellectuals (including researchers) are encouraged to work in the field. It is often suggested, for example, that professors of education take over public school classrooms from time to time in order to understand what schools are really like. While labor of this sort may be helpful to the individual, it does not alter the hierarchical relations between teachers and professors (not to mention those between teachers and students); neither does it alter the authority of certain ways of knowing. Again, since these relations are often authoritarian and oppressive, praxis of this sort fails to confront the status quo.

In contrast to the notions described above, educative research depends on what might be called a political sense of praxis, as developed by Gramsci (1971). This sense of praxis unites theory and practice in such a way as to 'put neither in a position of subservience to the other' (Gramsci, 1971, pp. 334–336). Researchers and those studied enter into a reciprocal relationship similar to the one advocated by Gramsci wherein 'the common work experience has to be as much a venue for intellectuals putting their point of view [forward] as it is for workers advancing theirs' (Entwistle, 1979, pp. 163–164). Further, the practice pole of the theory-practice dialectic is understood as conscious action in pursuit of a common goal. Praxis, therefore, is concerned not only with reciprocity between individuals but with the development of a political philosophy which commits actors to social change (Entwistle, 1979). But not just any action or change will do. Collective groups must 'seize upon those experiences and struggles in which there are still the glimmerings of solidarity and the promise of dialogical communities in which there can be genuine mutual participation and where reciprocal wooing and persuasion can prevail' (Bernstein, 1983, p. 228).

This suggests that researchers interested in emancipatory change must work *with* those studied and the wider community both in understanding what are problems and in interpreting reality. It is not enough to switch places with practitioners or, as some have suggested, to include their after-the-fact responses in research reports (e.g., Lather, 1986). The reciprocal relationship that develops must lead to conscious action directed toward a common goal, and that goal must in some way express the 'promise of a dialogical community'. What this means is that the educative researcher must take an openly political stance in considering what projects to approach and must push for issues of social justice and equality. However, the projects must be approached and developed such that decisions made with those studied and others reflect the power of persuasion, not the entrenched position of individuals or the legitimized status of particular types of knowledge. Further, the reciprocal relations must be expanded to the community level so that there can be a 'distinctive mediation between the universal [common goals] and the particular [practices] . . . yielding a type of ethical know-how in which what is universal and what is particular are codetermined' (Bernstein, 1983, p. 146). Only this type of praxis will serve emancipatory interests.

To begin this process, it is necessary that method not be viewed simply as a tool one uses to solve a problem. Vygotsky's (1978) work on tool use, carried out in another context, is apropos here. He concluded that there is *no* tool whose use does not shape the person using it just as it also shapes the external environment. Yet this is precisely the stance most leftist educational researchers take. They assume that the choice of method is similar to choosing the proper screwdriver. If the educational problem is such that a qualitative approach gives the best data, use a qualitative approach; if the problem is such that a quantitative approach gives better data, use that approach. What this position ignores is that all methods have a political moment which at a fundamental level expresses a relationship between people. Because those concerned with emancipatory change are interested in contesting relations of domination, it is essential that they use a method which does not reproduce the type of relations they so despise. In the same way that Shor (1980) argues that liberatory teaching cannot occur without the withering away of the traditional authority relationship between teacher and student, so too must the alienating relationship between researcher and researched wither if emancipatory aims are to be achieved. While most ethnographic research has looked back to show how it is as objective and therefore is as valuable as the dominant positivistic paradigm, educative research looks forward to the fulfillment of purpose.

If a concern of this type of research is the relation between method and purpose and, specifically, the relationship between researcher and those studied, then the researcher need not hide behind a curtain of objectivity. Emancipatory research puts the researcher back into the research. This means that the researcher does not have to pretend that she/he comes in with a 'blank slate' but rather acknowledges the embedded prejudgments and allows them to be *critically* scrutinized. Bernstein (1983) cites the American pragmatist C. S. Peirce on this point: 'We cannot begin with complete doubt. We must begin with all the prejudices which we can actually have when we enter upon [a study]' (cited in Bernstein, 1983, p. 128). Bernstein (1983) concludes that 'the problem is not to rid knowledge of prejudice[s] but to test them critically in the course of [substantive] inquiry' (p. 128).

One way to facilitate the scrutiny of prejudgments for both researchers and participants is to seek out alien or contrasting views within dialogical encounters. By doing so, potentially illuminating points of view will challenge the common sense notions of what is real. In other words, educative research encourages both researchers and participants to challenge each other's interpretations of reality. Bernstein (1983) summarizes Gadamer's thinking on this point, suggesting that 'It is only through the dialogical encounter with what is alien to us . . . that we can open ourselves to risking and testing prejudices' (pp. 128–129). It is not *that* our interpretations differ, therefore, that is significant; it is *how* and *why* they differ. And it is by challenging each other on these insights that we begin to have a shared lifeworld (Wittgenstein, 1974).

Discussing how researchers' and participants' histories reflect contradictions is another important way to unearth and critically discuss prejudgments. Whitehead (Whitehead & Lomax, 1987) argues that educators exist as 'living contradictions', that is, their work is framed by tensions between their values and their practices. These living contradictions influence what the researcher takes note of, how she/he understands events, and even how such understanding is expressed. If prejudgments are to be assessed, the tensions in personal histories and their relation to contextual structures must be made explicit and become an integral part of the process of educative research.

Putting the researcher back in the research is only part of an attempt to foster a more egalitarian relationship between researchers and the wider community. Educative research requires that research be transformed from a monological process to a dialogical process. In most research the researcher does not enter into a discourse about the focus of the study or potentially conflicting interpretations of reality. The focus and the interpretation are, instead, imposed and legitimized by the supposed expertise inherent in one's position as researcher. The result is an oppressive relationship; community members do not participate in these decisions and are therefore encouraged to accede to the researcher's notion of what is problematic or what phenomena mean. Educative research, on the other hand, encourages community members to argue the interpretation of reality and come to a mutual understanding. When successful, the researcher is 'united by a specific bond with the other, he thinks with the other, and undergoes the situation with him [the other]' (Gadamer, cited in Bernstein (1983) p. 164). The turn, therefore, in educative research is toward common effort to understand and transform reality. The image of a solitary researcher trying to study a subject gives way to one of a community bonded by discourse and action.

A dialogical approach does not suggest or require a sameness between researcher and community members. It is likely and even inevitable that the individuals will have different strengths and abilities. Its egalitarian nature results from the fact that the interpretation of reality is based on the persuasiveness of reason. As Arendt so powerfully argues,

> Authority . . . is incompatible with persuasion, which presupposes equality and works through a process of argumentation. Where arguments are used, authority is left in abeyance. Against the egalitarian order of persuasion stands the authoritarian order which is always hierarchical (cited in Bernstein, 1983, p. 220).

By furthering a more substantively critical and egalitarian relation between researcher and community members, a dialogical approach encourages an 'object-subject switch', to borrow a phrase from Shor (1980). This switch transforms the research participants from manipulated objects into active critical subjects. Not only does the researcher avoid imposing meanings on those studied but those studied are empowered in the sense of changing from 'reactive objects into society-making subjects' (Shor, 1980, p. 98). At the very least, this switch is a symbolic exodus from the oppression of the hierarchical relationship inherent in most communities.

CONCLUSION

At the heart of educative research is an attempt to escape what Bernstein (1983) refers to as the 'Cartesian Anxiety', the proposition that methods are either relativistic or objective. To escape this anxiety, we must reject the dichotomy itself and reconceptualize the canons by which research is judged. Typically the rightness of the method is understood as its ability to produce truths of some sort. For most ethnographers, these 'truths' are researchers' descriptions of the ways actors socially construct reality. This is why much of the debate over ethnography has focused on the procedures necessary to produce those truths. What links the various positions, however, is the assumption that the rightness of the method can be understood by looking at method in isolation – as technique. And this is the assumption that educative research challenges. The rightness of educative research is based on the *relation* between normative frameworks established by a dialogical community and the specific practices of the study. For those interested in emancipatory change, the normative framework of the community is the establishment of democratic and egalitarian relations. It is the relation of research approaches to this purpose which clarifies the rightness of the study. In defining the rightness of method as a relation between practices and purpose, educative research escapes the net of relativism. Clearly, all practices are not equal. Practices that reproduce or strengthen hierarchy are inappropriate for this type of research. Educative research does not claim to remove bias and produce objective accounts of reality. To the contrary, educative research is explicitly political and asks actors to acknowledge prejudgments and critically to assess them. The political moment inherent in all method is made explicit.

The political nature of educative research suggests that the type of relations we establish with other members of the educational community are of fundamental importance. Because researchers come into contact most directly with those studied, we have focused on this relation. Our arguments indicate that the categorical distinction is itself a reflection of the status quo and helps to legitimate relations of domination between these groups. This does not mean that we eliminate the difference between 'researchers' and those studied. Instead, we share with Gramsci the position that neither group inherently has a better way of knowing. The aim is to use the differences between groups in a way that increases *both* groups' understanding of schooling.

The promise of a dialogical community does not obtain simply by changing the nature of the relations between researchers and the actors under study. The dialogue must spread to other members of the educational community. It is clear from our previous discussion on the politics of change that most leftist educational research does not contribute to this goal and has for the most part produced proposals which tend to give the reader either little hope or are naively romantic (Bowles & Gintis, 1976; Giroux, 1983). The unsatisfying nature of such proposals is not idiosyncratic and cannot be rectified simply by calling for 'mid-range' or 'applied' work of the sort recently proposed by Michael Apple (1986, p. 200). Only when we reconceptualize method so that it explicitly embodies the purpose of emancipatory change can we know both the structural and the ideological constraints which inhibit this aim and the possibilities for such a change. It is more than a little ironic to ask others to challenge common sense notions about oppressive hierarchies if we as researchers are not also willing to do the same with our taken-for-granted role.

ACKNOWLEDGMENTS

We thank Stephen Kemmis and Philip Wexler for their comments on an earlier draft of this paper.

REFERENCES

Agar, M. (1980). *The professional stranger: an informal introduction to ethnography.* New York: Academic Press.

Anyon, J. (1981). Social class and school knowledge. *Curriculum Inquiry, 11*(1), 3–42.

Apple, M. (1979) *Ideology and curriculum.* Boston: Routledge & Kegan Paul.

Apple, M. (1986) *Teachers and texts: a political economy of class and gender relations in education.* New York: Routledge & Kegan Paul.

Apple, M., & King, N. (1979) Economics and control in everyday school life. In M. Apple, *Ideology and curriculum* (pp. 43–60). Boston: Routledge & Kegan Paul.

Aronowitz, S., & Giroux, H. (1985) *Education under siege: the conservative, liberal and radical debate over schooling.* London: Routledge & Kegan Paul.

Bernstein, R. (1983) *Beyond objectivism and relativism: science, hermeneutics and praxis.* Philadelphia: University of Pennsylvania Press.

Boon, J. (1981) Functionalists write too: Frazer/Malinowski and the semiotics of the monograph. Paper presented at the annual meeting of the American Anthropological Association, Los Angeles, CA.

Bowles, S., & Gintis, H. (1976) *Schooling in capitalist America.* New York: Basic Books.

Braverman, H. (1975) *Labor and monopoly capitalism.* New York: Monthly Review Press.

Carr, W., & Kemmis, S. (1986) *Becoming critical: education, knowledge and action research.* London: Falmer Press.

Cazden, C. (1983) Can ethnographic research go beyond the status quo? *Anthropology and Education Quarterly, 14,* 34–41.

Clifford, J. (1983) On ethnographic authority. *Representations, 1*(2), 118–146.

Clifford, J., & Marcus, G. (Eds) (1986) *Writing culture: the poetics and politics of ethnography*. Berkeley: University of California Press.

Drummond, L. (1981) Jonestown: A study in ethnographic discourse. Paper presented at the annual meeting of the American Anthropological Association. Los Angeles, CA.

Entwistle, H. (1979) *Antonio Gramsci: conservative schooling for radical politics*. London: Routledge & Kegan Paul.

Erickson, F. (1986) Qualitative methods in research on teaching. In M. Wittrock (Ed.) *Handbook of research on teaching* (3rd ed.) (pp. 119–161). New York: Macmillan.

Everhart, R. (1983) *Reading, writing and resistance*. Boston: Routledge & Kegan Paul.

Fay, B. (1977) How people change themselves. The relationship between critical theory and its audience. In T. Ball (Ed.) *Political theory and praxis: new perspectives* (pp. 200–233, 266–269). Minneapolis: University of Minnesota Press.

Geertz, C. (1973) Thick description: toward an interpretive theory of culture. In C. Geertz, *The interpretation of cultures* (pp. 3–30). New York: Basic Books.

Giroux, H. (1983) *Theory and resistance in education: a pedagogy for the opposition*. South Hadley, MA: Bergin & Garvey.

Giroux, H. (1981) Pedagogy, pessimism, and the politics of conformity: a reply to Linda McNeil. *Curriculum Inquiry, 11*(3), 211–222.

Gitlin, A. (1980) Understanding the work of teachers. Unpublished doctoral dissertation, University of Wisconsin, Madison.

Gitlin, A. (1983) School structure and teachers' work. In M. Apple & L. Weis (Eds) *Ideology and practice in schooling* (pp. 193–212). Philadelphia: Temple University Press.

Gramsci, A. (1971) *Selection from the prison notebooks*. New York: International.

Lather, P. (1986) Research as praxis. *Harvard Educational Review, 52*(3), 255–277.

LeCompte, M., & Goetz, J. (1982) Problems of reliability and validity in ethnographic research. *Review of Educational Research, 52*(1), 31–60.

McLaren, P. (1986) *Schooling as a ritual performance*. London: Routledge & Kegan Paul.

Marcus, G., & Fischer, M. (1986) *Anthropology as cultural critique*. Chicago and London: University of Chicago Press.

Metz, M. (1978) *Classrooms and corridors: the crisis of authority in desegregated secondary schools*. Berkeley: University of California Press.

Popkewitz, T. (1984) *Paradigms and ideology in educational research*. Lewes: Falmer Press.

Pratt, M. (1986) Fieldwork in common places. In J. Clifford & G. Marcus (Eds) *Writing culture: the poetics and politics of ethnography* (pp. 27–50). Berkeley: University of California Press.

Rabinow, P. (1977) *Reflections on fieldwork in Morocco*. Berkeley: University of California Press.

Rist, R. (1970) Student social class and teacher expectations: the self-fulfilling prophecy in ghetto education. *Harvard Educational Review, 30*(3), 411–451.

Shapiro, S. (1987) Educational theory and recent political discourse: a new agenda for the left? *Teachers College Record, 89*(2), 171–200.

Shor, I. (1980) *Critical teaching and everyday life*. Boston: South End Press.

Simon, R. (1983) But who will let you do it? Counterhegemonic possibilities for work education. *Journal of Education, 165*(3) 235–256.

Simon, R., & Dippo, D. (1986) On critical ethnographic work. *Anthropology and Education Quarterly, 17*, 195–202.

Spindler, G. (Ed.) (1974) *Educational and cultural process: toward an anthropology of education*. New York: Holt, Rinehart & Winston.

Spradley, J., & McCurdy, D. (1972) *The cultural experience: ethnography in a complex society*. Chicago: Science Research Associates.

Tyler, S. (1985) Ethnography, intertextuality, and the end of description. *American Journal of Semiotics, 3*(4), 83–98.

Valli, L. (1986) *Becoming clerical workers.* Boston: Routledge & Kegan Paul.

Vygotsky, L. (1978) *Mind in society.* Cambridge, MA: Harvard University Press.

Weiler, K. (1988) *Women teaching for change: gender, class and power.* South Hadley, MA: Bergin & Garvey.

Wexler, P. (1987) *Social analysis of education: after the new sociology.* London: Routledge & Kegan Paul.

Whitehead, J., & Lomax, P. (1987) Action research and the politics of educational knowledge. *British Educational Research Journal, 13*(2), 175–190.

Willis, P. (1977) *Learning to labour.* Farnborough, England: Saxon House.

Wittgenstein, L. (1974) *Philosophical investigations* (trans. G.E.M. Anscombe). Oxford: Basil Blackwell.

14

ON THE TEACHER AS RESEARCHER

M. Hammersley

In this chapter I want to examine an idea that has been widely advocated in recent years: that educational research should be an integral part of the work of teachers in schools rather than an activity carried out on schools by outsiders. This is the idea of the teacher-as-researcher engaging in action research in classrooms or schools (what I will henceforth refer to as teacher research, TR for short). It is an idea that arose from a number of sources, and shares similarities with attempts to reconcile research and action in other fields.[1] It draws on arguments about the nature of research and teaching that have wide significance.

The idea of encouraging teachers to do research on their own schools or in their own classrooms is not a new one. There was a strong teacher action research movement in the USA in the 1950s.[2] Corey, one of its most influential advocates, defines action research as research undertaken by teachers, administrators and others to improve their own practice (Corey, 1949). At that time it was strongly associated with a widespread commitment to using scientific method to solve educational problems, and was inspired in particular by the work of Dewey and the progressive movement. Dewey believed that scientific recommendations could only be tested through practice, and saw the teacher as a research worker testing out educational theory (see Hodgkinson, 1957, pp. 138–9).

In Britain the idea of the teacher-as-researcher seems to have emerged in the 1960s and 1970s, largely independently of the American action research movement.[3] It arose partly from curriculum reform within schools (Elliott, 1991), but also from a shift within the community of curriculum developers and evaluators away from a bureaucratic model, in which new curricula were developed centrally by experts, adopted by local authorities, schools and teachers, and their success assessed by specialized evaluators using quantitative assessment of outcomes. This model was criticized both because it was ineffective in practice and because it was judged to contravene important educational and political values. It was ineffective because often, even when schools and teachers were committed to the curricular proposals, they used them in ways that departed from those intended by the curriculum developers. The result was that although the innovation had effects, perhaps even desirable ones, these were not those that were anticipated and therefore were often not measured. By focusing only on what was intended, evaluators failed to understand what had and had not (and what could have) been achieved. Furthermore, it was argued that this narrow focus reflected an inappropriate conception of human life, one modelled on the presuppositions about physical phenomena built into natural scientific method. At the same time, attention came to be given to the diversity of perspectives to be found amongst those with an interest in the curriculum development process. The result was the emergence of a variety of new approaches to evaluation.[4] These changes in perspective led many curriculum researchers to reject one of the basic presuppositions of the bureaucratic model – that teaching involves the specification of objectives to be achieved and the selection of effective means to achieve those objectives. More emphasis was placed on the *process* of teaching, as a skilled and locally managed activity. Associated with this was a reassertion of the value of the professional autonomy of teachers and renewed emphasis on their key role in curriculum change; this sometimes being located within a wider political framework advocating democracy and/or radical social transformation of some kind.

Curriculum development came to be seen by some, therefore, as primarily concerned with enhancing the professionalism of teachers. It was emphasized that the teacher is (or ought to be) a skilled practitioner, continually reflecting on his or her practice in terms of ideals and knowledge of local situations, and modifying practice in light of these reflections, rather than a technician merely applying scientifically produced curriculum programmes. Given this shift in perspective, the role of curriculum developer and evaluator changed. For some the distinction between the two, which had often been blurred, largely disappeared; and the curriculum researcher now came to be seen as someone charged with helping teachers to improve their practice through developing their capacities for self-reflection.

An important element of this shift in curriculum studies was the move away from quantitative to qualitative methodology, the latter being adapted from anthropological, sociological and historical research. This was motivated by the concern with processes rather than outcomes, and by the switch in audience from the research community and higher-level policy-makers towards teachers and the public generally. Qualitative method, it was argued, could deal better with local circumstances, and presented findings in terms that were accessible and useful to teachers, parents and others. In addition, it was more attuned to the distinctive character of human social life, compared with the previously dominant quantitative methods that had been adopted from the physical and biological sciences (Parlett and Hamilton, 1977).[5]

It seems likely that, in some degree at least, the move within curriculum studies from bureaucratic to professional conceptions of teaching, and from the researcher as developer and evaluator to facilitator, also arose from the application to the researcher–researched relationship of broadly progressive ideas about the teacher–pupil relationship; ideas that were at the heart of many of the early curriculum development projects. The latter were often concerned with encouraging more discovery-based or inquiry-led approaches to teaching, where the role of the teacher was to facilitate learning rather than to transmit knowledge. It is easy to see how such ideas would raise doubts about the validity of a relationship between curriculum developer or evaluator and teachers that seemed closer to the traditional teacher–pupil relationship than to that which was embodied in the curriculum projects being promoted and assessed. There is a sense here in which history was repeating itself. In a critical evaluation of educational action research in the USA, published in 1957, Hodgkinson (p. 139) remarked that action research is a direct logical outcome of the progressive education movement: 'After showing children how to work together to solve their problems, the next step was for teachers to adopt the methods they had been teaching their children and learn to solve their own problems cooperatively'.

One of the most important figures in these developments in the field of curriculum research in Britain was Lawrence Stenhouse. At the core of Stenhouse's work is a view of the learner, whether child or adult, scholar or teacher, as producing knowledge, and knowledge which is always tentative, and open to debate. This reflects commitment to a particular conception of the essential character of humanity, a form of humanism. Stenhouse used at least two models for this ideal, which he saw as corresponding in their basics despite superficial dissimilarities. The first was the humanist scholar (notably but not exclusively the historian). The second was the natural scientist, conceptualized in the terms made popular by Popper (Stenhouse, 1975, pp. 124, 125; 1983, pp. 17, 19).[6] Stenhouse argues that we are constrained by assumptions and habits built up in the past and that it is the business of education to make us freer and more creative (Stenhouse, 1975, p. 82). He applied this ideal to pupils in his advocacy of inquiry learning, exemplified in the discussion-based lessons encouraged by the Humanities Curriculum Project (HCP). He also applied the model to the teacher, not just in that the latter was to take the role of a senior learner rather than of an intellectual authority in these discussions, but even more importantly in that he conceived teaching as a process in which the teacher learns how to improve his or her teaching. Furthermore, while Stenhouse denies that there is an epistemological base for the discussion-based approach in HCP (ibid., p. 93), it seems clear that his position does involve epistemological presuppositions: he sees inquiry learning as teaching the epistemological lesson that knowledge is a human product, not simply a reflection of the world (Stenhouse, 1983, pp. 179–81). For him this seems to have been as important as, if not more important than, the more substantive knowledge which forms the school curriculum.

As regards the teacher as reflective practitioner discovering how to improve his or her teaching, Stenhouse's ideas draw on Hoyle's (1972) 'extended professionalism' but go beyond this to involve:

—the commitment to systematic questioning of one's own teaching as a basis for development;
—the commitment and the skills to study one's own teaching;
—the concern to question and to test theory in practice by the use of those skills;
—readiness to allow others to observe your work and to discuss it with them on an honest, open basis.

(Stenhouse, 1975, p. 144)

For Stenhouse, then, the professionalism of the teacher is based on expertise in seeking to understand the world, including one's own practice, not on superior knowledge already gained (Stenhouse, 1983, p. 185). Thus, curricular ideas are to be tested through action, as the continually developing product of invention and reflection. Closely related to this is the idea of the teacher as artist (ibid. p. 157).

On the basis of these ideas, Stenhouse criticizes approaches to curriculum development and evaluation that run counter to this model of the teacher, for example by specifying curricular objectives to be pursued. He also criticizes research that studies classroom interaction for purposes extraneous to the improvement of the teaching in that classroom, as irrelevant and/or ineffective (Stenhouse, 1975, Ch. 6). It is not clear how far this criticism is intended to run. It is directed primarily at curriculum research and evaluation, though it applies to other kinds of educational research as well. Yet Stenhouse does not seem to extend it to theoretical or basic research. Thus, at one point he envisages a division of labour between teacher researchers and professional researchers in which the existence and role of a more theoretically oriented form of research seems to be preserved. Here teachers would carry out case studies on the basis of the collaborative development of a common language, while professional researchers would seek to 'master this material and scrutinize it for general trends'. And Stenhouse comments that it is out of this synthetic task that general propositional theory can be developed (ibid. p. 157).

Many subsequent advocates of TR have tended to extend both the role of the teacher as researcher and to reduce the role of the non-teaching educational researcher to a subordinate one, at most. An example is Carr and Kemmis's book *Becoming Critical* (1986). They draw on critical theory, taking over Habermas's typology of approaches to inquiry, in which each approach is constituted by different fundamental interests. First there is research based on a technical interest, in which the researcher produces knowledge that is then applied to practice. The natural sciences conform to this model, being concerned with the instrumental control of nature. And, like Habermas, Carr and Kemmis claim that this technical interest has been overextended in the case of much quantitative research in education, which treats human relationships as subject to bureaucratic manipulation and control. The second form of inquiry, the interpretive approach, is based on a practical interest. Here the aim is to understand and describe the perspectives of the people involved in the events studied. This is more appropriate to the investigation of human social life than the instrumental model, Carr and Kemmis argue, but it fails to take adequate account of the ways in which practical thinking and practice may be distorted by ideology. It is suggested that what is necessary, therefore, is a critical approach. This shares much in common with the practical approach, but at the same time uses science to understand how practical perspectives may be ide-ologically distorted. Above all, rather than being committed to human under-standing alone it is directed towards bringing about emancipation, it is aimed at the construction of a rational, just and democratic society. Indeed, accord-ing to Carr and Kemmis, it should exemplify this in its practice. They recognize different forms of action research, but see emancipatory action research as the superior form and claim to detect a historical shift in this direction.[7]

The work of Stenhouse, Carr and Kemmis, and others has provided the basis for a sustained critique of conventional educational research, and has led to widespread advocacy of collaborative and practitioner research. And while it is not always clear whether the latter is intended to replace the former, this often seems to be implied by the arguments employed. In the remainder of this paper I want to examine these arguments as they relate both to research and to teaching.

CRITICISM OF CONVENTIONAL EDUCATIONAL RESEARCH

We can identify several criticisms of conventional educational research de-ployed by advocates of TR, though these are given varying emphasis by dif-ferent critics:

1. That it is largely irrelevant to the practical concerns of teachers.
2. That it is often invalid because it is separated from the object that it claims to understand: notably, the classroom practice of teachers.
3. That it is undemocratic in that it allows the views of educational researchers to define the reality in which teachers are forced to work.
4. That it amounts to a process of exploitation.

I shall consider each of these arguments.

Irrelevance

The claim that educational research is irrelevant to the work of teachers is often supported by the argument that teachers do not read educational re-search and that even then they do they find it of little interest (Burgess, 1980, p. 171; Kemmis, 1982, p. 11; Hustler, Cassidy and Cuff, 1986, p. 8). It is almost certainly true that most teachers do not read much educational research; indeed most of them probably read it only when it is set reading for in-service courses. However, it is not clear that this is because they have found it irrelevant and uninteresting. And even where there is a negative reaction we must be aware that, as Cope and Gray (1979, p. 241) remark: 'genuine confusion and uncertainty may be mistaken for suspicion and hostility'.

Furthermore, these empirical arguments about teachers' responses to educational research cannot provide the basis for a judgement about the relevance of the findings of educational research. After all, how people respond depends on what they expect and want; and those expectations and desires may be well- or ill-founded. For instance, teachers may expect research to provide solutions to the problems that face them in the classroom. Indeed, educational researchers sometimes present their work as solving those problems; doing this perhaps out of a desire to help, but also no doubt because this seems to be increasingly necessary to obtain research funds. But there are good reasons to believe that research cannot solve teachers' problems; certainly not in the sense of providing a set of behavioural rules which, if followed, will avoid or resolve the problems. There are at least two reasons for this.

First, even if we research a problem we are by no means guaranteed a solution. Progress in research is often slow or nonexistent, even in the natural sciences. There is no scientific method that guarantees results. Often a problem is investigated for a long time without much being achieved, and discoveries that are made may owe as much to good fortune and to intuition as to method.

Second, the circumstances that teachers face in their work and the considerations that must inform their decisions are diverse and variable, and therefore seem unlikely to be amenable to action in accordance with an abstract set of rules. Here I am adopting the view that sound practice cannot amount to the straightforward *application* of theoretical knowledge but is an activity that necessarily involves judgement and draws on experience as much as (if not more than) on scientific knowledge.[8]

However, that educational research cannot provide *solutions* to practical problems does not imply that it is irrelevant to practice. Information may be relevant and useful to teachers without providing them with solutions to their problems. I do not pretend that there are no difficulties with the provision of such information. For example, if the circumstances in which individual teachers work are highly variable, how can generalizations about such situations, or theories about them that abstract away the particularities, be of value? These problems are not easy to deal with (Hammersley, 1992, Chs. 5 and 11), but they face the teacher-as-researcher as well as conventional researchers; at least to the extent that he or she is concerned with generalizing from past experience to the future and/or with developing collective professional knowledge.

Of course, what I have said here may be accepted, but the argument for TR still pursued by the suggestion that conventional researchers tend to investigate problems of their own formulation rather than those of teachers.[9] This, it seems to me, is only partly true; and even to the extent that it is true it is not necessarily a negative feature of educational research. The assumption here seems to be that the value of the products of educational research resides solely in their value for teachers. For example, 'the value of [researchers'] contributions lies in the extent to which they support the practical judgment of teachers and increase their capacity to reflect systematically upon the complex situations they confront' (Elliott, preface to Nixon, 1981, p. 1). Yet teachers are not the only audience for educational research, there are other sorts of practitioners involved in the education system as well. Furthermore, many of the topics that educational research has focused on – the effectiveness of different teaching styles, the consequences of class size for pupil performance, the effects of streaming and banding, the potentially self-fulfilling character of teachers' expectations, etc. – are of concern to many teachers. And, over and above this, they probably should be of potential concern to all teachers. What teachers *ought to be* concerned about cannot be decided by what they are *in fact* concerned about. Teachers do not have any uniquely privileged position in deciding what are important educational issues. Thus we should not dismiss those topics pursued by educational researchers on the grounds that no teachers are concerned with them, even if this is true.[10]

In my view, then, the case for the irrelevance of the findings of conventional educational research has not been established. It is clear, too, that the issue of relevance is more complex than it might at first appear. This is not to say, of course, that it is not an important issue and that the relevance of educational research could not be improved.

Invalidity of educational research

It is sometimes claimed not just that the findings of educational research are irrelevant, but also that they are often invalid, and that this results from the fact that they are carried out by outsiders.[11] There is only limited force in this argument.

Sometimes it is argued that only those actually involved in a social situation can truly understand it. This argument is founded on the idea that direct experience of, or closeness to, a phenomenon gives one valid knowledge of it. Ironically, this is an argument that has often been used by qualitative researchers themselves in claiming the superiority of their methods, and particularly participant observation, over quantitative work. In doing so, of course, they open themselves up to the criticism that because they are not as close to the situations they study as are the participants, their knowledge is less likely to be valid than participants' knowledge. In my view, however, while closeness to and involvement with the phenomena being investigated can be of value, the epistemological assumption that seems to underly this argument – that knowledge comes from contact with reality – is unsound. This is because all knowledge is a construction: we have no direct knowledge of the world.[12]

There are, though, some more specific and defensible methodological arguments on which the claim that practitioners are best able to understand their own activities and situations could be based:

1. That teachers have access to their own intentions and motives, thoughts and feelings, in a way that an observer does not, and so have a deeper understanding of their own behaviour than an outsider could ever have.
2. That the teacher-researcher will usually have long-term experience of the setting being studied, and will therefore know its history first hand, as well as other information that may be required to understand what is going on. It would take an outsider a long time to acquire such knowledge; indeed, this may never be possible.
3. That the teacher already has relationships with others in the setting and can use these in order to collect further data. Once again, an outsider would need to spend a considerable time in the field building up such relationships.
4. That because teachers are key actors in the settings studied in educational research, they are in a position to test theoretical ideas in a way that a mere observer can never do.

Each of these arguments points to an advantage that insiders may have in the sources of information available to them, and I think they have some validity. However, for each of the advantages listed above there is a countervailing disadvantage:[13]

1. People can be wrong even about their own intentions and motives; self-knowledge is not immediately given and therefore valid. Furthermore, people can deceive themselves about their intentions, motives, etc. Indeed, they may often have an interest in such self-deception where an outsider has less reason to prefer one account over another. Also, understanding often requires seeing a phenomenon in its wider context, and this may be particularly difficult for those closely involved in it. It is for this reason that ethnographers stress the importance of maintaining some (at least intellectual) distance from the activities they observe.
2. The information that practitioners have about the situations they operate in is a product of experience deriving from a particular role (or a limited number of roles) that will have given access to some sorts of information but not to others. In particular, their understanding of the perspectives of other categories and groups of people involved in the setting may be superficial or distorted. An outside researcher may be able to tap a wider range of sources of information than an insider, and will usually be more able to process that information for the specific purposes of inquiry, and (to some extent at least) in an explicit way that allows for checking by others. The knowledge teachers have will have been processed implicitly and to a large extent on the basis of practitioner concerns, and may involve misconceptions that serve, or are relevant to, those concerns.
3. Again, the relationships available to the practitioner will exclude as well as

include, and may not include what is necessary for research purposes. Furthermore, some of those relationships may place constraints on the inquiry (for example on what can be observed, what questions can be asked, what conclusions can be published, etc.) that an outside researcher would be able to avoid. For example, a teacher doing research in the school in which he or she works is likely to operate under more serious threat of control by senior management or governors than is an outside researcher. This may even extend to what lines of investigation can and cannot be pursued.

4. What is required to test theoretical ideas may well conflict with what is needed for good practice. (To deny this is to conflate what is true with what works in a particular situation.) The practitioner may therefore be faced with a dilemma, and as a result may not be able to test his or her ideas. In any case, quasi-experimentation is only one possible research strategy, one with characteristic disadvantages (notably potentially high reactivity) as well as advantages.

In short, I do not believe that being an established participant in a situation provides access to valid knowledge that is not available to an outside researcher. In general, the chances of the findings being valid can be enhanced by a judicious combination of involvement and estrangement. However, no position, not even a marginal one, guarantees valid knowledge; and no position prevents it either. There are no overwhelming advantages to being an insider or an outsider. Each position has advantages and disadvantages, though these will take on slightly different weights depending on the particular circumstances and purposes of the research.

Educational research as undemocratic

'Democracy' is a term that can mean many different things, but what often seems to be assumed in criticisms of educational research as undemocratic is some notion of participatory democracy. The complaint is that the voices of educational researchers are heard at the expense of those of teachers. This is presumably the sense in which Elliott describes some educational research as involving the 'disenfranchisement' of teachers (Elliott, 1988, p. 157), and what Nixon (1981, p. 9) has in mind when he refers to the 'paternalism' of traditional educational research. Rudduck (1987, p. 5) hints at the same point: 'there is an urgent need to analyse the structures that govern the production and distribution of research knowledge and the right to engage in research acts. Teacher research is, at one level, a means of countering the hegemony of academic research which teachers are often distanced by.' It is claimed that researchers are in a position to publish their views about the nature of education, schooling, teachers and pupils in a way that teachers are not; and that, as a result, researchers contribute to defining the reality in which teachers work in a much more powerful way than teachers can themselves.

This argument seems to me to suffer from several defects. First, it ascribes an implausible amount of power to the written word in relation to teachers and their work situation. While teachers have by no means total control over what goes on in the classrooms and schools in which they work, their power in these domains is substantial, and is certainly far greater than that of most outside researchers. Furthermore, the influence of research on the local and national policies that shape schools is extremely limited. If this were not so, the educational reforms of the late 1980s would not have occurred, since they involve assumptions that run counter to the results of most research over the previous thirty years (Gipps, 1993).[14]

Beyond this, though, I think the model of participatory democracy presupposed by this criticism is open to challenge. In everyday life we do not treat everyone's opinions on all topics as of equal value, and therefore as worth hearing; and with good reason. We judge the likely validity of views on a variety of grounds, and among these we certainly take account of their source. We assign certain sources of information a degree of intellectual authority on particular sorts of topic, on the grounds that there is reason to believe that they are less likely to be subject to error of significant kinds. In the case of research this authority derives from the fact that it is held to be governed by norms of systematic investigation and rigorous analysis. Of course, this authority is fallible and is recognized to be so; and it is limited to particular areas and types of issue. Furthermore, researchers are not the only ones who can legitimately claim intellectual authority. The same is also true of teachers, on the grounds of their first-hand experience in schools and their understanding of what is involved in the process of education. That, surely, is a crucial element of what it means for teaching to be a profession. It is true that the intellectual authority of research has sometimes been exaggerated in comparison with that of teachers and other practitioners; but this should not lead us to deny the intellectual authority of research, simply to treat it more circumspectly.

Educational research as involving exploitation of teachers

The final criticism I will consider in this section is to the effect that conventional research is exploitative, in that it serves the interests of researchers rather than those of the people studied: 'much educational research, both in principle and practice, remains an activity indulged in by those *outside* the classroom for the benefit of those *outside* the classroom' (Nixon, 1981, p. 5). One point that it is important to make in response to this is that researchers typically have to request and negotiate access to the settings and groups they study, and this may be blocked at any point. Of course, the extent to which the people studied are able to block access will depend on their position in society generally, and in the particular setting, and on who (if anybody) is sponsoring the researcher. Thus, when (as is common) a researcher negotiates access to a school via the headteacher, teachers may feel pressure to co-operate. However, it is rare, I suspect, for participants to be forced into co-operation in this manner; there are usually ways in which they can be less than co-operative without incurring the wrath of their superiors (and it is unusual for superiors to be very strongly committed to research). In any event, most educational researchers would respect the wishes of subordinates to refuse access. More often than not, I suggest, researchers are in a relatively weak position *vis-à-vis* most of the people they study, in terms of gaining access to sites and to information in order to do their research. This is not a position that facilitates exploitation.

Very often the charge that researchers exploit teachers amounts to the claim that the sole, or primary, function of research is to further the careers of researchers. Of course, there is no doubt that some researchers (like some teachers) are motivated primarily by careerism; but it does not follow from this that even what *they* produce is of no value. Fortunately or unfortunately, what is of value does not always spring from good intentions; nor do the latter guarantee beneficial results. There is an important difference between the motives that individuals may have for becoming researchers and the function of research as an institution. In many ways this argument returns us to the question of relevance, which I discussed earlier.

Another element of the charge of exploitation is that researchers simply take over the knowledge of teachers and present it as their own. Thus, Carr and Kemmis talk of conventional educational research as expropriating the experience and work of teachers (1986, p. 162). However, while there may be a legitimate question in the case of any study about the 'value added' over and above what teachers already know, anybody who has been involved in research will realize that there is always a considerable amount of work added. The value of that work cannot be easily measured, but of course exactly the same is true of the contribution that teaching makes to children's learning (Lortie 1975).

CRITICISM OF TRADITIONAL TEACHING

Advocacy of TR does not just involve criticism of conventional educational *research*, but also of traditional conceptions of *teaching*: 'it seems probable that a teacher can assume the role of a researcher, but that this will be possible only in an "open" classroom . . .' (Stenhouse, 1975, p. 155). In many ways TR is an extension of some of the ideas of the progressive and radical education movements of the 1950s, 1960s and 1970s. In particular it is based on a rejection of what has come to be called transmission teaching, a form of pedagogy which presupposes that education involves the *transfer* of knowledge and skills from teacher to pupils. At the same time, it involves a rejection of what Elliott (1991) calls the craft culture of teaching, in which teaching is treated as an activity whose character is fixed and known. It is argued that traditional teaching should be replaced by a form of pedagogy that is closer in nature to research; and this is proposed on epistemological, pedagogic and/or political grounds.

There are two aspects of the inquiry-based conception of teaching, then. The first relates to the learning in which teacher and pupils engage in the classroom, dealing with substantive curricular topics. The second concerns what we can call the process of practical inquiry in which the teacher reflects on and modifies his or her classroom practice. In relation to the first, TR involves advocacy of learning as inquiry; in relation to the second, a conception of teaching as an activity that must be subjected to continual monitoring and improvement. Discussions of TR vary in how much emphasis they give to these two aspects, though generally there is more emphasis on the second than the first. I shall look at each in turn.

Learning as inquiry

Associated with TR is a minimization, if not a denial, of any fundamental difference in role between teacher and pupil. Thus, Stenhouse sees both pupils and teachers as researchers. At the same time, though, TR is dedicated to extending the professionalism of teachers by involving them in research. In short, advocates of TR seem to combine elements of what can be broadly described as progressivism with a commitment to teacher professionalism. However, we must ask whether these two tendencies are mutually compatible, and also whether TR offers a convincing account of the nature of teaching.

The first issue can be dealt with more rapidly than the second. There seems to be a tension, to say the least, between the promotion of teacher professionalism by advocates of TR, on the one hand, and their playing down of the difference in role between teacher and taught on the other. Of course, how sharp this tension is depends on the extent to which the minimization of differences between teacher and student is carried and the form it takes. Advocates of TR are often not very clear about this, and no doubt they differ considerably in their views about it. For these reasons we can do little more than point to the problem.

The criticism of traditional teaching that is implicit, and sometimes explicit, in TR centres on the treatment of knowledge and of pupils by the teacher. First, there is rejection of the assumption, said to be built into conventional forms of teaching, that knowledge is something produced elsewhere by experts whose validity is certain. Stenhouse, in particular, emphasizes the tentative and personal character of all knowledge. He does not deny the role of specialist research communities in producing knowledge (albeit knowledge that must be tentative in its status), but he emphasizes that what should take place in the classroom is a collective exploration of issues into which knowledge from outside would be fed, and in a way that does not take its validity for granted. Furthermore, particularly on issues about which there is no general consensus, the discussion should be open ended, not guided by the teacher to some foregone conclusion. More than this, no intelligible conclusions should be ruled out by the teacher.[15]

Despite a personal preference for this mode of pedagogy, I believe it is a mistake to see it in terms of learning as a form of inquiry. There may often be great value in putting children and students in situations that are analogous in key respects to those of scientists or historians, both because of what this can teach them and because it may increase their motivation. However, this remains a simulation; as those who are involved are often only too aware (Atkinson and Delamont, 1976). Indeed, that it is a simulation is what allows it to be a fruitful learning experience. By setting up the parameters of the simulation in particular ways the tasks facing students can be made both manageable and fruitful given the time, skills, knowledge and other resources available to them. In this respect, even in discovery-based approaches the teacher remains a teacher rather than simply a senior learner (as in Stenhouse's formulation). And, contra Stenhouse, the teacher's authority in this respect must be recognized by learners. A teacher must be 'an authority', not just 'in authority'.[16]

More than this, though, at the root of Stenhouse's ideas about inquiry learning, and indeed of those of some other advocates of TR, there seems to be a conception of inquiry as completely open and 'democratic', in which nothing is fixed, everything is and should be open to question and investigation. And yet the import of much recent work in the history and philosophy of science has been to stress the extent to which, and respects in which, scientific research is relatively closed, in which its pursuit depends on much being taken for granted until further notice. This is one of the messages, for example, of Kuhn's (1970) book *The Structure of Scientific Revolutions*, a message that has tended to be overlooked by many social scientists.[17] In short, the advocacy of inquiry learning, by Stenhouse and others, may be based on false assumptions about the nature of inquiry.

Teaching as practical inquiry

The other aspect of the criticism of traditional teaching by advocates of TR is that concerned with the attitude that teachers adopt towards their classroom practice. Again, I want to question both the extent to which teaching should be seen as a form of inquiry and the model of inquiry assumed.

There is, of course, a sense in which teaching, as a form of practical activity, does involve inquiry. When faced with a problem in their work, teachers may collect and process information about it with a view to finding out why it arose and how it can be handled. This may be done on the spot in the classroom or later when there is a respite. Similarly, teachers may sometimes reflect on their work in a less problem-oriented way, asking questions of a kind that are similar to those which preoccupy the various social-science disciplines and philosophy. It is not unreasonable to see this as a form of inquiry, though it may differ from what a researcher would do in tackling the same questions.[18]

Two points are worth making about this. One is that inquiry in this sense is by no means restricted to teachers. From this point of view, we are all researchers, to one degree or another, in the various roles we play. In fact, interpreting inquiry in this way, it becomes difficult to distinguish it from human perception and cognition in general. Consequently, it is not clear how this concept of inquiry can provide the basis for an extension of teacher professionalism. Of course, to some degree what is involved in TR is a desire to make this kind of everyday inquiry among teachers more systematic and rigorous. This may be valuable, but caution is required. First, reflection and inquiry, however 'systematic' and 'rigorous', are not guaranteed to produce advances in useful understanding. The outcome of all research is uncertain. Furthermore, the products of systematic inquiry will not necessarily be better than the presuppositions built into traditional ways of doing things. It is a modernist fallacy to assume otherwise.[19] Second, the desirability of reflection and inquiry on any particular occasion is a matter of judgement. They are not automatically of value. For one thing, inquiry involves opportunity costs: it takes time and resources that could be used for other things.[20] Moreover, there seems to be implicit in TR a conception of rational action that is highly intellectualist in character, as if the rational response to a problem is always to seek to resolve it through inquiry. This is by no means always the case (Lindblom and Cohen, 1979), and especially not given that teachers operate under great pressures of immediacy and complexity (Doyle, 1977).

Another danger is that the conception of rigour that is applied to teachers' practical inquiry by some advocates of TR is derived from disciplinary research and is not necessarily appropriate. In the context of different activities, for example research as against teaching, different things will be treated as fixed and as open to question, and often quite rightly so. For example, there will be different evaluations of the costs of different sorts of error. This raises a paradoxical possibility: that rather than TR being an extension of teacher professionalism at the expense of researchers, as I suggested earlier, in practice it could represent a form of researcher imperialism: the inappropriate imposition of research considerations on the practice of teaching. There is a hint of this when Carr and Kemmis (1986, p. 2) suggest that the professional development of teachers requires that they adopt 'a research stance' to their teaching; or when Stenhouse (1975, p. 142) proposes 'an educational science in which each classroom is a laboratory, each teacher a member of the scientific community'. Part of the appeal of TR is probably that it gives teachers access to a high-status label for their work. Given the extent to which teaching as an occupation has been degraded in status terms, coming to see oneself as not just a teacher but a researcher could be appealing. Indeed, one can see it as a professionalizing strategy, as the advocates of TR clearly do.[21] However, it is worth noting that this strategy effectively involves at least an acknowledgement of the low status of teaching, as conventionally understood, if not a reinforcement of it. In my view we should be concerned with raising the status of teaching as an activity directly, rather than seeking to do so by appeal to the status of research (whose status is, in any case, equivocal).

Finally, while some elements of teaching may constitute a sort of inquiry, there is much more to teaching as an activity than these, and the other parts ought to be valued more highly. There are skills involved in managing class-room relationships, in diagnosing learning difficulties, in knowing when to press on with an activity and when to call a halt, etc., etc., that are not in any simple sense inquiry skills. I suspect that it is not so much that advocates of TR overlook these other aspects of teaching as that they believe that for teaching to be rational these must all be founded on principles that have been subjected to systematic reflection and justification; that they must be part of a rationally comprehended whole. Carr and Kemmis (1986, p. 124) come close to this in the following, despite qualifications:

> A primary task for any research activity concerned to adopt a scientific approach to educational problems is to emancipate teachers from their dependence on habit and tradition by providing them with the skills and resources that will enable them to reflect upon and examine critically the inadequacies of different conceptions of educational practice . . . This does not mean that 'practical' ways of thinking must be abandoned in favour of some 'theoretical' mode of thought. What is being abandoned is an unreflective attitude so that a more critical, scientific attitude can be adopted towards established educational creeds. Hence, science does not *replace* existing theories of educational practice so much as *improve* them, by subjecting the beliefs and justifications which sustain them to criticism. For it is only by so challenging current educational certainties that the interpretations and judgments of educators will become more coherent and less dependent on the prejudices and dogma that permeate unreflective educational thinking.

In a similar way, Stenhouse (1983, p. 158) argues that much teaching is habit-ual and that what must be developed are cultural habits that 'we can defend and justify'. Yet the idea that to be rational, desirable, etc., practices must have been subject to reflexive examination and proven to be justified is by no means obviously true. Indeed, it is a point of view that has been rejected even as it applies to research (Tully, 1989). There are good reasons to believe that no practice can be founded on explicitly formulated and justified assumptions. As Wittgenstein remarked, at the bottom of any practice is action not knowledge (Wittgenstein, 1969; Morawetz, 1978).

Furthermore, what is involved sometimes in TR is not just an overly intel-lectualist conception of teaching as a practical activity that extends teacher professionalism into the realm of research but also a proposed transforma-tion of teaching in other directions as well. One of the most extreme ex-amples of this is to be found in the work of Carr and Kemmis (1986), who see critical action research as effectively part of a counter-hegemonic struggle designed to transform society in the direction of participatory democracy, which they seem to regard as the most rational form of political and social organization. Here the role of the teacher is extended much further than in the case of Stenhouse. He or she becomes a member of an expanding action research community, incorporating parents and others, that is committed to transforming society:

> Action research can thus establish conditions under which it can identify and expose those aspects of the social order which frustrate rational change, and provide a basis for action to overcome irrationality, injustice and deprivation. It does so by creating conditions in which the self-critical communities of action researchers commit themselves to rational communication, just and democratic decision-making and access to an interesting and satisfying life for all.
>
> (Carr and Kemmis, 1986, p. 197)

The authors themselves describe this proposal as Utopian, but they claim that there is no justifiable alternative (*ibid.* p. 223). It is certainly Utopian in the sense of being of doubtful feasibility, but whether it is Utopian in the sense of being desirable is another matter; and Carr and Kemmis provide little explicit argument in support of that claim.

CONCLUSION

In this chapter I have examined the idea that educational research should take the form of teachers carrying out research in their classrooms and schools, this being seen not as an extra activity added on to their teaching but rather as a transformation of that teaching. In the first part of the paper I argued that while teacher research might be useful, it is no substitute for educational research of a more conventional kind. I looked at each of the arguments directed against conventional research: that it is irrelevant to practice, that it is invalid, that it is undemocratic and that it involves exploitation of teachers. In each case I argued that these are not convincing.

In the second part I looked at the other side of TR: its implications for teaching. I suggested that it represents a broadly progressivist critique of traditional teaching, yet that there seems to be a potential conflict between this and the conception of TR as extending teacher professionalism. I examined the two respects in which TR portrays teaching as a form of inquiry: as discovery learning or discussion-based lessons in the classroom, and as a form of practice involving and perhaps founded on critical reflection and inquiry. I argued that in neither respect can teaching be usefully regarded as isomorphic with inquiry. While simulation of inquiry is one useful technique that teachers may use, it is only one of many, and its value is crucially tied to the fact that it is a simulation. Similarly, I argued that while, like other activities, teaching does involve processes of reflexive inquiry, these often, and rightly, take a different form from conventional educational research. Furthermore, they by no means exhaust what is involved in teaching. Nor is the idea that teaching must be fully self-reflexive, forming a coherent whole founded on explicit and justified principles, a convincing one.

It has not been my intention to argue that teachers should be discouraged from engaging in reflection and inquiry. Far from it. To some degree, and in some forms, this is likely to be of value from both a practical and a research point of view; though it must be said that the space for it in the lives of teachers is probably even less now then when it was originally proposed. Rather, my aim has been to counter the proposal that the roles of teacher and educational researcher should be integrated, which is at the core of TR. In my view this is undesirable from the point of view both of research and of teaching.

ACKNOWLEDGEMENTS

Thanks go to John Elliott, Peter Gates, Roger Gomm, Jack Whitehead, and Peter Woods for comments on an earlier draft of this paper. There will still be much in it with which many of them disagree. I'm also grateful to May Pettigrew for correcting some of my misconceptions, and for supplying relevant literature of which I was unaware.

NOTES

1. Similar ideas are to be found in applied anthropology (van Willigen, 1986), 'new paradigm' research in social psychology (Reason and Rowan, 1981), in feminist methodology (Mies, 1983), in some areas of industrial sociology (Gustavsen, 1986) and of management studies (Torbert, 1983), and in the field of adult education and development studies (Hall, Gillett and Tandon, 1982; Latapi, 1988).

2. Norris (1991) traces the idea of the teacher-as-researcher even further back, to the early work of Ralph Tyler.

3. The American movement was part of a broader tradition of action research that is still influential in other fields, see for example Argyris, Putnam and Smith (1985, Ch. 1). An early article in British sociology of education advocating teacher research, which was influenced by the work of Argyris, seems to have had little impact in that field or elsewhere (Bartholomew, 1973). However, Kemmis (1988) suggests that there may have been a link between the American movement and developments in Britain via the influence of the Tavistock Institute in London. For a useful discussion of the British teacher as researcher movement, see May (1982).

4. See Hamilton *et al.* (1977), Simons (1987) and Norris (1991). Given my focus here on TR, I will not be giving attention to the changes that resulted in the field of educational evaluation. See Elliott (1991b) for a useful discussion of the relationship between democratic evaluation and the teacher action research movement.

5. In this respect recent versions of TR contrast with the older American action research tradition, which as I noted relied on a more traditional quantitative conception of research method. This difference parallels changes in educational research generally, and in the social sciences as a whole, where quantitative method has come under increasing criticism and qualitative method has become more widely advocated and adopted.

6. Skilbeck (1983) sets Stenhouse's humanistic methodology in a wider context.

7. John Elliott takes a similar view to Carr and Kemmis in some respects, balancing the idea that teachers must be empowered to investigate their own practices and circumstances with a recognition of the cultural and social constraints on the development of such investigations. However, he criticizes the critical research model for its privileging of the position of the researcher and failure to recognize the scope for radical reconstruction within the practical tradition (Elliott, 1988, 1991). There are still other variants of TR; some of which emphasize the professional development of teachers more in terms of their personal development, see for example Whitehead (1989), McNiff (1992, 1993).

8. This is an idea to be found in much recent writing about education, for example Schwab (1969), Schon (1983, 1987), Hirst (1983), and Carr (1987). It is worth emphasizing that, contrary to what is sometimes implied, conventional educational researchers do not typically assume that practice is the mechanical application of research findings. Some come close to this, for example Lieberman in his discussion of *Education as a Profession* (1956); though even he recognizes that teachers may need to engage in practical research themselves (Lieberman, 1956, pp. 192–5). Others, for example Gage (1963) and Van Valen (1962), see a continuum between educational research and the practical inquiries carried out by teachers.

9. See for example Carr and Kemmis (1986, pp. 108–9 and 117).

10. Kelly (1985, p. 144) makes the same point, in the course of advocating action research. She comments: 'The issues which teacher researchers study tend to be questions of classroom management rather than socially or sociologically important problems. I do not accept that action research should be restricted to the questions which are important to practitioners, or that the practitioners' viewpoint is necessarily "right".' Carr and Kemmis formulate their argument in terms of educational problems arising out of or being grounded in educational practice. Yet, given that they share Kelly's 'critical' orientation it is not clear what would and would not count as an educational problem for them, or even what are legitimate grounds for deciding this.

11. See, for example, McNamara (1980) and Kemmis (1988, p. 45). See also Hammersley (1981).

12. For a discussion of what I take to be the implications of this point, see Hammersley (1992, Ch. 3).

13. See Burgess (1980) for a discussion of some of these problems.

14. Of course, one might argue that present times are exceptional, that at other times educational research has been more influential on policy. This is true to a degree, but I think it is clear that research has rarely if ever been the decisive factor in shaping educational policy, and it is probably a mistake to think that it ever would be.

15. It should be noted that Stenhouse, who is one of the most explicit of the advocates of TR on this issue, does not claim that discussion-based or inquiry-based lessons are the only element of teaching. Indeed, he argues that there is even a role for transmission of factual information.

16. For a discussion of this distinction and its significance, see Flathman (1989).

17. But not by philosophers: it was the focus of the debate between Popper and Kuhn, the former being closer to what I have called here an open view of science. See Lakatos and Musgrave (1970).

18. Of course, schoolteachers, like teachers in higher education, do sometimes work as researchers in a more conventional sense. This highlights that what is at issue here is not so much teachers-as-researchers but teacher research as practical inquiry: the key issue is the nature of the research rather than who does it.

19. This fallacy is even to be found in writers, like Elliott, who stress that teaching always takes place within a framework of practical understandings (compare Elliott, 1988 with Elliott, 1991a).

20. To believe that reflection and inquiry are always good is another common fallacy, a fallacy to which researchers are especially prone.

21. See, for example, Carr and Kemmis (1986). Though this strategy relies on a rather old fashioned and much criticized conception of professionalism; see, for example, the discussions in Becker (1970) and Johnson (1972).

BIBLIOGRAPHY

Argyris, C., Putnam, R. and Smith, D. M. (1985) *Action Science*, San Francisco, Jossey Bass.

Atkinson, P. and Delamont, S. (1976) 'Mock ups and cock ups: the stage-management of guided discovery learning', in P. Woods and M. Hammersley (Eds) *School Experience*, London, Croom Helm.

Bartholomew, J. (1973) The teacher as researcher, *Hard Cheese*, no. 1, pp. 12–22.

Becker, H. S. (1970) The nature of a profession, in H. S. Becker *Sociological Work*, Chicago, Aldine.

Burgess, R. G. (1980) Some fieldwork problems in teacher-based research, *British Educational Research Journal*, Vol. 6, no. 2, pp. 165–73.

Cane, B. and Schroeder, C. (1970 *The Teacher and Research: a study of teachers' priorities and opinions on educational research and development*, Slough, NFER.

Carr, W. (1987) What is an educational practice?, *Journal of Philosophy of Education*, Vol. 21, no. 2, pp. 163–75.

Carr, W. and Kemmis, S. (1986) *Becoming Critical*, Lewes, Falmer.

Cope, E. and Gray, J. (1979) Teachers as researchers: some experience of an alternative paradigm, *British Educational Research Journal*, Vol. 5, no. 2, pp. 237–51.

Corey, S. M. (1949) Action research, fundamental research and educational practitioners, *Teachers College Record*, No. 50, pp. 509–14.

Doyle, W. (1977) Learning the classroom environment, *Journal of Teacher Education*, No. 28, pp. 51–5.

Elliott, J. (1988) Educational research and outsider-insider relations, *Qualitative Studies in Education*, Vol. 1, no. 2, pp. 155–66.

Elliott, J. (1991a) *Action Research for Educational Change*, Milton Keynes, Open University Press.

Elliott, J. (1991b) Changing contexts for educational evaluation: the challenge for methodology, *Studies in Educational Evaluation*, Vol. 17, no. 2, pp. 215–38.

Flathman, R. (1989) *Towards a Liberalism*, Ithaca, Cornell University Press.

Gage, N. (1963) Paradigms for research on teaching, in N. Gage (Ed.) *Handbook of Research on Teaching*, Chicago, Rand McNally.

Gipps, C. (1993) The profession of educational research (presidential address), *British Educational Research Journal*, Vol. 19, no. 1, pp. 3–16.

Gustavsen, B. (1986) Social research as participative dialogue, in F. Heller (Ed.) *The Use and Abuse of Social Science*, London, Sage.

Habermas, J. (1987) *Knowledge and Human Interests*, Cambridge, Polity Press.

Hall, B., Gillett, A. and Tandon, R. (Eds) (1982) *Creating Knowledge: a monopoly?*, New Delhi: Society for Participatory Research in Asia.

Hamilton, D., Jenkins, D., King, C., MacDonald, B. and Parlett, M. (Eds) (1977) *Beyond the Numbers Game: a reader in educational evaluation*, London, Macmillan.

Hammersley, M. (1981) The outsider's advantage: a reply to McNamara, *British Educational Research Journal*, Vol. 7, no. 2, pp. 167–71.

Hammersley, M. (1992) *What's Wrong with Ethnography?*, London, Routledge.

Hirst, P. H. (1983) Educational theory, in P. H. Hirst (Ed.) *Educational Theory and its Foundation Disciplines*, London, Routledge and Kegan Paul.

Hodgkinson, H. L. (1957) Action research: a critique, *Journal of Educational Sociology*, Vol. 31, no. 4, pp. 137–53.

Hoyle, E. (1970) Educational innovation and the role of the teacher, *Forum*, no. 14, pp. 42–4.

Hoyle, E. (1972) Creativity in the school, unpublished paper given at OECD Workshop on the Creativity of the School, at Estoril, Portugal, cited in Stenhouse (1975).

Hustler, D., Cassidy, A., and Cuff, E. C. (Eds) (1986) *Action Research in Classrooms and Schools*, London, Allen and Unwin.

Jackson, P. (1968) *Life in Classrooms*, New York, Holt, Rinehart and Winston.

Johnson, T. (1972) *Professions and Power*, London, Macmillan.

Kelly, A. (1985) Action research: what is it and what can it do?, in R. G. Burgess (Ed) *Issues in Educational Research: Qualitative Methods*, Lewes, Falmer.

Kemmis, S. (1982) Introduction, in Action Research in Curriculum Course Team (Eds) *The Action Research Reader*, Deakin, Deakin University Press.

Kemmis, S. (1988) Action research, in J. P. Keeves (Ed.) *Educational Research, Methodology, and Measurement: an international handbook*, Oxford, Pergamon.

Kuhn, T. S. (1970) *The Structure of Scientific Revolutions*, Chicago, University of Chicago Press.

Lakatos, I. and Musgrave, A. (Eds) (1970) *Criticism and the Growth of Knowledge*, Cambridge, Cambridge University Press.

Latapi, P. (1988) Participatory research: a new research paradigm?, *Alberta Journal of Education*, Vol. 34, no. 1, pp. 310–19.

Lieberman, M. (1956) *Education as a Profession*, Englewood Cliffs, NJ, Prentice Hall.

Lindblom, C. and Cohen, D. (1979) *Usable Knowledge*, New Haven, Yale University Press.

Lobkowicz, N. (1967) *Theory and Practice*, Notre Dame, IL, University of Notre Dame Press.

Lortie, D. (1975) *Schoolteacher*, Chicago, University of Chicago Press.

MacDonald, B. and Walker, R. (1977) Case study and the social philosophy of educational research, in D. Hamilton, D. Jenkins, C. King, B. MacDonald, and M. Parlett (Eds) *Beyond the Numbers Game: a reader in educational evaluation*, London, Macmillan.

McNamara, D. (1980) The outsider's arrogance: the failure of participant observers to understand classroom events, *British Educational Research Journal*, no. 6, pp. 113–25.

McNiff, J. (1992) *Creating a Good Social Order through Action Research*, Poole, Hyde Publications.

McNiff, J. (1993) *Teaching as Learning: an action research approach*, London, Routledge.

May, N. (1982) The teacher-as-research movement in Britain, in W. Schubert and A. Schubert (Eds) *Conceptions of Curriculum Knowledge*, College of Education, Pennsylvania State University.

Mies, M. (1983) Toward a methodology for feminist research, in G. Bowles and R. Duelli Klein (Eds) *Theories of Women's Studies*, London, Routledge and Kegan Paul.

Morawetz, T. (1978) *Wittgenstein and Knowledge: the importance of On Certainty*, Amherst, MS, University of Massachusetts Press.

Nixon, J. (Ed) (1981) *A Teacher's Guide to Action Research*, London, Grant McIntyre.

Norris, N. (1990) *Understanding Educational Evaluation*, London, Kogan Page.

Parlett, M. and Hamilton, D. (1977) Evaluation as illumination: a new approach to the study of innovatory programmes, in Hamilton et al. (Eds).

Reason, P. and Rowan, J. (1981) *Inquiry: A Source Book of New Paradigm Research*, Chichester, Wiley.

Rudduck, J. (1987) Teacher research, action research, teacher inquiry: what's in a name?, in J. Rudduck, D. Hopkins, J. Sanger and P. Lincoln, *Collaborative Inquiry and Information Skills*, British Library research paper 16, Boston Spa, British Library.

Schwab, J. (1969) The practical: a language for curriculum, *School Review*, no. 78, pp. 1–24.

Schon, D. (1983) *The Reflective Practitioner*, New York, Basic Books.

Schon, D. (1987) *Educating the Reflective Practitioner*, San Francisco, Jossey Bass.

Simons, H. (1987) *Getting to Know Schools in a Democracy*, Lewes, Falmer.

Skilbeck, M. (1983) Lawrence Stenhouse: research methodology, *British Educational Research Journal*, Vol. 9, no. 1, pp. 9–20.

Stenhouse, L. (1975) *An Introduction to Curriculum Research and Development*, London, Heinemann.

Stenhouse, L. (1983) *Authority, Education and Emancipation*, London, Heinemann.

Torbert, W. R. (1983) Initiating collaborative inquiry, in G. Morgan (Ed.) *Beyond Method*, Beverly Hills, Sage.

Tully, J. (1989) Wittgenstein and political philosophy: understanding practices of critical reflection, *Political Theory*, Vol. 17, no. 2, pp. 172–204.

Van Dalen, D. B. (1962) *Understanding Educational Research*, New York, McGraw Hill.

Whitehead, J. (1989) Creating a living educational theory from questions of the kind, How do I improve my practice?, *Cambridge Journal of Education*, Vol. 19, no. 1, pp. 41–52.

van Willigen, J. (1986) *Applied Anthropology: an introduction*, Massachusetts, Bergin and Garvey.

Wittgenstein, L. (1969) *On Certainty*, Oxford, Blackwell.

INDEX OF NAMES

INDEX OF SUBJECTS